Morphology of Towns

Perspectives in Urban Geography

- New Directions in Urban Geography
- Comparative Urban Research 1986
- Comparative Urbanisation: City Growth and Change 1986
- Models in Urban Geography (Theoretical) 1987
- Models in Urban Geography (Mathematical) 1987
- Urban Research Methods: Central Place, Hierarchical and City Size Models
- Contemporary City Ecology 1987
- Slums, Urban Decline and Revitalization 1987
- Contemporary Urban Issues 1987
- Rural-Urban Fringe
- Morphology of Towns
- Cities and Housing
- Perceptual and Cognitive Image of the City 1987
- Urban Economics 1987
- City Planning : Problems and Prospects 1987
- City Planning : Administration and Participation 1987
- Urban Planning and Policies: Reorientation of Policy Norms
- Urban Planning and Policies: Cross-Cultural Urban Policies

Concept's International Series in Geography No. 3

PERSPECTIVES IN URBAN GEOGRAPHY

VOLUME TEN

Morphology of Towns

Edited by
C.S. YADAV

CONCEPT PUBLISHING COMPANY PVT. LTD.,
NEW DELHI-110059

ISBN 81-7022-80-7 (Set)
ISBN 81-7022-31-7 (Vol. X)

First Published 1987
Reprinted 2011

Published and Printed by

Concept
Since 1974

Concept Publishing Company Pvt. Ltd.
Regd. Office:
A/15-16, Commercial Block, Mohan Garden
New Delhi-110059 (India)
Phones : 25351460, 25351794, *Fax* : 091-11-25357109
Email : publishing@conceptpub.com,
Website: www.conceptpub.com

Editorial Office:
H-13, Bali Nagar, New Delhi-110 015, India.

Preface

NATURE OF URBAN GEOGRAPHY

There are several studies on urban geography which reveal that, as a major sub-discipline, it has a long tail but a short body. However, the spectrum is so vast and broad that researchers are able to make general statements in defence of its conception, philosophy, nature and orientation. Urban geography today encompasses and interfaces with various disciplines which are interested in urban studies. As an introduction to this series, our task here is to make an attempt to briefly review the development of geographical interest in various aspects of cities.

There are several reviews of the early development of urban geography which have been dealt with by Berry and Harton (1970)[1] and Carter (1974).[2] Berry and Harton in their book, **Geographical Perspective on Urban System**, have made an attempt to introduce readers to its present-day status. They have clearly resolved that "the formative years of the social science in the late nineteenth century and early twentieth century were also the years in which urban studies first developed,"[3] thus providing the context for geography's emerging interest in cities. However, the emergence of urban studies dates back to the writing of Greek scholars, but as a sub-discipline, it has reached its present-day status only in the past 30 years.

In their historical perspective the works on urban geography show that the pre-20th century studies primarily concerned themselves with themes of location, size and shape of the cities. The initial findings were strongly subjective, descriptive and dependent more on observation such as the works of Hassert (1907)[4] and Blanchard (1911).[5] In the succeeding years the conceptual framework of site and situa was criticized by Aurousseau (1924)[6] and Crowe (1938)[7], their conception being that cities were not inanimate objects in landscape, but also organic elements which involved people and their movements. The morphologist, later in 1960, truly brought the indigenous line of evolution in the sphere of urban geography and studies on the build-up fabric of cities (Conzone, 1960).[8] Smails (1955)[9] constituted the prime base of urban geography, which remained articulated without any major conceptual change till early 1960s. The studies on the morphological aspects of the urban system were influenced by external forces, consequently the methodological frameworks got impetus within the discipline. At this juncture the evolution of concepts was not based on environment but took shelter under the umbrella of economics of location, and incorporated analysis of land values and rents, and the concept of nodality and accessibility. These concepts were derived from the economic theories of Cooley (1894)[10], Weber (1899),[11] and Hurd (1903).[12]

The Chicago School of Urban Ecology hastened the evolution of urban geography. In his monumental work Park (1925)[13] developed the idea of order and analysis of towns. Further, a powerful thrust and much of the rationale was provided to the studies of urban geography by the Central Place Theory of Christallar (1933).[14]

The impact of the statistical method was powerful and it brought rapid and enormous changes in the field of urban geography. It also brought new insights into the development and application of urban geography towards increased quantification. Brian J. Berry, a pioneer in the field, analysed the spatial order, size and location of towns and cities. There was widespread use of innovative techniques to explore the nature of urban problems, hypotheses were tested, new theories propounded and old theories remodelled. The statistical methods were put to a variety of uses. Smith (1965)[15] evaluated the classification of settlements; Berry and Garrison (1956)[16] examined the utility of the rank-size rule for urban populations. The models of Park and Burgess (1925),[17] Harris and Ullman (1945)[18] and Homar Hoyt (1939)[19] were tested and re-examined by various geographers.

A new impetus to urban geography came from social area analysis which was initially propounded by Shevky and Bell (1955)[20] and later on this provided a basis for factorial ecology. The collaboration of this stream in urban geography was offered by Berry (1971)[21], Herbert (1972)[22] and Johnston (1971).[23] As a consequence of these thrusts in geography after 1960, the techniques of investigation were sharpened and this has provided the basis for a scientific explanation of cities. Attempts were made to introduce new theories and frame laws to make the explanation of events more rational and logical. Sophisticated models were propounded as urban geography entered a new era of rationalizing the subject matter of urban studies on the basis of new philosophies, new concepts, new theories, new methodologies and applications.

However, the status of contemporary urban geography has been elevated only recently by the behavioural approach. The studies of perception and cognition which have a long tradition in physiology were first introduced into the field of geography by Lynch (1960)[24] Dowson and Stea (1973)[25], Gould and White (1974).[26] At present there is a sudden spurt in the studies on the subject with a new paradigm. But the full impact of behavioural approaches upon urban geography has yet to be realized.

The aim of this series is to seek reorientation of the discipline strengthened by new philosophies, methodologies, subject matters or application. The series has been arranged in such a way that all contemporary viewpoints are covered comprehensively. Hopefully, this series will inspire researchers to appreciate the work already done by geographers in studying cities. Geography by nature seems to be a synthesizing field of inquiry. As such we have made an endeavour to combine some of the otherwise disparate facts garnered by other disciplines in such a manner that we can gain a better understanding of the urban system. The study of urban geography is essential if we are to analyse the human consequences of the settlements in which we live. It is useful to planners, decision makers in government and corporations and also to each one of us as citizens. Finally, it gives us a perspective on what may be happening to our cities and to the nature.

To achieve the above goal only those contributions with originality and contrasting viewpoints were selected for inclusion in this series. In doing so the editor does not wish to compete with the journals in the field in which innovative research and methodological aspects are presented. But he does wish to convey, and convey with conviction, that significant researches are being undertaken in the different branches of urban geography and in other allied disciplines. The present series is an attempt to provide a selective reappraisal and rigorous examination of the assumptions and the urge to disseminate new knowledge created by the mutual interaction. Emphasis is also placed on the conceptualization and theorization of the subject matter so that general laws may emerge. A conscious effort has been made to organize the series in such a way that it reflects the philosophical approach parallel to that of the behavioural school. Finally, a vigorous attempt has been made to demonstrate throughout the series how geographers are basically involved in solving the urban problems.

C. S. YADAV

REFERENCES

1. Berry and Harton, **Geographic Perspectives on Urban Systems: With Integrated Readings**, New Jersey, Prentice Hall, Inc, Englewood Cliffs, 1970.
2. Carter, **The Study of Urban Geography**, Edward Arnold, London, 1974.
3. Berry and Harton, 1970.
4. Hassert, K., **Die Stadte Geographisch Betrachect**, Leipzig, 1907.
5. Blanchard, R., **Grenoble: Etude de Geographic Urbanine**, Paris, 1911.
6. Aurousseau, M., "Recent Contributions to Geography: A Review," **Geographical Review**, 1924, 14, p.444.
7. Crowe, P.R., "On Progress in Geography," **Scottish Geographical Magazine**, 1938, 54, 1-19.
8. Conzone, M.R.G., "The Plan Analysis of an English City Centre," In Norkorg (Ed), **Proceedings of I.G.U. Symposium on Urban Geography**, C.W.K. Gleerup, Lund, 1962.
9. Smails, A.E., "The Urban Mess of England and Wales," **Transactions and Papers**, Institute of British Geographers, 1946, 11, 85, p.101.
10. Cooley, C.H., "The Theory of Transportation," **Publications of the American Economic Association**, 1894, 9, p.5-7.
11. Weber, A.F., **The Growth of Cities in the Nineteenth Century: A Study in Statistics**, New York, 1899.
12. Hurd, R., **Principles of City Land Values: New York Record and Guide**, 1903, p. 19-21.
13. Park, R.E., "Suggestions for the Investigation of Human Behaviour in an Urban Environment," in R.E. Park, E.W. Burgess, R.D. Mackenzie (eds), **The City**, University of Chicago Press, 1925.
14. Christallar, W., **Central Place in Southern Germany**, Gustar Fischer, Teno, 1933.

15. Smith, R.M.T., "Method and Purpose in Functional Town Classification," **Annals of the Association of American Geographers**, 1965, 55, pp.539-548.
16. Garrison, W.L., "Applicability of Statistical Inference to Geographical Research," **Geographical Review**, 1956, 46, 427, 429.
17. Burgess, E.W., "The Growth of City," in R.E. Park, E.W. Burgess and R.D. Mackenzie (eds), **The City**, University of Chicago Press, 1925.
18. Ullman, E.L., "The Nature of Cities," **Annals, American Academy of Political and Social Science**, 1945, 242, 7-17.
19. Hoyt, H., **The Structure and Growth of Residential Neighbourhoods in American Cities**, Washington, Federal Housing Administration, 1939.
20. Shevky, E. and Bell, W., **Social Area Analysis**, Stamford University Press, Stamford, 1955.
21. Berry, B.J.L. (ed), "Comparative Factorial Ecology," **Economic Geographic (Supplement)**, 1971, 47.
22. Herbert, D.T., **Urban Geography: A Social Perspective**, David and Charles, Newton Abbot, 1972.
23. Johnston, **Urban Residential Pattern**, Bell, London, 1971.
24. Lynch, **Image of the City**, Massachusetts, Cambridge, 1960.
25. Dowson and Stea, "Image and Environment", Chicago and London, 1973.
26. Gould and White, R., **Mental Maps**, London, 1974.

Acknowledgements

We are highly thankful to Prof. David G. Dickason Western lMichigan University Kalamazoo (U.S.A.) who guided us whole heartedly during the initial stage of the Project. We regret that his name was not acknowledged in earlier volumes.

We also thank Editors Gerd-Michael Hellstern, Frithjof Spreer Hellmut Wollmann, **Heft 2, Vol. II** and **Vol. III** for their permission to use material from "Applied Urban Research", Proceedings of the European Meeting on Applied Urban Research, Essen, 2-4, Oct. 1981.

Contents

SECTION TWO
COMMERCIAL USE OF URBAN LAND

SECTION THREE
RECREATION USE OF URBAN LAND

SECTION FOUR
URBAN LANDUSE IN HILLY TOWNS, INDIA

List of Contributors

A.S. Morris: Department of Geography, University of Glasgow, Glasgow G128QQ

Antal Lehmann: Pecs, Tolbuhin IIT 172, 7628, Hungary

Asel Floderus: The National Swedish Institute for Building Research, Post Box 785; 5-80129, Gavle

B.K. Roy: Deputy Registrar General (M) India, office of the Registrar General, R.K. Puram New Delhi-110066 (India)

Bela Gertig: Pecsi Janus Pannonius Tudomanyegyetem, Tanarkepzo Kara Foldrajz Tanszeke, H-7624 Pecs, Ifjusagu 6

Donald A. Fraser: Department of Geography, Concordia University, Montreal, Quebec, Canada

Francoise Burn: Professeur de geographie, Faculte des Lettres, Avignon - France, 25 Boukvard Bwno de Marechal 13090. Aix-en - Provence, France

H.M. Saxena: Department of Geography, Government Post Graduate College, Sriganganagar Rajasthan, (India)

J. Donald Hughes: Prof. of History, University of Denver, University Park, Denver, Colardo-80208

J.P. Singh: Lecturer in Geography, Regional College of Education, Bhopal-462013 (India)

Jagdish Kaur: UGC Teacher Fellow at the Institute of Himalayan and Regional Development Studies, Garhwal University, Srinagar Garhwal, (India)

James B. Kenyon: Associate Professor, Department of Geography, University of Georgia, Athens, Ga.30602

Jyotirmoy Sen: Lecturer in Geography, Siliguri College, Siliguri, North Bengal, Assam

K.G. Willis: Department of Town and Country Planning, University of Newcastle upon Tyne, Newcastle upon Tyne, NEI 7RU

Kent A. Robertson: Assistant Professor Urban Affairs Program, State University of New York at Purchase, N.Y. 10577 U.S.A.

Mahadeb Pal: Jalpaiguri Zilla School, Jalpaiguri, Assam

Nandeshwar Sharma: Reader and Head, Department of Geography, L.N. Mithila University, Darbhanga-846004 (India)

P.C. Sharma: Principal, Kendriya Vidyalaya, (Central School) Sambalpur, Orissa (India)

Pranab Kumar Chakravarti: Reader, Department of Geography and Applied Geography, University of North Bengal, Darjeeling (India)

FIRST

C.S. Yadav

Introduction

There is an increasing number of contemporary geographers who have been focusing their attention on the study of urban areas. The object under the lens of the urban geographers is the analysis of the activities of man, the physical forms of structures developed for these activities and their association and arrangements with one another and with the land. This is expected to provide theoretical notions regarding the morphology of the towns, that is, study of the layout and build of towns viewed as the expression of their origin, growth and function (Dickinson, 1984).[1] He concludes that much work of the inferior quality has appeared in this field, and although investigation of the town plan and build began to be systematically undertaken about 50 years ago, it has received virtually no serious attention from geographers. However, there is evidence that some attempt was made to study the individual town layout of its streets and blocks which were analysed in relation to public buildings, and natural and planned growth. It seems necessary, therefore, that geographers should pay more attention to the physical ground plan on which the city rests. As a matter of fact towns with their appreciable size have an internal geography that is full of interest and significance. The physical forms and arrangements of spaces and buildings which consist of urban landscapes provide an ample opportunity to geographers to investigate and analyse their nature, their relative disposition and their social interdependence.

URBAN LAND USE

The urban land use is a term which denotes urban space:

land area of cities, water areas in the cities and three-dimensional spaces above the surface of the city, or "the land we are concerned with can be described as land now used for purposes that are characteristically urban" (Bartholomew, 1955).[2] In essence the term "urban land use" broadly refers to spatial distribution of city functions, its residential communities or living areas, its individual commercial and retail business districts or major work areas, and its institutional and leisure time functions (Chapin, 1957).[3] The past urban studies have clearly revealed that the broad geographical pattern of these functional areas, their characteristics, how they developed and how they change have been the burning topics of research from a variety of related fields, such as architecture, land economics, geography, human ecology, sociology and others. Nevertheless some of this work is highly subjective and speculative, some of it is documentary and descriptive and some of it is experimental. However, scientifically oriented systematic attempts at theoretical explanation of land use arrangement is made by scholars such as Burgess (1925)[4], Hoyt (1939)[5], McKenzie (1933)[6], Harris and Ullman (1945)[7], and Firey (1947).[8] An examination of the work of these pioneers in the field of urban land use clearly indicates that there are significant variations in their emphasis. For example, Homer Hoyt sought an explanation of the city structure and its land use patterns primarily in terms of universal economic forces which were essentially responsible to govern the make-up and change in this configuration. On the other hand Walter Firey's work demonstrates that land use arrangements are determined by values and attitudes held by city residents and the resultant actions in the selection of locations to satisfy these values and attitudes. The generalizations made by Burgess, Hoyt, Harris and Ullman reveal heavy emphasis on economic determinants of land use, with the assumption that human value systems and group actions are self-regulating and are contained by dominant economic forces (Chapin, 1957)[9], whereas Firey, quite contrary to this notion, found these elements of human behaviour as key variables in the make-up and change of urban land use patterns.

Economic Determinants of Land Use

The rationale behind the economic explanations of the urban land use pattern is based on the assumption that economics acts beyond the immediate environs of any particular urban centre which involves consideration of the structure and functioning of the urban economy as it fits into the larger economy of the region and the nation. Both regional and localized forces interact to shape the land use patterns. Most of the land economists view urban land use in a broader framework of the Equilibrium Theory which states that each land parcel is determined by the urban land market. Accordingly, the land is considered as a commodity traded in the market subject to the forces of supply and demand. In its essence the Equilibrium Theory states that price is both a function of the costs of making land productive and a function of the net income or return realizable after the development of that land. The decision to buy or sell a parcel of land in the urban setting is prompted by the opportunities which maximize the return from a transaction in the market in which land is put. Thus urban land is considered to have value because of its potential to produce income in future. Alonso (1964)[10] correctly recognized that, "The patterns of land uses and land values will be mutually determined". Hurd (1924)[11] propounded the principle that "value in urban land . . . is the resultant of economic or ground rent capitalized". As a matter of fact in a city economic rent is determined by superiority of location and the functional use of the land, so that any utility of the land may compete for any location within a city and all land goes to the highest bidder. The efficiency of a parcel of land use is measured by its rent paying ability. Ratcliff (1949)[12] says that,"The utilization of land is ultimately determined by the relative efficiencies of various locations. Efficiency of use is measured by its rent paying ability, the ability of a use to extract economic utility from a site. The process of adjustment in a city structure to a most efficient land use pattern is through the competition of uses for various locations. The use that can extract the greatest return from a given site will be the successful bidder". From this there emerges an "orderly pattern of land use spatially organized to perform most efficiently the economic functions that characterize urban life" (Ratcliff, 1949).[13]

Thus to the economist land is pressed into use by the existence of a value as established by the alternatives of land development, and the use of a particular parcel is finally determined in the operations of market forces by the price paid and the decision as to what alternative will yield the highest return. Thus the land use structure of the city is determined plot by plot, parcel by parcel by the forces of the urban land market. It is the competition of land uses in the market that distributes the use types in an arrangement that approaches the most efficient pattern.

Socially Rooted Determinants of Land Use

The social action in a particular city influences the location and arrangement of land uses although they are less understood and frequently confused with the economic determinants. Most research in this aspect of urban development lacks an operational slant (Chapin, 1957).[14] Although both kinds of influences interact with each other and it is difficult to differentiate the effects, social scientists in order to provide a coherent framework for interpreting the urban land use structure, are increasingly directing their attention to the role that social values and ideals play in determining the land use patterns in cities. In essence, the behaviour patterns of individuals, institutions and forms which occur in the spatial patterns largely determine the physical structure of a city. Chapin (1957)[15] postulated that, "Looking at urban land use patterns as the aggregate product of many individual and group actions in occupying and improving the land, we may view those actions as a form of human behaviour activated by certain human needs and wants." Chapin provided a stimulating framework, consisting of values, behaviour patterns and outcomes. Fig. 1.1 indicates some of the sequences Chapin tries to invoke. "Certain individual-or group-led values concerning the use of a particular parcel or area set in motion a four-phase cycle of behaviour which culminates in the parcel or area being put to a particular use" (Chapin, 1957).[16] These phases are part of the cycle of human behaviour or of the behavioural pattern (Carter, 1976)[17], which are classified as (i) experiencing of needs and wants, (ii) defining goals, (iii) planning alternatives, (iv) deciding and acting. Carter has appropriately summarized the findings in this way: "From these values, both conscious and subconscious or explicit or implicit, of individuals or groups of individuals, patterns of behaviour are generated, leading to those actions in the urban setting which are the determinants of the land use patterns".

Social Values and Land Use

It is a truism that values held by an individual motivate his behaviour resulting in a certain organized form of action. This is so in the case of people or groups also. Chapin (1957)[18], has recognized that these values may be latent, or subconscious, or they can be articulated or conscious, they may be economic, political, social, religious, authentic and so on, but they play an important role in the evolution of land use patterns. Walter Firey's[19] empirical investigation on Boston also supports this conviction in which he analysed how values and ideals determine the existing land use patterns.

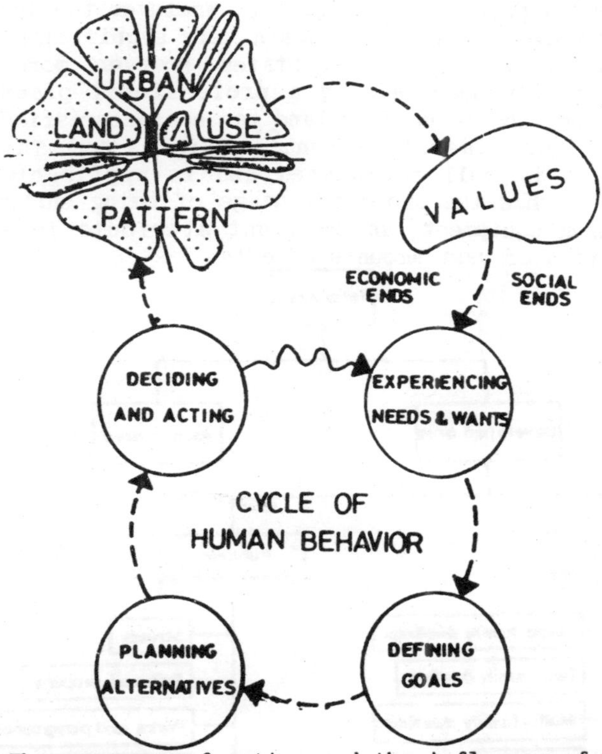

Fig. 1.1 : The sequence of action and the influence of values in bringing about a change in the urban land-use pattern.

Measurement and Classification of Urban Land Use

Classification is vital and most significant to the study of urban land use, because it provides an easy key to understand the complex character of the city structure. The classificatory scheme prevalent points out that groupings or classes of land uses are not arbitrary, they are rational and empirical, and have some basis for their development and have some measure of extended applicability. As a matter of fact, it is realized that no single land use classification can cater to all needs of all cities, but in general there should be some basic structure of the classifications which is applicable to many if not most cities.

Since most of the land use classifications have been formulated by urban planners, they are generally accepted as formulized land use classifications. One of the earliest attempts to formulize land use classification in the U.S.A. was made by Harland Bartholomew (1955)[20]. The system of Bartholomew is presented in Fig. 1.2. Whatever the drawbacks of the Bartholomew system, it has a very significant impact on land use study in the United States. However, more recently, an attempt has been made by a professional planners' organization, who focused on land use characteristics alone as a basis for classification.[21] (Fig. 1.3.) This classification is well formulated and is applicable to most cities. It has the added advantage of being suited to data processing equipment, an important attribute in an era of utilization of vast amounts of data.

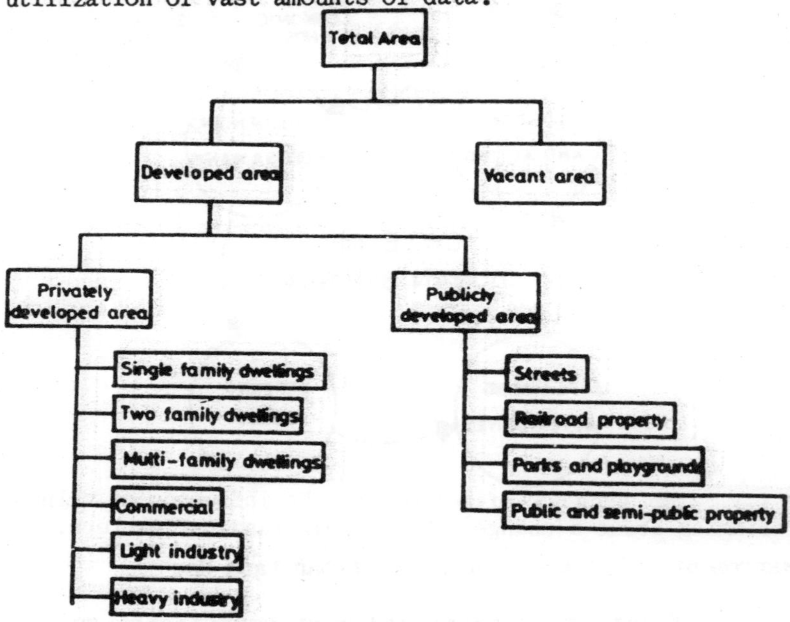

Fig. 1.2 : Classification of uses of urban land.

The land use pattern of any urban area is a reflection not of the immediate and current space requirements of a community but rather of their cumulative needs over a period of years. The urban areas are complex systems which have created myriads of problems and the need for adjustment and modification in the physical form of the urban environment. This physical form is called morphology of the towns. As a matter of fact many diverse forces are consistently reacting upon urban society, creating pressures for growth and

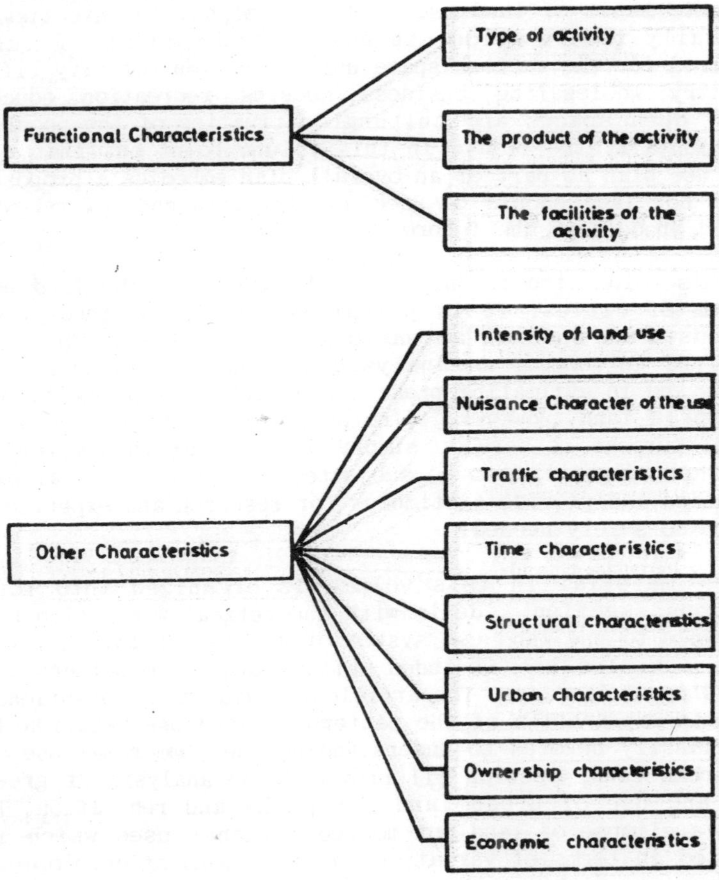

Fig. 1.3 : Structure of a land use classification system based on land use characteristics.

renewal in the physical form of the urban environment. The present volume is designed to fulfill local objectives of social, economic and physical well-being. It examines the economic basis of land uses. It is designed to investigate basically the location, intensity and amount of land required for the various space using functions of city life-industry, wholesaling, business, housing, recreation, education, open spaces and cultural activities of the people. Fundamentally the essays in this volume point out that the land use plan as part of an overall plan embodies a proposal as to how land should be used as expansion and how renewal should proceed in the future.

This volume treats only limited aspects of the land use system of cities. It is primarily focused on theory and methods with special attention given to the techniques required in making an analysis of land use, in measuring trends and in estimating present and future requirements for the use of land. However, if nothing more is accomplished, a useful purpose is served, simply by bringing this material together where it can be subjected to a more critical examination and provide a stimulus for research and experimentation so sorely needed.

The material in this volume is organized into four sections: section I deals with theoretical work which has relevance to the land use system of a city. In this section those articles are included which explain the pattern and intensity of land use. The articles provide the conventional economic explanation of the pattern of land use, section II is primarily devoted to understanding the commercial use of the urban land; section III provides the analysis of green belt and use of urban land for parks and recreation. It gives a glimpse of land put to recreational uses which is analysed in terms of variation in size, form of development and location within the city. It also analyses the functional and spatial hierarchy of urban parks; section IV deals with the comprehensive plan of urban land uses in the hilly towns of India.

The operation and analysis of urban land markets are a highly complex matter in the present day situation. There is no doubt that land by definition is considered to be a scarce commodity in cities, consequently the conventional economic explanation of the pattern of land use depends on the well-known and familiar concept of production function and utility function. R. K. Wilkinson in his article, "Urban Structure: Theory and Application", identifies that the purpose of analysing the structure of cities and urban areas is to explain the pattern and intensity of land use, that is, the location of different activities and the relative density of population. In essence most of the researchers are concerned with explaining the location of residential and non-residential land use. The author agrees with the principle that urban areas are largely the outcome of an economic process, and therefore the model of urban structure is that of a land market which explains the profile of land values use. In this paper the author makes a vigorous attempt to explain a theory of the allocation of urban land use; location decision; some limitations for the theory of urban structure and zoning and land use controls; and finally he suggests the procedure of planning of land use which determines the best allocation of land.

From the beginning of the 1970s, the pace of urbanization has slackened considerably. The supply of housing and services in some regions and sectors is greater than the current demand. In this situation the consumer priorities play an important role. However, the local authorities make efforts to control the process of urbanization that is generated by forces outside their domain of influence. They have a decisive influence on the supply of sites, housing and public services, but they have a very little say so far as the demand for these utilities is concerned. When it is considerably greater than the supply, it causes them trouble, as there is a constant pressure on them to meet the demand. A. Floderus in his article, "Negotiating for Development or Change of Urban Land Use", clearly reveals that the right to determine land use is divided according to various principles. The elected bodies of the municipalities make decisions based on the authority inherent in their political supremacy and are responsible to the municipalities or the electorate. Municipal agencies function as administrative authorities and use their power or laws and regulations. Property owners or those with the right to use property have authority and economic responsibility for the use and maintenance of the property. Changes in the use of land necessitate coordinated decisions from these three parties, and the decision makers are dependent on each other's actions. Political, administrative and property economy decision making are put in principal opposed to each other. Political credibility, justice and economic feasibility are criteria which must in one way or the other be satisfied. In specific cases, however, opposing interests can become relevant, when there are limitations for fulfillment of policies. The credibility of a politician rests upon his ability to live up to the expectations of his voters. The credibility of an administrator rests on his impartiality. In spite of the incompatibility of the political and administrative aspects of public power, local authorities are expected to behave as a united organization.

Cities' existence and evolution may be taken for granted to be an all-time reality. The urban evolution did mark, and even does so now, the creation of the visual event. Nandeshwar Sharma through his article, "On Aspects of Master Plan in City Planning Context", has also tried to prove that the main issue which confronts the city planners is connected with the events of building or rebuilding or making over cities. He has, besides, tried to explore the nature and character of a master plan, where should it aim, what should it constitute, what operational philosophy should it involve.

In recent years, especially after the introduction of the town and country planning movement in India, some interesting trends in the regularization of environment and related aspects of local and regional areas were initiated. In this planning process the Third Five Year Plan has emphasized the importance of urban development and provided assistance in the preparing of master plans for selected areas. Sometimes the guidelines were drawn up to analyse either in a descriptive system or cartographic system to establish various trends within such regions. This clearly indicates that there is a wide scope for an evaluatory study to reveal a mosaic of landscape in the local areas of towns and urban agglomerations in Indian census. B. K. Roy in his article, "A Census Oriented Study of Carto-Spatial Model on Temporal Land Use in a Million City-Case of Lucknow Urban Agglomeration", has given thought to the construction of land use maps of such areas, with reference to time. The author in the paper presents a census-oriented study of a spatial model in temporal land use within the jurisdiction of an urban agglomeration of Lucknow. This study has been constructed with time reference of 1971 and 1981 Censuses. It is based partly on the concept of "Markov Chains". A study on these lines, if considered for a larger number of towns, can help establish a forecasting trend. Again, the present concern for developing towns and city conditions may need evaluation of the jurisdictions of towns and cities for which a great deal of census data is available, which would also help in further researches. Certain issues of technical transformation have been raised in such a study which demand constant research by technicians to streamline the internal and peripheral structure of a townscape which may be able to provide a healthy rural-urban continuum.

Most cities experience expansion problems in the transition areas between their different functional zones, the best known examples being the areas of transition between CBD and the remainder of the city, and between the urbanized and rural areas. These transition problems may be the economic and administrative ones of mixed and incompatible land uses, speculative land holding or derelict land, or the social problems associated with a rootless, unhomogeneous poor population, unadapted to the problems of inner city life. Intergroup tensions are also created between long established residents in old houses and newer residents seeking cheap rental housing, or between residential land users and advancing commercial users.

A.S. Morris in his article, "Mendoza: Land Use in the Adobe City", makes an effort to define and examine what may be termed a transition area. The author convincingly evaluates its problems and distinctive character as compared to the traditional transitional area. In Mendoza, an Argentine city of half a million inhabitants, it is contended that the problem affects a major section of the city because, like other cities of the dry north-west, this city was built in adobe. The author discerns three structural elements: a centre of modern reinforced concrete; a ring of adobe in process of replacement; and a new outer post 1940 ring of anti-seismic construction. He concludes that the size of adobe area, the presence of the new outer ring, and the lack of planning control have created patterns which are distinctive, such as diversity of land use in the old city, urban expansion and a low density of residential land use.

The city centre, variously referred to as the central business district, down town and urban core has recently been of rather sporadic interest to American geographers. Most of urban geographers have focused their attention upon function—the array of activities present in terms of form, the stock and arrangement of brick and mortar containment space available. Functional concentrations have also been mapped for a number of U.S. cities. Movement—local shift of the central core over time—and identification of zones of assimilation and discards have been natural adjuncts to this line of investigation in the general search for underlying forces and processes. But the structure of the urban core in terms of its functional differentiation into specialized subdistricts has constituted perhaps the major thrust of recent interest. All of these studies evaluate the intensity of activities and land uses in the central cores, but no study in the geographic literature has devoted attention in which a flow of pedestrian traffic within the district has been used as a direct basis for an analysis of the functional arrangement or process of development. The paper entitled "Land Use Associations versus Centrality in the Distribution of Pedestrians in the Urban Core: Atlanta" by James B. Kenyon fills this gap. He, in this article, hypothesizes that pedestrian volumes, by intersection within an urban core, are in part externally conferred and in part internally generated. External generation is tested through a gravity model which analyses the pedestrian load in terms of the location of the intersection among other intersections in the district. Internal generation, or direct attraction of pedestrian traffic, is seen as a function of the intensity and combination of land uses within the intersection area. This is tested by stepwise regression of pedestrian volumes against nine land-use combinations. Together, the external and internal explanations account for 70 per cent of the variance in pedestrian distribution and provide a basis for comment on new development within the area.

The morphological pattern of a market town is a complex areal phenomenon consisting of the features of the market places and other infrastructures. The past studies have clearly indicated that it is rather difficult to establish whether marketing activity determines the man-made geographic structure of towns or the structure of the town determines the marketing activity. As a matter of fact, the market infrastructures are the product of marketing activity and the structure of the town. The obvious fact is that it is a reflection not of the immediate and current space requirements of the community but rather of the cumulative needs over a period of years. Thus many a scholar believes that the study of morphological patterns is not only necessary for understanding the present pattern but also for providing a guideline for its better planning. Dr. H.M. Saxena in his article, "Morphological Form and Typology of Market Towns in Rajasthan", analyses the form and typological pattern of market morphology of the market towns in Rajasthan State. The study is based on field work done by the author while studying market towns in Rajasthan. He identifies four distinct forms of market morphology such as: (i) Rectangular Pattern; (ii) Linear Pattern; (iii) Crossroad Pattern; and (iv) Complex or Irregular Pattern. According to the findings of the author, the market morphological patterns become more and more complex as towns grow in size. He says that the growth of market morphology in Rajasthan is very much related with the growth of settlements. In their initial stage only a few shops cater to the minimum demands of a small village, but when it becomes a town, a series of shops develop along the main roads, or at crossroads. The growth of population and settlements leads to formation of complex market morphological units and other infrastructures. Finally, the author concludes that there is a direct relationship between growth of population, urban development and growth of market morphology.

Hotels have historically been a vital component within the structure of American central business districts, both from a functional prospective and in terms of competition. In physical terms, it has been noted that hotels have consistently been among the grandest buildings in large American cities. Hotels have also been important in cultural terms as they have been traditionally utilized as centres for a variety of social and public affairs, thereby prompting the label "Palaces of the Public". Despite the obvious importance assigned to hotels in the evolution of downtowns, little has come from an attempt to descriptively or empirically document the current status of this activity. It is surprising and disappointing that social scientists and historians should have conducted infrequent research pertaining to historical, locational and social aspects of American hotels. Kent A. Robertson in his article, "The Downtown Hotel: Evolution and Recent Trends in the Large American City", criticizes social scientists and reminds them that this lack in scholarly attention is somewhat curious in that the hotel has played such a significant role in the historical development of American cities. The author points out that hotels appear to be constituting a major component of many CBD redevelopment plans across the country. He asserts that a better understanding of the role and magnitude of the downtown hotels, in both the past and present tense, should be acquired in order to facilitate the effectiveness of future policies and plans. Accordingly the author illucidates the purpose of this paper as (i) to briefly describe the evolution of the downtown hotel since the early 19th century and (ii) to document and analyse some of the trends exhibited by downtown hotels between 1968 and 1979.

Eating out in French towns is a fact just as old as the town itself and meets the basic needs. The need to eat outside your home is what one calls "necessary meal". The festival meal is an intended break from routine and such a "sociable meal" gathers several guests around a table or a meal meant for pleasure time, this being sometimes the very goal of their outing. Here the author poses a question, how can we resist all those tempting institutions and new styles which since the beginning of the seventies have played a great part in changing the outside appearance of towns. Attractive to the customer, the multiplicity is in fact the visible part of a deep reorganizing process which Francoise Brun in his article, "Old and New Restaurants in French Towns", has tried to analyse. The author concludes that the first generation cafeterias are located in shopping centres and along the main roads. The second generation cafeterias try to find their place in the middle of the ladder. They are already in a successful competition with traditional restaurants and also with ethnic cooking restaurants. The author clearly reveals that the proliferation of different types of restaurants is more a sign of a transition period than of a healthy situation.

The public land in the city is largely utilized for recreation, education, cemeteries and religion which are significant users of the public land for the efficient functioning of the urban society, although they use relatively small amounts of urban space. The urban parks that comprise most of the land utilized for recreation in the city exhibit considerable variation in size, form of development, facilities provided, location within the city and extent of the service area.

To bring city dwellers closer to the country, since the image of the countryside and village life was held to be idealistic, Howard proposed a series of garden cities, each surrounded by a green belt-ring. It was no Utopia, but a realistic blueprint which would integrate all the advantages of town and country life, in which all the advantages of the most energetic and active town life, with all the beauty and delight of the countryside can be secured. K. G. Willis in his article, "Green Belts", propounds the same idea. The author in this article analyses the evolution of green belts in the U.K. According to him green belts are conceived as rough rings of land, usually several kilometres around a number of developed areas. Within the green belts no future development is permitted and as a consequence the further expansion of cities and urban agglomerations is halted. He provides us an explanation of the functions and effects of green belts, and tells us that a number of problems still remain to be solved before any proper evaluation of green belts can be made. First, since amenity is income elastic demand for amenity is expected to be much greater in future. perhaps growing faster than the demand for housing in Western Europe and the USA. The author realizes that this will have implications for the future size and distribution of green belts, and that there is the question of who has the right to amenity in the green belt land. In the present analysis, the author has assumed that amenity rights accrue to householders around green belts. But amenity rights are not recognized in English planning law. As such, the author offers an alternative assumption that householders would need to buy green belt lands to secure amenity rights to them. And he also finds that willingness to buy is much less than willingness to sell.

Since it is a basic attribute of society to function in a permanent and close relation to its physical environment it transforms it according to the requirements of society keeping in view the mode of production and the level of development of the productive forces. Antal Lehmann in his article, "A Phyto-Geographical Method for the Investigation of Agglomeration: Example of Pecs and Its Vicinity", convincingly argues that changes in the physical environment within a given area reflect the quantitative and qualitative impacts of the social activity inducing change. As a consequence the process of urbanization, and agglomeration, so characteristic of our day, must be well indicated in the alterations in the physical environment of the area involved. According to the author, of all factors the biota factor of physical environment is the most sensitive to these influences. Man first alters the natural vegetation of the area. He then transforms the vegetation in an unconscious way to various extents. He completely exterminates normal vegetation and creates a new type of vegetation or creates or leaves behind a completely barren ground where grows the so-called ruderal weed associated with low number of species and specimen, spontaneously or by conscious human action as in the case of buildings, yards, industrial establishments, mines, transport, etc. The author analyses the character of this type of vegetation as an indication of the spatial and temporal extension and intensity of social economic processes. In this paper the author has knowingly applied the quantitative indicators of ruderal weed association, their spatial ratio, and its temporal change in order to delineate agglomeration or to determine the degree of agglomeration.

The importance of trees in the urban milieu was first recognized in 1882 by Sir Henry Joly de Lotbiniere who sponsored the first law related to the tree festival in the city. Different propositions have been put forward every year to celebrate the occasion when trees are planted in front of homes. Donald A. Fraser in his article, "Plants and Parks of Montreal", makes a brief survey of parks and trees in Montreal and illustrates the importance of trees in the urban milieu. The author recognizes that the residents of Montreal have made a choice of the natural hard woods, American elm, silver made ashes, poplars and black coca and some important species scattered all over the city. Apart from the trial listing of new species for their adaptability to an urban environment is a continuous process. Thus today one can find in parks and streets plantation, the house chestnut, asscilus hippocastannum, honey, locust, gliclitsia triacanthos, tantaniam maple, white ash and mulberry. According to the author there are eight regional parks, 12 golf courses, two natural reserves, one bird sanctuary and two airports within the Montreal area. He says Montreal is a dynamic, ever changing urban development of some two million people, and the Archipel Scheme when implemented may alter the face of the city. The project could even exert human control over all water flowing for metropolitan Montreal. Up to six dams, five canals and four lakes could be united for this purpose to prevent flooding, to improve water quality.

The great cities of antiquity, creative Athens, imperial Rome and a hundred others such as commercial Corinth and Marseilles, templed Jerusalem and polyglot Alxandria were dependent on the forests that were within their reach even more than the modern cities that stand on their ancient sites. The process of urbanization in the littoral was accompanied by a process of deforestation and the two stood in direct relation to one another. J. Donald Hughes in his article, "Forests and Cities in the Classical Mediterranean", has made an attempt to review classical works on the relationship of forests and the cities.

Dr. Bela Gertig in his article, "The Effect of Urbanization & Tourism in Hungary", has clearly explained the development of tourism in Hungary. While explaining the Hungarian tourism the author finds that in the 1930s it was poorly developed. However, after 1945, the frontiers of tourism started spreading slowly. Before this tourism was confined to Budapest and was largely seasonal. It was an interesting feature of tourism in this period that only members of the ruling and the middle classes could participate. Majority of workers or peasants would not even think of having a holiday let alone a little leisure. Hungary had also a little share in international tourism during this period. However, after 1945, with the growth in industrial productivity the Hungarian Government paid greater and greater attention to the development of national and international tourism. The author finds that tourism in Hungary is limited to a season. Both Hungarian tourists and visitors from abroad during the past 35 years under survey arrived in the main season. He further finds that due to heavy rush of tourists in one season, the number of beds available does not meet the demand and therefore strongly recommends immediate increase in them. The author also suggests that additional places of tourist interest should be established keeping in view the demand. Besides, geographical, territorial distribution should also be altered.

In India the morphology of hilly towns has been influenced by the physical factors, site, climate, geological structure, natural beauty, availability of water and cultural settings. Dr. P. C. Sharma in his article, "Factors Affecting the Morphological Patterns of Hilly Towns: A Case Study of Himachal Pradesh", thinks that the analysis of the morphological patterns of hilly towns makes it clear that the towns of Himachal Pradesh resemble dynamic organisms constantly in the process of evolution. The layout and structure of these towns may be taken as an expression of their origin, growth and evolution of functions. Some old established functions of these towns are being modified while the new functions are being added to them under the influence of various physical and cultural forces which are in many cases interwoven. The author in this paper provides a comprehensive survey of Himachal Pradesh towns in terms of physical controls, such as climatic controls, geological controls, natural beauty and availability of water. The role of cultural control is also vividly highlighted in terms of impact of transport and communication, functional impact, impact of educational institutions on the morphology, impact of trading and commercial establishments, impact of industries, impact of administrative functions, impact of policy of government and impact of the teaching of regionalism.

Siliguri standing on the banks of Mahananda river is a fast growing town today, the largest town of North Bengal. There have been both high growth of population and commercial activities of the town during the past few years. Urban growth of the town has brought with it some problems. Authors Mahadeb Pal and Jyotirmoy Sen in their article, "Siliguri: A Study in Urban Land Use", have dealt with the land use plan of Siliguri in a comprehensive way. According to the impression of the authors the town itself was not built to any plan; it is really an "overgrown village". From the study it becomes quite obvious that there is an unbalanced land-man ratio and to get ample space in the core of the town attention should be paid to the development of the other fringes of towns and the authors feel happy to note that the Government has accepted for implementation the proposal to develop a satellite town in the Western part. The authors foresee that it will lessen congestion in the town.

J. P. Singh has taken the initiative to provide a comprehensive survey of Shillong. He finds Shillong to be the "Queen of hill stations", "Scotland of the East". In his attempt the author provides a survey of physical setting, evolution of the city, demographic structure, patterns of land use and problems of planning. He finally suggests a tentative plan for the development of Shillong for a period of 25 years. According to him it would be a wise step to develop new residential colonies with neighbourhood facilities within the present urban limits in the suburbs. In order to provide uniform marketing facilities some community and neighbourhood civic centres are proposed to be established in and around Shillong. The author also suggests marginal shifting of government offices and defence establishments. According to him decentralization of schools and colleges to equate educational opportunities to different areas. Two areas in the Jowar Road and another in the Gauhati-Shillong Road should be developed into industrial districts. The fish dale should be converted into a park. In order to develop tourism in the city, large, cheap hotels and more rest-houses are required.

Badrinath, essentially a religious destination, is a focus of attraction for both religious and secular visitors. The latter are steadily on the increase. Jagdish Kaur in her article, "Badrinath: Hindus' Super Pilgrimage Resort on the Himalayas; A Study in Site Character, Pilgrim Patterns and Process of Modernization", finds that with the process of modernization and better facilities in transport and accommodation, Badrinath, with its multiple outdoor recreation resource endowment, promises an upcoming tourist destination. Jagdish Kaur assigns the cause of opening of the area for tourists to Badrinath yatra. She feels that the Badrinath recreational-cum-religious resource may well be studied in two parts, within the township and immediate surroundings and the other that may be developed as a tourist complex planning base on a timescale. The author has realized that it is pertinent to discuss the first one here for inclusion in the tourist itinerary. She then analyses the pilgrim traffic patterns, accommodation facilities and the master plan of the city.

Darjeeling resting among the Himalayan foothills is undoubtedly a tourist's paradise. It commands a thrilling view of the glowing snow-capped peaks like Kanchenjunga. Pranab Kumar Chakravarti in his article, "Darjeeling: The Queen of the Hill Stations", attributes many qualities to the city, and says the town is modern, elegant and sophisticated by all standards, offering all the amenities of civilized life, rich flora and fauna and this all has attracted tourists, holiday makers, health seekers, adventurists, and globetrotters. Pranab provides a comprehensive survey of the city. He feels that Darjeeling's recognition as an international hill resort is a post-independence phenomenon. Increased leisure, better educational facilities, fast transport media have added to its development. Tourism has changed the physiognomy of the urban landscape a great deal though in the process much of its original flora and fauna have been destroyed by human encroachment.

NOTES

1. Robert E. Dickinson, "The Scope and Status of Urban Geography", **Land Economics**, 1948, XXIV, 221-38.
2. Harland Bartholomew, 1955, **Land Use in American Cities,** Harvard University Press, Cambridge.
3. F.Stuart Chapin, Jr. 1957, **Urban Land Use Planning,** Harper and Brothers, Publishers, New York.
4. Ernest, W., Burgess, 1925, "The Growth of the City", in R.E Park et al., (Ed.)., **The City,** University of Chicago Press.
5. Homer Hoyt, 1939, "The Structure and Growth of Residential Neighbourhoods in American Cities, Federal Housing Administration", in Arthur M. Weimer and Homer Hoyt, **Principles of Real Estate,** The Ronald Press Company.
6. R. D. Mckenzie, 1933, **The Metropolitan Community,** McGraw Hill Book Company, Inc.
7. Chawney D. Harris and Edward L. Ullman, "The Nature of Cities", **The Annals of the American**

Academy of Political and Social Science, November, 1945.

8. Walter Firey, 1947, **Land Use in Central Boston,** Harvard University Press.
9. Chapin, 1957 op. cit., P.4.
10. W. Alonso, 1964, **Location and Land Use,** 16 (Cambridge, Man).
11. R. M. Hurd, 1924, **Principles of City Land Values,** New York.
12. R. V. Ratcliff, 1949, **Urban Land Economics** 369, New York.
13. R. V. Ratcliff, op. cit.
14. Chapin, op. cit., 20
15. Chapin, op. cit.
16. Chapin, op. cit., 30
17. Carter, op. cit.
18. Chapin, op. cit.
19. Walter Firey, op. cit.
20. Harold Bartholomew, op. cit.
21. Land Use Classification Committee, North Carolina Section, South East Chapter, American Institute of Planners, "A Proposal for a Standardized land Use Classification System", 1960.

SECTION ONE

LAND USE SYSTEMS

TWO

Asel Floderus

Negotiating for Development or Change of Urban Land Use

THE AIMS OF THE STUDY

When I started research on the community planning process in 1974 at the National Swedish Institute for Building Research the aim of my work was to design a model for comprehensive planning in order to integrate physical, economic and social planning of a municipality. I started to design a manual, a kind of check-list to be used by Local Authorities continuously in the planning and budgetary processes. Later on I found that the Swedish Association of Local Authorities had developed a very similar model independent of ours, so this kind of thinking about planning seems to have been very common at the time.

The manual was tested in a municipality of average size, an industrial town of about 28,000 inhabitants. Interviews with politicians and local officials of the planning administration revealed, however, that crucial decisions concerning land use were not encompassed by the planning model. For instance, decisions on municipal acquisition of land, exploitation of land for housing or industrial plants, and the granting of planning permissions were taken after negotiations with participants outside local government. These decisions were seldom, if ever, foreseen in comprehensive plans, made up years ahead. Instead, the results of negotiations for development or change of urban land use determined the content of the plans for other branches of local government.

Paper presented at the "European Meeting on Applied Urban Research," Essen, Oct. 2-4-1981.

This experience totally changed the aim of my research project (Floderus, 1981). The question I put myself was: can Local Authorities control urban development and, if so, how do they carry it out? The method of research was to work alternately with observations of Local Authority actions and construction of a frame of reference for better theoretical understanding of what they were actually doing.

Changed conditions for urban planning

Local Authorities make efforts to control a process of urbanization that is generated by forces outside their domain of influence. They have a decisive influence on the supply of sites, housing and public services, but they have very little to say about the demand for these utilities. When the demand is considerably greater than the supply, this will cause them trouble, as there is a constant pressure on them to meet the demand. From the point of view of control, however, the situation is not very complicated. They have to draw up plans for new projects and implement them as fast as they can. As far as implementation is dependent on the provision of state loans and municipal land, regional governmental bodies and Local Authorities can control the urban development by giving higher or lower priority to projects.

From the beginning of the seventies, the pace of urbanization has slackened considerably. The supply of housing and services in some regions and sectors is greater than the current demand. In this situation the priorities of consumers will play a larger role. Households migrating to urban regions of southern and central Sweden during the fifties and sixties that were accommodated in the new suburbs, are now attempting to the best of their ability to realize their own ideas of a good home. This is often a small house outside or on the fringe of the urban area or a summer house which the owner can rebuild for permanent use himself.

The present situation offers Local Authorities another kind of negotiation than they had to handle during the sixties. Instead of an agreement with a developer or a contractor to produce, for instance, 100-500 dwellings, there is in some communities a session of negotiations for every other new dwelling. The applicant is less often than before a building owner, acting on the part of anonymous consumers; it is more often the head of a household who is just on the point of realizing his dream of a good home for himself and his family. This situation is not foreseen in the so-called rational process of physical planning, where urban development is determined by long-term comprehensive plans.

Preparatory project planning and strategic planning

The idea of a planned urban environment, in which the development of the urban area is supposed to be outlined in comprehensive development plans ten to twenty years ahead and implemented in detailed town plans and project designs, was codified in the Building Act of 1947. The intention of the legislators was that master plans should be granted by the Government before implementation. In practice master plans were very seldom given this firm authority, and only then in strictly limited parts. The concept of a hierarchy of plans has nevertheless played a large role in normative thinking regarding urban planning.

The concept of comprehensive planning, as it was introduced in the Building Act, can be characterized as a preparatory project planning process. The total urban area is regarded as a large "project' for the authorities. It is presupposed that the principal of the plan disposes of the resources necessary for the implementation, or that all bodies with influence on the implementation will come to an agreement regarding the content of the plan. In order to reduce the uncertainty of the planning process, the planner has to gain more information on and better control over the operating environment, the evaluations of the constituency and the intentions of contiguous policy systems (Friend et al., 1974).

A different concept of planning can be characterized as a strategic planning process. The planner is aware of the fact that he has not all the means necessary for the implementation of a comprehensive plan at his disposal. Uncertainty regarding the intentions of other policy systems is inevitable. The area of uncertainty includes the market behaviour of households and firms. The strategic plan will not be an image of a future state that is very unlikely to be realized, but a frame of reference for Local Authorities and other bodies to identify current public interests and work out strategies for how to use the means available for them to look after these interests in a continuous process of negotiating and bargaining.

Political, administrative and financial domains of influence

The elected bodies of the municipality make decisions based on the authority inherent in their political supremacy and are responsible to the municipality's electorate. Certain of the municipal authorities, e.g., the Building Committee, function as judicial administrative bodies and base their power on laws and regulations. Property owners and beneficial owners have authority and financial responsibility for the use and maintenance of the property. Major changes in the usage of land necessitate coordinated decisions from these three parties, and the decision-makers are interdependent of each others' +actions. Political and administrative decisions are taken by public bodies. Financial decisions on the usage of property are taken by public bodies only to the extent that they are landowners themselves. The main part of urban and rural land is privately owned.

The fields of political, administrative and financial decision-making concerning property are not in principle opposed to each other. Political credibility, lawfulness and economic feasibility are criteria which must in one way or another be fulfilled. In specific cases, however, opposing interests can become relevant, when there are limitations on the fulfillment of policies. The implication of the statement that neither political, nor administrative or financial criteria can be given general priority in decisions on land use is that all efforts to design generally applicable manuals for such decision processes are doomed to fail. The limitations on the fulfillment of criteria are always related to the specific situation. When an interested party claims a change of, for instance, land use a state of instability occurs. The role for the planning administration is to negotiate and find solutions that, at least temporarily, restore a stable state with due observance to the criteria relevant to the specific situation. The concept of the public administration as a controlling and stabilizing system in a cybernetic sense is discussed in detail with special reference to urban issues by McLoughlin (1973).

The course of the negotiations

Negotiations for development or change in the use of urban land take place between representatives of those claiming a change and of those interested in preserving status quo. Instigators of change, as far as buildings are concerned, are private or public building owners. The authorized representative of conservative interests is the

Building Committee, in some cases regional or national state bodies. In the following these parties will be named the "builders" and the "authorities". When the preferences of builders and authorities as to type and location of building projects do not completely coincide, the initial state of negotiation can be illustrated as in fig. 2.1. The efforts of the authorities to control urban development are aimed at hindering undesired projects from being realized and promoting the realization of desired projects (Floderus, 1979).

In order to implement a project, it is necessary to find a solution that can be accepted by both builders and authorities (Fig. 2.2). The minimum requirements of a positive result are that the builder will find the approved project at least better than no project at all, and the authorities will find it less costly to approve the project than to forbid it. The parties can, of course, also agree on solutions which both find quite satisfactory, though they differ from the initial preferences of any or both of them.

It should be noticed that the word "negotiation" is used here in a wide sense. An application from a builder which is immediately approved by the authorities, can be said to have passed without negotiation. The coincidence of preferences may, however, be due to the fact that either the builder or the authorities, or both, have at an early stage of their own planning processes foreseen and taken into account the presumed preferences of the opposite party. Thus "negotiations" can be said to have taken place without formal contacts between the parties. In this wider sense, "negotiations" can also be said to occur between, for example, producers and consumers on the market.

Means of local authority control

When the authorities succeed in promoting projects that would not otherwise have been implemented, they do this either by effectively constraining all other projects or by making desired projects more attractive in the eyes of the builders. In reality, Local Authorities combine these methods. In areas where they wish to prevent building, they apply restrictive legal means of control. They have also certain means of making building outside urban districts less attractive by raising the charges for technical services, such as clearing snow or emptying sewage pits. In areas where Local Authorities prefer development, they acquire land, make investments in a service network and offer building sites at prices that the buyers may find attractive enough to change their initial preferences.

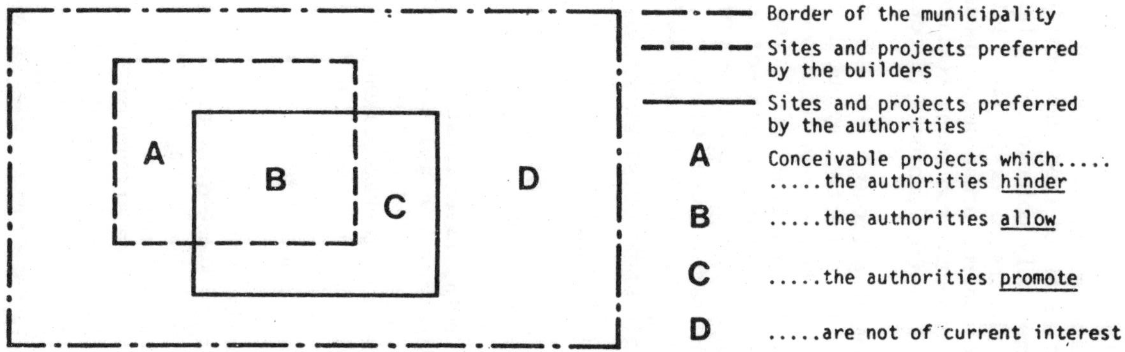

Fig. 2.1 : The attitudes of builders and authorities towards conceivable projects in defferent locations.

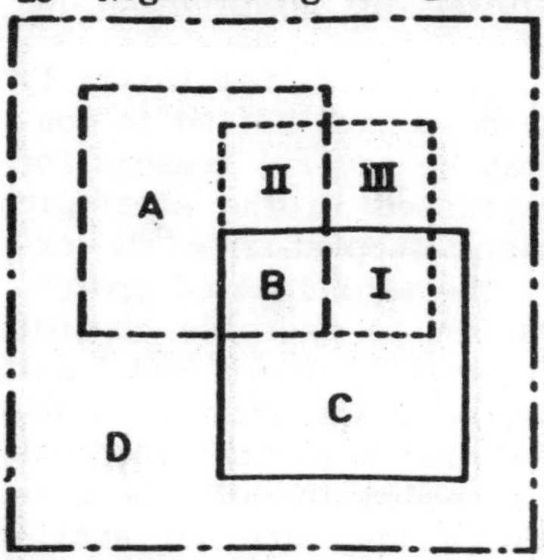

2 A

A feasible project has to be accepted by both the builder and the authorities, which means that it has to belong to category B (See fig. 1). Conceivable projects in any of the categories C, A or D (I, II or III) can after negotiations be included in category B, if either the builder, the authorities or both parties change their attitudes.

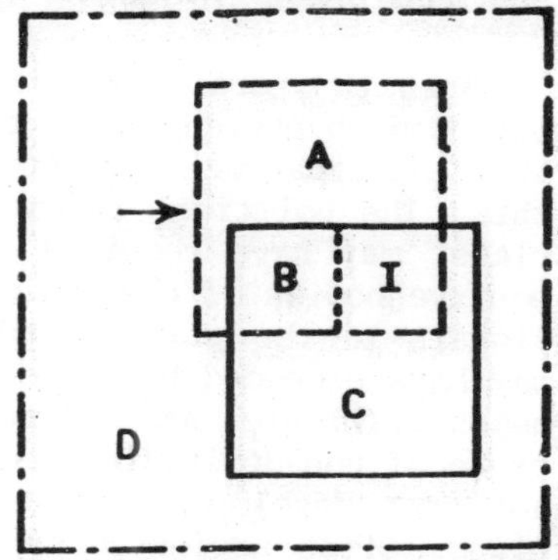

2 B

If the <u>builder</u> changes his attitude as a result of the negotiations, this means that the authorities have succeeded in promoting a project that would not otherwise have occurred. Projects that earlier belonged to category C (I) have been included in category B.

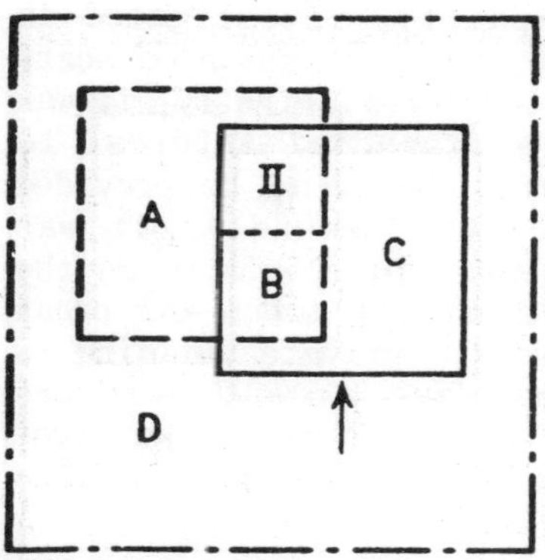

2 C

If the <u>authorities</u> change their attitude, this means that they give permission to a project which they tried to hinder at the beginning of the negotiations. Projects that earlier belonged to category A (II) have been included in category B.

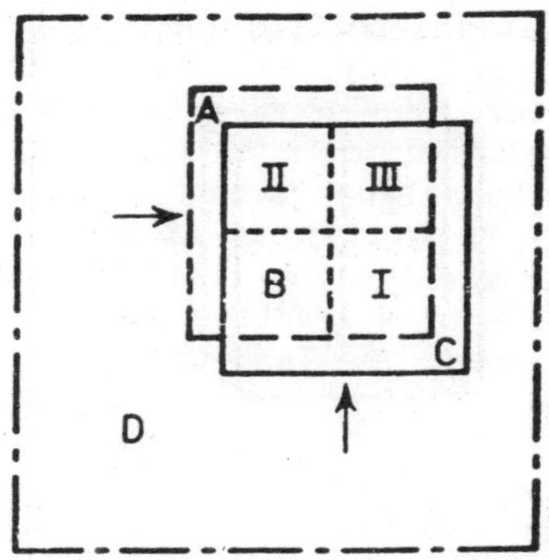

2 D

If the possibility of a new site or project comes up during the course of the negotiations, both the <u>builders</u> and the the <u>authorities</u> may change their initial preferences. Projects that earlier belonged to category D (III) have been included in category B.

Fig. 2.2. Alternative results of negotiations between builders and authorities.

When the Local Authorities allow projects they initially intended to prevent, they can be said to have failed to control the urban development. There may be several reasons for this. The political intentions, expressed in the strategic plans, may have received insufficient support from the executive bodies of the municipality. The ambitions of professionals in the planning administration to exercise control may have exceeded both the aims of the politicians and legal means available. Another reason for Local Authorities to approve of non-desired projects may be that municipal land has not been developed to the extent intended in comprehensive plans. Sites preferred by Local Authorities are not available when the demand for new housing is acute. However, a change in priorities on the side of the Local Authorities should not always be regarded as a failure. A reason for the authorities to constrain location of new housing outside the urban area may be a fear of claims for expensive public investment. In the negotiations they may, however, have come to an agreement with the developer or the building owner regarding the financial conditions for an exploitation.

Local authority control in practice

The politicians of the municipality, investigated in this study, saw two main reasons to restrict unwanted scattered development outside the built-up area. Firstly, it was claimed to be in the municipality's financial interest to channel new urbanization into areas that could be provided with utilities at foreseeable costs. Secondly, it was claimed to be in the communal interest to economize on the use of attractive land on the outskirts of towns and urban areas. The land primarily in demand for private building is also attractive for recreational purposes. In a planned expansion of urbanization it is this land that is in the first place likely to be reserved for parks and other public utilities.

The politicians in power deemed it in the interest of the majority of citizens in this municipality to constrain what they regarded as urban sprawl. They made a basic decision to forbid new construction outside planned areas within a zone approximately covering an area that could be reached by car from the central community within ten or twelve minutes. The restriction on building in this zone was based on the regulation in the Building Act which states that urban exploitation of land should be preceded by a development plan.

All applications received during one year for building within the restricted zone were examined in the study. Most of the applicants refrained from building or applied in other areas, either at a greater distance from the urban core or in areas subject to a plan. A large proportion of the applicants, however, argued their cases energetically and put forward specific reasons for their wish to build on the site they had selected. In many cases, the Building Committee finally approved to their applications. Sometimes the applicants appealed against the Building Committee's decision to the Regional Council or even to the Government. In most cases, but not always, these higher courts of appeal supported the decision of the Building Committee. The variable and inconsistent application of the law was regarded as unsatisfactory by both politicians and local government officials.

It is obvious that if a political decision to channel all new construction into planned areas is to be implemented by legal means of control in each individual case, it must be given the form of an unambiguous prohibition. A general intention to economize on land use is not sufficient as a basis for decisions in the individual case. It must be implemented in the form of an authorized plan.

A plan differentiating between land that may or may not be built on will affect the property market assuming, of course, that there is a demand for the land. The greater the importance placed by Local Authorities on the need to economize on the use of attractive land and to maintain control over public investment, the more they are obliged to limit access to new building sites. If the supply of approved sites is at all times considerably greater than the demand, it will not be possible to channel new construction into the areas given highest priority by the Local Authorities.

When Local Authorities at the directing level of the planning administration decide to, very strictly, channel the demand for new housing into certain areas, the pressure from applicants at the implementing level increases. In addition, when the restrictions against new construction cover a large, sparsely built-up area, the effect of a single approved building permit seems insignificant. We find that the more restrictive Local Authorities are at the directing policy level, the weaker seem their arguments to justify these restrictions in each individual case, and the stronger is the applicant's interest in having his site approved. So the municipal defence against urban sprawl caves in at the implementing level of planning administration.

Local Authorities have the possibility of counteracting the effects of a restrictive application approval policy by taking over land themselves, planning it and offering new building sites in sufficient quantities to satisfy demand. This is, in fact, what a majority of Swedish municipalities do. By acquiring land at a relatively low "undeveloped" land price, they have been able to offer new building sites at regulated prices, and in most areas become price leaders for building land where it, nota bene, is a question of sites of equal quality to those offered on the open property market. In their attempts to maintain control over land prices, Local Authorities have co-operated with the Regional Housing Boards, who via mortgage policies control construction costs for housing based on state loans.

The municipal reserves of land consist primarily of rural property outside previously built-up areas, mainly suitable for large scale exploitation. It is obvious in the study, however, that builders' preferences are directed to sparsely built-up rural areas, such as vacant sites in old villages. To meet this demand Local Authorities would have to make development plans not on undeveloped land but for sparsely built-up areas.

There exists in the municipality investigated sparsely built-up areas where there is no current need for e.g., common water supply or a sewage purification plant. Some of these areas are, however, approaching a state when the need for such amenities is becoming acute. The Local Authority is reluctant to prepare development plans in such areas, for the following reasons.

A plan that differentiates between land that may be built on and land that may not, creates differences in land values not existing before the plan was established. The higher values of land favoured by the plan cannot be equally distributed among landowners. There will be "windfalls and wipeouts", and those treated disfavourably will object to the plan and most often appeal to higher courts (Hagman et al., 1978). It will take years to finally have the plan approved. If the plan is approved the Local Authority will be obliged to provide the planned area with a water and sewage network and charge the landowners according to current rates. These rates, however, are calculated and approved by the administrator of government housing loans on the basis of costs in new urban areas. In these comprehensively planned areas, common amenities can be introduced more economically than in areas which have grown dense over a period of time. The Local Authorities therefore have to bear a larger proportion of the costs.

The price for a site in a municipally owned area, or in an area where the construction is implemented according to a contract between the Local Authority and a developer, includes the price of surrounding open space and public facilities. In previously sparsely built-up areas the price of a site on the property market will be at least equal to, and often higher than in municipally owned areas. If open space and public facilities are, however, to be provided the Local Authority will have to purchase additional land.

New sites on municipally owned land are usually distributed between private building owners according to a waiting list. In built-up areas where the land is privately owned, Local Authorities do not have the possibility to control the distribution of building sites. They have usually not the financial and administrative capacity to act on the property market in built-up areas in favour of those who have difficulties in obtaining an approved site. The establishment of a plan in a built-up area would therefore not entirely relieve the pressure on the Building Committee to approve applications for scattered construction outside the urban areas.

Parties interested in the use of land

Studies of Local Authority action in practice and interviews with local politicians and officials gave insight into the motives for municipal policies. The next step of the research work was to analyze the roles of the participants in the context of interests in the development and management stages of urban areas and the existing rules of the game balancing these interests.

The negotiations between Local Authorities and building owners or land developers take place during the stage of development. How the participants define their interests and evaluate acceptable or not acceptable offers depends on the roles they will play and the responsibilities they will have to take on during the stage of management, when the urban environment is used and maintained.

During the latest decades the responsibility of Local Authorities for the provision of services in urban areas has increased considerably. As owners of public housing companies they have also obtained a vested interest in the housing market. This has led to claims for stronger means of control on the part of Local Authorities when decisions of critical importance for urban development are taken. The legislators have met these claims by gradually changing the rules of the game at the stage of development.

Participants and opposing interests at the development and management stages are illustrated in Fig 2.3 Both the presumptive users of new buildings, such as households and companies, and those with an economic and professional interest in building activities, such as developers and contractors, are identical with or allied to the building owner as instigator of change of land use. The Building Committee with the charge to look after that conservative interests be paid attention to, as far as these interests are observed in current legislation, is the opponent. Allied to the Building Committee, there are those who in a specific case prefer status quo, e.g., participants in current land use and owners of existing housing and other premises, who have reason to fear that the implementation of a new project would adversely affect the value of their property. This will occur if new construction spoils the environment, but property owners can also fear new construction for the reason that they determine the demand for new housing or other premises being already satisfied.

It should be noticed that the participants scheduled in the table represent opposing interests in principle. In practice, the range of states of negotiation may vary from full understanding to direct confrontation between the parties.

At the management stage, providers and consumers of housing and public services represent opposing interests. These interests are adapted to each other through political processes, market mechanisms or formal negotiations. Examples of services the price and quality of which is decided entirely through political procedures, are technical services in housing areas, such as streets and sewers. In other sectors, e.g., public transport, the behaviour of the consumer on the market influences to some extent the supplier. Formal negotiations take place between the landlords and tenants' associations in order to arrive at agreements on rents for housing.

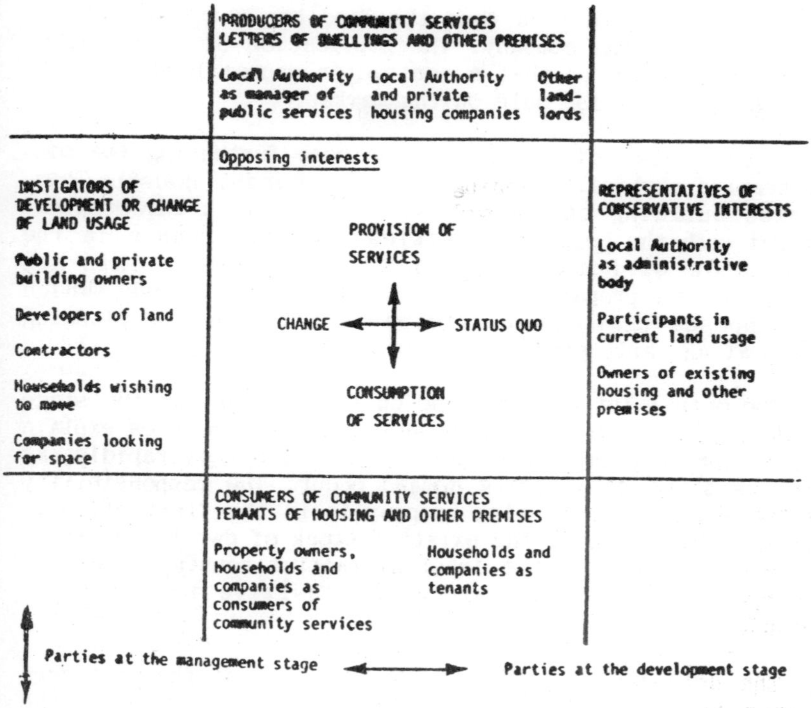

Fig. 2.3 Participants and opposing interests at the development and the management stages of the built-up environment

According to the Building Act of 1947, Local Authorities have the right to claim that urban development shall be preceded by a development plan. Before granting a plan, Local Authorities can draw up a contract with the developer to carry his share of the costs of providing the new area with necessary utilities. This means, as far as the configuration of interests is concerned, that the opposing participants at the stage of development unite themselves as providers of public services at the management stage. The land developer and the Local Authority have a common interest in the economic efficiency of the development plan.

Another step was to unite the interest of the building owner with that of the housing company. According to an amendment in 1975 to the rules governing the granting of state housing loans, such loans are granted only for building on land leased or sold by the municipality for development. In addition, state loans are only granted when tendering contractors have offered the building for purchase. Exception is made, however, for single-family houses built by the owner, on condition that the land has not been sold to him by a building company. The implication of these amendments to the law is that a contractor cannot build a house with state loans for sale on the market.

These rules of the game have been furthering the comprehensive physical planning of new suburbs. Housing companies building on undeveloped land are to a large extent united with the Local Authorities as participants in the provision of housing and public services. This has facilitated a preparatory project planning process, which presupposes that the participants agree on the planning goals at an early stage of the process.

The mutual interests of the building owners at the stage of development and the established housing companies explain why the production of new housing decreases very rapidly, as soon as signs of yielding demand occur. The responsibility of the owners of a housing company is in the first place to maintain the value of the existing stock of dwellings. Those companies managing the least attractive housing stock, in the eyes of the tenants, are most sensitive to a fall in demand.

The decline in activity on the part of the providers leaves the initiative of change in the hands of the households acting on the property market. These households are not liable to share the interests of Local Authorities and take part in a preparatory project planning process on these conditions. During the stage of management, households will be entirely on the consumer's side in negotiations.

Political and administrative credibility

An initiative on the part of a building owner brings Local Authorities into a state of negotiation. The goal of the building owner is quite clear. He wishes to implement his project within the range of his resources. But what is at stake for the negotiators on the opposite side of the table?

In the more elaborate normative descriptions of the process of physical planning, the goals of public administration are often exemplified in the form of a checklist. It is said to be a public responsibility to preserve the value of the natural and the built-up environment, to further health, security and comfort, to watch over the urban development so that built-up areas are provided with sufficient public services at reasonable costs and so on.

These lists give some information regarding current issues in discussions on urban quality but no good answer to the question; "What's at stake for Local Authorities?"

Local Authorities have nothing to gain in these negotiations as the claims on them are ultimative. They are supposed to bring the best to all and everybody at the lowest possible costs. All they can obtain by bargaining is to minimize their losses. These losses are not only, not even in first place, of an economic nature. What is at stake for the local politicians and officials is the credibility of their wielding of political and judicially administrative power.

The credibility of a politician rests upon his ability to live up to the expectations of his voters. As far as urban development is concerned, these expectations have to do with a well functioning housing and property market, healthy and attractive surroundings, sufficient public services at the cost of reasonable taxes. These concepts are interpreted differently by different groups of citizens. By conflicting goals in a situation of bargaining, the politician must correctly determine the strength of opposing interests and make the sacrifices that cost him the least of credibility among his own voters.

The credibility of an administrator rests on impartiality. His reputation will suffer if the public has cause to suspect that similar cases are not treated similarly. The administrators require unambiguous instructions of how to distinguish between lawful and unlawful changes of land use. From the administrator's point of view, there shall be no discrimination with regard to the various goals of different groups of citizens.

Further studies of conflicts on land use

In spite of the incompatibility of the political and judicial aspects of public power, Local Authorities are assumed to behave as a united organization. I think that there are two main reasons why the schizophrenic nature of the claims on Local Authorities is so clear in situations of conflict on the use of land. Firstly, the interests of the participants on both sides are very strong. Investments in housing and other premises are of utmost importance for both the private households and the taxpayers. Secondly, the participants on both sides are often strong enough to articulate their claims, which draws the attention of the public to these conflicts.

My further studies will be aimed at the exploration of a sample of documented conflicts on land use, handled by political and administrative bodies at different levels of authority. The outcome for the different parties of a conflict will be explained by analyzing resources and motives of public and private actors, seen in the light of prevailing social and institutional conditions and in relation to the specific issue and situation in which their interests are at stake.

REFERENCES

Floderus, A., Local Authority Control of Urban Development. In: **Research Into Local Planning Processes** (A report from a Colloquium in Sweden 1979), pp 215-225. Swedish Council for Building Research, Stockholm, 1979.

Floderus, A., **Kan Kommunen styra bebyggelseutvecklingen?** (Can Local Authorities Control Urban Development?) Byggforskningsradet, Stockholm, 1981. (Available in Swedish only.)

Friend, J. K., Power, J. M., Yewlett, C. J. L., **Public Planning, the Intercorporate Dimension**, Tavistock Institute of Human Relations, London, 1974.

Hagman, D. G., Mysczynski, D. J. **Windfalls for Wipeouts; Land Value Capture & Compensation**, ASPO Press, Chicago, 1978.

McLoughlin, B, **Control and Urban Planning**, Faber & Faber Ltd, London, 1973.

THREE

Nandeshwar Sharma

On Aspects of Master Plan in City Planning Context

MASTER PLAN AS ALL INCLUSIVE A TERM

Planning happens to be at all stages in its variegated standard. It frequents the actions at individual, family, regional, national and international stages with its due honour. It acquires the nature of differing standards, in accordance with the intensity and dimension of purpose, in being of short-term or long-term duration, of advocacy, structure or strategy, new or action and system, plan approach nature, Master plan assumes the nature of all inclusiveness in the sense that it tends to master mind the task of striking a balance of various and often conflicting considerations as associated with different plan approaches. It justifies its all inclusiveness by virtue of its ability to include all aspects and facts of human life and action: whether it be a plan for impounding deep sea fishes, whether it be a plan for penetrating into the womb of the earth to extract the 'liquid gold'–petroleum, 'black diamond'–coal and other minerals of concern, whether it be a plan for launching satellites into space, whether it be a plan for directing action to any direction among many ones.

MASTER PLAN AS AN EXCLUSIVE TERM IN CITY PLANNING CONTEXT

Master plan as an exclusive term stands to refer to its application to the art and science of building and rebuilding or making over of urban centres. In its spirit and contents it tends to assume the dimension of all comprehensiveness and the term is often identified interchangeably with comprehensive city plan and general plan. It, however, shows inclination to confirm its identity with comprehensive city plan, but distinguishes its separate identity from a general plan, in incorporating varied non-governmental applications which absent from the latter signifying a long-range, comprehensive planning exclusively by or for a government agency within specific corporate limits. In definitive perspective master plan may be accepted as all exclusive a term to refer to all inclusive a design for city's making over in respect of its physico-social and politico-economic conditions of workability and habitability assuming the ever containing dimension and complicity of time motion and space. It is in this exclusive form that the term master plan in its various manifestations of issues and tasks has found deliberations in city planning context.

CITIES' DAYS' CRISES AND CONCERN

Urban evolution did mark, and even does so, the creation of a visual event. Cities - the physical outcome of the visual event_signify today to be the fair game to the creative mind. The game lured human mind for quite a long time. The present modern technology geared, however, such an acceleration to the pace of urbanisation in terms of dimensions of time, motion and space that cities proved to be elements of not merely unmixed blessings. They signify a visual event leading to maximisation of structures, minimisation of open spaces and elimination of **Nature** plaguing themselves by physical congestion and socio-economic deterioration. It seems, therefore, nothing astonishing that traditionally attached to the **Nature** or wide open environment most men have started thinking cities as places "nice to visit but not to live in" as places "pestilential to the morals, the health and the liberties" of their inmates and as places signifying "pandora's box of ills and evils"; the visual event in terms of "Urban crisis" and "Urban chaos" and the urbanisation as "a major international problem". The descriptions referring to the visual event at stake or the fair game to the creative mind add possible note of pessimism. Already afloat are dire predictions that by the time the present century rolls itself the conditions of habitability and workability will go the extent of unbearability and unless ameliorative steps are taken soon, the pessimists may well withhold the belief.

Cities' existence and evolution may be taken for granted to be all time reality. The issue of concern remains, thus, connected with the events of building and rebuilding or making over of cities_the events again being fair game to creative mind. The concern of concern that emerges, however, pins into issues of building cities to what number, of what dimension and of what quality? and those of making over of cities to what degree? to what nature? and to what direction? City considered to be the elemental emit 'of planning and the object of planning being the adequate dramatisation of communal life' makes it obligatory not to think of "one goal, but a direction": "One plan, once for all, but the conscious selection by the people of successive plans" while planning the master plan making process in city planning context.

PLANNING OF THE MASTER PLAN MAKING PROCESS IN CITY PLANNING CONTEXT

Planning being 'mental preparation for action' and visual events 'for game to creative mind' make it plausible for plan making process to think the issues and tasks of planning before the master plan is created and to rehearse its implications before the plan is enacted. The gamut of master planning making process envisages action to initiate with the stage of perception, to emulate with the stages of diagnosis and prescription and to terminate with the stage of evaluation. The gamut contemplating the actions at stages has been attempted to be portrayed with the help of diagrammatic model (Fig. 3.1).

WHERE SHOULD A MASTER PLAN AIM AT

Following the dictum "it must be thought before it is created" it approaches rationality in deciding where should a master plan aim at? It, thus, becomes the task of making search for plan objectives, which are in no case few but many, simple but complex and universally contained but subjectively framed. People and facilities combine to frame what may be termed as urban anatomy. Central objectives underlying a master plan in city planning context should strive for a townscape in physical through either creation or correction, so as to meet the ego of optimists and to desist the belief of pessimists of city environment. This means a master plan must centrally aim at providing a person an environment of highest order amenity, beauty, safety, convenience and serenity to glorify the city conditions of liveability and workability.

From such an intrinsic central objective emits an array of general objectives bearing relevance to actions of plan maker. The urban anatomy that a city develops, largely becomes the result of behavioural interplay of various use claimants of its land: place of habitat, place of work and place of leisure dominating the scene. These claimants usually come into use conflict in time and space dimension proving detrimental to the cause in meeting the spirit of central objective. The condition necessitates for the master plan to aim at use space rapprochement among dominant groups of aspirants for land occupancy. General objectives of use conflict elimination by applying both preventive and corrective measures should be comprehended in the perspective of use space rapprochement model (Fig. 3.2).

In apperceive term a master plan should aim at: (1) creative actions in making provisions for adequate scope for the development of new areas in conformity with the need of accommodation of ever increasing dimensions of users of land; (ii) corrective and preventive actions to guide an orderly, efficient and attractive development of the city under the effective role of regulation and control, (iii) suggestive actions to release the maximum comfort for community by augmenting and improving public facilities and (iv) applicative actions to weigh its rationality with reference to issues of implementation, folk-value implication, use conflict elimination and resource provision. The essence of a master plan lies, therefore, in its being in a position to determine the city's desirable future development exhibiting an appropriate relation among different users of land, people and facilities and all that in a scale with the expected growth of the community and its financial resources.

WHAT SHOULD A MASTER PLAN CONSTITUTE

Having such broad-based objectives a master plan necessarily turns into a comprehensive scheme in city planning context. In its comprehensive frame it should constitute: (i) a wholesome and reasonably spacious lay out of the sites and structures to accommodate people, functions and facilities; (ii) a co-ordinated programme of development over fixed period of time so as to ensure the longevity and continuity to existing city elements; (iii) a pragmatic legal frame-work for the successful accomplishment of the programme with reference to (a) a sensible control over existing elements, (b) co-ordination between public and private interests, (c) conservation of valuable elements in the urban texture, (d) elimination of use conflict within the framework of proper standards of development and (e) comprehension of a well defined fiscal programme; (iv) a specific layout indicating problem areas and identifying priority of actions and (v) a regional frame of the plan to ensure provision for balanced and appropriate distribution of services and resources to put city into regional scale.

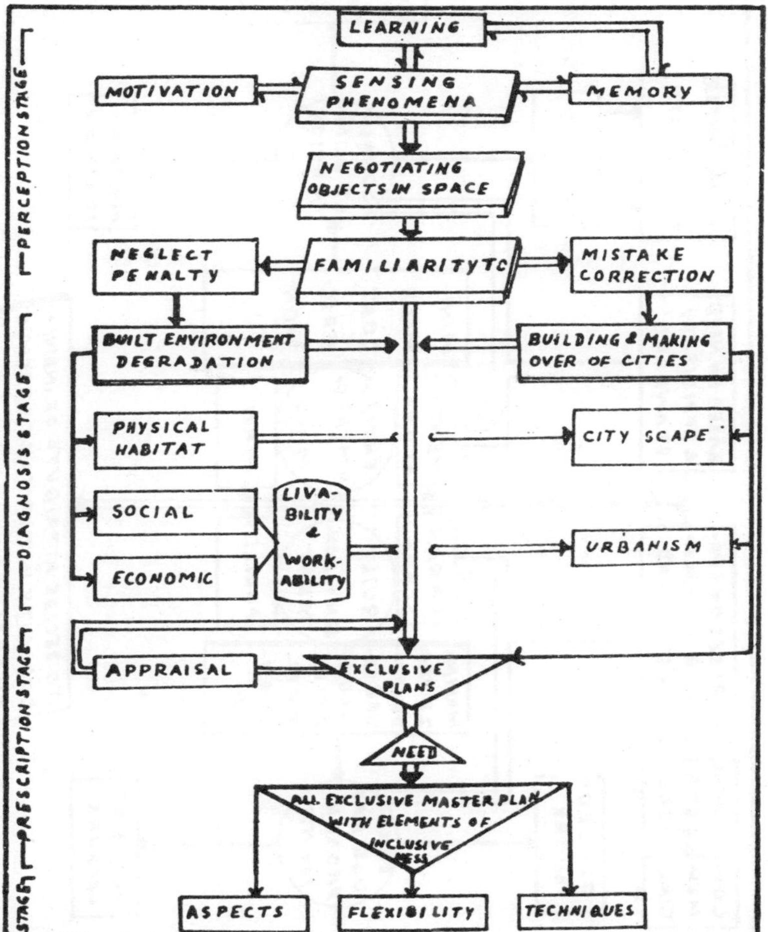

FIG. 3.1

PLANNING THE MASTER PLAN MAKING PROCESS

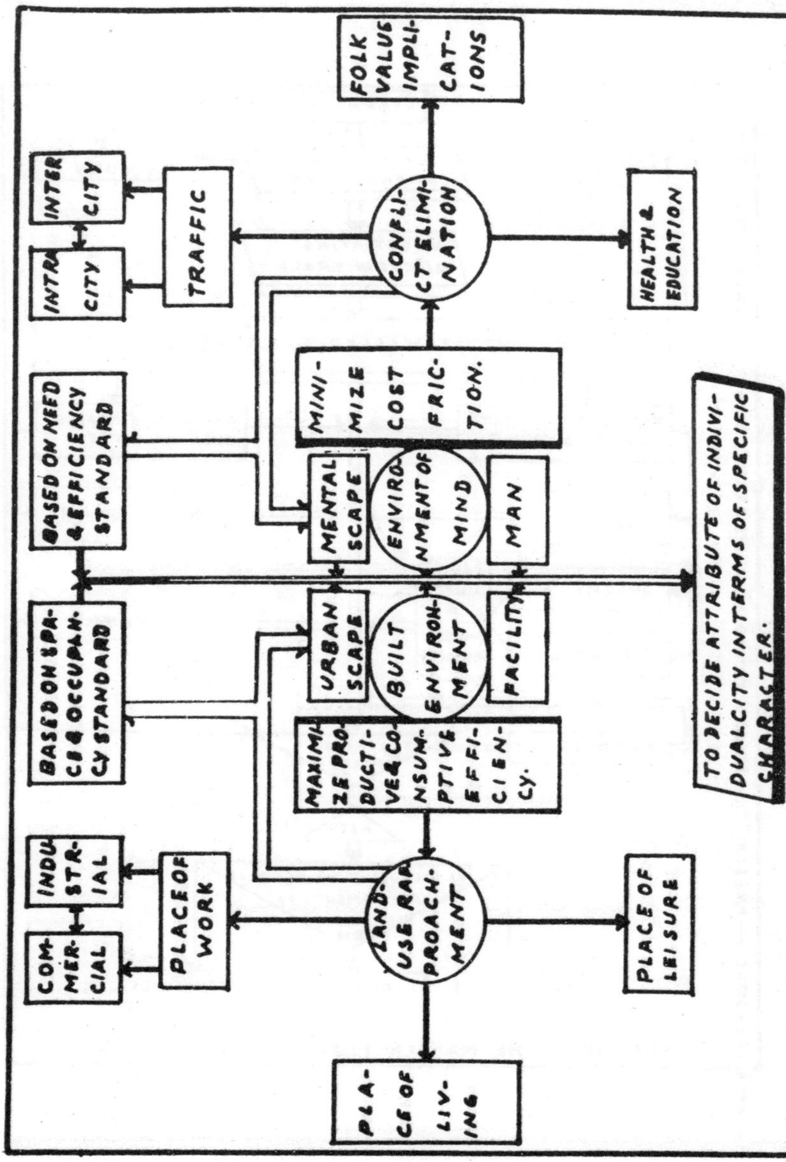

FIG. 3.2 USE SPACE RAPPROACHMENT MODEL

WHAT SHOULD A MASTER PLAN BE LIKE

Different constituents of a master plan as framed in perfect consonance with the objectives combine to suggest some definite form of it which is comprehended to be: (i) a balanced design suited to present and desirably future needs; (ii) in scale with the population and economic prospects of the community; (iii) in scale keeping with both the present and prospective financial resources; (iv) in a position to show the unsatisfactory conditions of today and way of correction to satisfy needs of tomorrow; (v) equipped itself for effective operation of the plan and (vi) a reasonably stable but not inflexible guide towards the development of the community.

WHAT OPERATIONAL PHILOSOPHY A MASTER PLAN INVOLVES

Most cities are by and large diseased. They deplorably lack productive and consumptive efficiency. They need a treatment which must involve some operational philosophy. The comprehensiveness of a master plan in terms of its objective, constitution and appearance attaches significance to it to be reckoned with in city planning context for all time to come and for all places to occur. The importance of master plan makes it imperative, therefore, to conceptualize the operational philosophy of it. The operational philosophy that a master plan should involve has been grafted to evolve a conceptual model (Fig. 3.3).

The model attempts to mastermind the sequential operations involved in the formulation of a master plan in city planning concept. The operational philosophy, as the model conceptualized, involves: (i) confirmation of the disease; (ii) resolution to treat the disease; (iii) dissection through the symptoms of the disease in temporal perspectives; (iv) treatment through prescription and operation in the creation of the master plan in question and suggestion for evaluation and effectuation of the plan.

The model, thus framed, involves a planning mechanism in which issues as related to decision making, fact finding and action receive due weight. The disease being recognised and the treatment being decided, the master plan formulation, in its methodological frame, must reasonably be preceded by a detailed survey into physical, demographic and economic attributes, in terms of the degrees of adequacies and inadequacies, i.e., personification of individual city with reference to its attribute possessed with specific character. Survey, thus, happens to be the essence of the plan formulation because it represents a way of bringing a system into the impression, gained empirically, of the city.

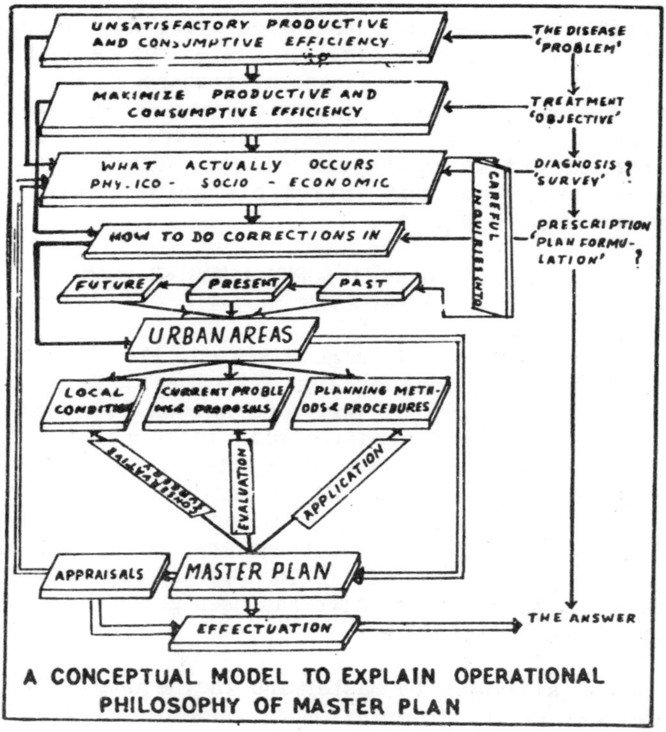

FIG. 3.3

The effectiveness of any plan tends to be the function of the composition of survey which is to be outlined anew for different cities in accordance with the nature of the unit which is the replica of its physical conditions, social behaviour, economic traits and its orientation towards functional activities. Survey, however, as proposed to assist a development plan of the nature befitting a master plan in city planning context may be outlined to be envisaged to encompass a scope comprising information on:

(i) **Base Map**: sectional as well as regional will maps_up to date in all respects;

(ii) **Urban setting**; site_geological, structural, lithological sub-terranean and topographical; situation—climatic and regional setting;

(iii) **Demographic**: characteristics as relevant to population and demographic attributes and trends in such characteristics;

(iv) **Economic Base**: basic and non-basic functions—the relative importance of, and trends in, income producing activities, productive and service industries, their location, type and growth;

(v) **Land Use**; use classes—compatibility and conflict, land occupancy and structures, adequacies and inadequacies, land values and trends in land utilisation, vacant land study;

(vi) **Intra-city and inter city movement**: traffic, transit and transportation—volume, pattern, conditions, adequacies and inadequacies;

(vii) **Utilities and facilities**; leisure-time facilities, educational, health, safety, household amenities and

(viii) **City legislation**; Zoning legislation, subdivision legislation, control regulations and local administration.

The set of informations will release the picture of the city in concern reflecting its conditions in terms of what exists. This provides the stage the master plan formulation begins at. A condition where most of what exists on the surface happens to be amicable, facilitates a start on what is practically a clean sheet. These cases the task. In most cases, however, things have drifted into an appalling muddle posing a serious challenge to the plan formulation action. The plan formulation action involves, therefore, tasks of (i) the creation of a design on practically a clean sheet on the one hand and (ii) the correction of things in existence with reference to community of interest and purpose on the other. The plasticity of the action yields a few philosophical phrases. A master plan has been, on the basis of which, advised to be a characteristic design having the qualities of adaptability or flexibility under altered conditions, economy, and practicability or feasibility. The veracity of the design is, however, often fraught with the dangers from such platitudes in view of the physical structure of any city being neither flexible nor mobile. The applicability of a master plan can not always be decided with reference to its economy because the plan's prime concern rests with the facilities and men put to change in temporal dimension. This concern allows any master plan to stand the test of applicability only when it encompasses the nature and volume of creation, correction and suggestion to complete the city environment in the light of the need and efficiency standards on the one hand and the space and occupancy standards on the other. Any completed environment will have to be subjected to diverse stress during its life cycle. This causes the same to cease to function as system, subsystem and space adaptable to new demands. Means at this point must be found to facilitate its timely replacement. Budgeted economy often has been seen to affect the implementation of plan directions in the form of patchwork with limited need-oriented decisions. This does not often prove economical. A master plan is after all to make over a city to function to meet a set of demands thrust upon it in its central role to acquire eminence in a region on the one hand and to improve its quality to reverberate as place in which men are to live and work on the other. The efficiency to which the effectuation of a master plan is to be linked must adequately be examined with reference to the very nature of the plan to be a process and not just a conducive statement.

FOUR

B. K. Roy

A Census Oriented Study of Carto-Spatial Model on Temporal Land Use in a Million City

A Case of Lucknow Urban Agglomeration (India)

PROLOGUE

In recent years especially after the introduction of the town and country planning movement in India some interesting trends in the regularisation of environment and related aspects of local and regional areas were initiated. In this planning process, the Third Five Year Plan had emphasised the importance of urban development and provided assistance to prepare master plans of selected areas.[1] Sometimes the dimensions were set to analyse either in a descripti.e system or cartographic system to establish various trends within such regions. Both the techniques sometimes rendered either way supplementary or in cases explanatory of the nature of problems where the reasoning of time and growth relation is difficult to support the pattern and trend of status of such areas.

Considering the scope of an evaluatory study to reveal a mosaic of landscape in local areas of towns and urban agglomerations in Indian census, a thought was given to construct land use maps of such areas with reference to time; in this case, this reference was 1st April, 1971 in the Indian census context. A mapping effort with this view was taken up in the 1971 census of India to prepare and publish maps for towns having population 50,000 and above on uniform land use classification in defined boundaries of each area.[2]

In the present census of 1981, this attempt is revived to construct urban land use maps with reference date of 1st March, 1981. These materials will again be published in the programme of the Town Directories of 1981. Latest census data and a series of non-census statistics would also be provided to the users of research and planning in the publication cited above.

With this background an exercise has been conducted to work out a carto-spatial model of land use change in Lucknow, the capital city of the State of Uttar Pradesh as a case study; a city which has attained million mark population in 1981. The growth of this city between 1971-81 stands at 23.66 per cent with an absolute population of 1,006,538 persons in 1981. The demography of the urban Lucknow is not too complex because it is situated in an undynamic environs of the Gangetic plain. The growth of population is small in Lucknow due to weaknesses in the attraction of migrants.[3] Even the environs in the neighbourhood of Lucknow have traditional agricultural activities and has mostly small and medium market towns with its sphere of influence except Kanpur.[4] It is peculiarly noted that excluding Calcutta, Bombay, Delhi, Madras, Bangalore, Hyderabad and Ahmedabad, the density of population in Lucknow is highest (6897 persons/km^2) among the other million cities. The reason is that Lucknow urban agglomeration is congested and only 27.57 per cent of variation of occupied houses in 1971-81 has occurred. Within this economic influence, the urban agglomeration of Lucknow is indicating certain expansions and the jurisdiction has extended at the census of 1981. The boundaries of towns and cities are defined in each census considering the nature and pattern of local areas to conduct census in India to delimit and enumerate population. With the existing development as gained by a town over time, this aspect required redilimitation of the existing boundary as fixed in the preceding census. The census takes into account the development forces reacting in the rural-urban environs. This connection is basically functional linkage or functional integration. This is established entirely on the subjective and field considerations in a major way. The applied aspect of urban growth is best manifested through the landscape changes in the local areas. Naturally, mapping effort to satisfy this need is enormous. Taking a clue to such resource materials, a model is envisaged here to fix up guidelines to investigate and highlight the nature of urban land uses in a definite time span to assess internal structure of townscape. A pair of maps of Lucknow urban agglomeration is presented with an analysis to diagnose the trend in the urban area in defined categories to help researchers working in the field to take up such studies and bring about patterns for many more urban areas for which resource materials are available so that the consciousness of such vital variables convey attention to planners to establish trend studies.

CONCEPT

The concept of the problem is based on deterministic and probabilistic foundations as a great deal of reverse mapping considering the dynamic patterning of a city organism is involved in this study. In this process, the two most important factors are involved: (i) extension and nature of town and its sub-regions and their relations with fringe in a defined time period in view of the population of non-agricultural occupations and (ii) the inherent population needs for various demands at a local level.[5] Therefore, the strategy of the model as worked out is based on the following considerations: (a) time span of a decade 1971-81 (census years) for temporal explanation and (b) classification and generalisation of land use categories in regions of the local area and its influence on development of the boundary margins resulting in establishing a carto-spatial model for assessing mapping of temporal changes in land use in an area of approximately 141 km^2 of Lucknow urban agglomeration.

To satisfy the above requirements, this study is conditioned by various other traditional formalities such as reconstruction of a base map and generation of date as outlined below to arrive at the testing of the model as presented.

THE BASE

One of the difficulties in the country is the availability of base maps with latest corrections. Besides, invariably, the components of outgrowth (in most cases unplanned) do not have blue prints to work out a general mapping device for analytical studies. Therefore, census faces a problem of constructing full mosaics of the core-regions of the local areas alongwith fringes, outgrowths and new developments. This has to be taken into consideration during the preparatory stage of the conducting of the census to delimit urban areas and urban agglomerations.

The base maps, sometimes very crude, are made to suit census operations and block formation. After a great toil such sheets are worked out and with the cooperation of the technical or public service departments of the corporate bodies convincing base maps are accepted for census operations in general.

With this procedure, a definition, classification for land use are taken by field observations and areas marked to prepare land use maps for selected towns and urban agglomerations with a reference of time as introduced in the foregoing.

DATA GENERATION

One of the drawbacks in such studies is the gap in data recording which is not available for all the land use categories in many cases of towns. The attempt to overcome the difficulty in the present design of investigation compels to calculate data by planimetric measurements on scaled maps by transposing field maps as far as possible giving a scientific cartographic foundation for data generation. In the case of Lucknow, 1:29,800 scale map was worked out and has been utilised for data generation for land use categories as referred to in the text. It is a matter of some anxiety how well this procedure delivers data reliability in calculation but it is claimed that certain degree of consistency is ensured.

On these considerations of map design and data generation, uniform scales have been constructed by mechanical process for narration of land uses with matched classification for census years of 1971 and 1981 in nine categories. This model can be designated as a simple 'Markov Chains' analysis on this theme.

MODEL HYPOTHESIS

(1) Let the proportions of land use categories to total area falling in each class in 1971 and 1981 be represented algebraically as follows :

Classification	Proportion to total area	
	1971	1981
C_1	$.p^1$	$1p^1$
C_2	$.p^2$	$1p^2$
C_3	$.p^3$	$1p^3$
C_9	$.p^9$	$1p^9$

(2) For a matrix with traditional probabilities

$$p_{i_j}$$

where p_{i_j} is the proportion of area moving to the jth classification from the ith. Now let total area 'A' be partitioned into different classifications as per 1971 census against 1981

$$C_1 \quad - \quad A_1$$
$$C_2 \quad - \quad A_2$$

$$C_9 \quad - \quad A_9$$

then $\quad A = \sum_{'i' = 1}^{9} Ai$

considering now the area 'A' under different classification in 1981. Let A_{11} A_{14} .... A_{19} be component area of A_1 falling under these classifications in 1981.

Accordingly, we can derive transitional matrix (Table 4.1) which will provide us with net gain or net loss of areas in respect of each class for 1971 and 1981. A_2 - A_9 should be split up accordingly;

Then

$$p_{i_j} = \frac{A_{i_j} \quad 'i' = 1, \ldots.. 9}{A_i \quad 'j' = 1, \ldots.. 9}$$

These p_{i_j}s will be elements of transitional matrix. From the matrix the maps deduct how different classifications are gaining or losing, i.e., wherefrom and whereto. It may be noted here that the compilation of maps will precede the computations for the matrix as above. It can be even modified as per the suitability of the classifications and need for generation of data for similar analysis.

THE TREND

According to the derivation of mapping and computations through statistical analysis as referred to above, a good deal of trend of adjustment of land uses in Lucknow city can be established. The transitional matrix (Table 4.1) as generated shows (compare Figs. 4.1 & 4.2) that the areas in various land use classifications in the city of Lucknow have been indicating gain or loss and some stationary classes which have not altered for use due to obvious reasons. The numbers indicated on the diagonal of the matrix are of areas of no change with that amount of dimension.

It is noteworthy that open areas of 20.88 km^2 have been used for residential purposes by 1981 out of open spaces of 1971 and additional areas also included alongwith which were not in the jurisdiction of the city in the preceding census. These are new residential areas of Ram Sagar Mishra Nagar and H.L. Colony, Aliganj Extension, and Hind Nagar Colony. These are all outgrowths of the city taken in the urban agglomeration in 1981. About 0.55 km^2 area has been utilised in addition in the use for industrial function during the decade. The open space which was added from other areas at the set up of 1981 were being used basically for residential and to certain extent business and educational purposes in view of the need of that zone.

If the total picture is considered at the set up of 1981 jurisdiction, 72.41 per cent variation is noticed in residential development. The development of public services has been static considering the area occupied under this function. A marginal increase to give the support to the inhabitants has taken place in administrative areas. There is no development sighted in the construction of recreational zone which indicates poor urban facilities to this million city in this regard. In fact due to enlargement of urban agglomeration a decline in this proportion of use has occurred. The actual area under this category at present in the city is only 1.45 per cent of the total area. This proportion in this use places Lucknow far behind the national average of 4 per cent.[6]

Another explanation of the evolution of land uses can be taken when the situation is compared at independent boundary as existed in 1971 and 1981 censuses of Lucknow urban agglomeration. As outlined earlier, the current census has redefined the boundary of Lucknow urban agglomeration by adding about 13.16 km^2 causing 10.31 per cent of additional area over 1971. Table 4.2 supports how these two years respond the functional areas as independent sectors in the mosaic of functional areal system of the city. In principle, the trends as available through this exercise indicate a neglect in public service, recreational, encroachment on open space or arable areas and miscellaneous area[7] development causing to greater extent an ecological disbalance. On the other hand, it seems that such attractions in the city's land use system are mainly for physical improvements.

TABLE 4.1

Transitional matrix showing partitioning of areas under each class of 1971 into different classes in 1981 (km^2) categories of landuse in Lucknow agglomeration

1981 / 1971	1	2	3	4	5	6	7	8	9	Total
1.	35.19	0.27	-	0.16	0.22	0.62	-	(-20.88)	(-6.83)	36.46
2.	-	5.49	-	-	-	-	-	(-0.10)	-	5.49
3.	-	-	3.46	-	-	-	-	-	-	3.26
4.	-	-	-	1.74	-	-	-	(-0.25)	(-0.03)	1.74
5.	-	-	-	-	3.12	-	-	-	-	3.12
	(-0.55)							(-0.10)	(-0.53)	
6.	0.07	-	-	-	-	1.17	-	-	-	1.24
									(-0.41)	
7.	-	-	-	-	-	-	2.92	-	-	2.92
8.	20.88	0.10	-	0.25	-	0.10	-	21.52	-	42.85
9.	6.83	-	-	0.03	0.53	0.41	-	-	-	7.80
	62.97	5.86	3.26	2.18	3.87	2.30	2.92	21.52	-	
	(+26.51)	(+0.37)	(0.00)	(+0.44)	(+1.06)	(0.00)	(-21.33)	(-7.30)		

Notations to category numbers:

1. Residential
2. Business
3. Public Services
4. Educational
5. Administrative
6. Industrial
7. Recreational
8. Open/Arable
9. Miscellaneous

N. B. Figures in brackets indicate net gain (+)/net loss (-) from one class to another for the decade 1971-81.

* Measured on the base map scale 1:29,800.

TABLE 4.2

Changes in Landuse of Lucknow Urban Agglomeration

Categories	1	2	3	4	5	6	7	8	9	TOTAL
Census Boundaries 1971										
% of total Area	28.56	4.30	2.55	1.36	2.45	0.98	2.29	24.05	33.46	100.00
Area in ks^2	36.46	4.59	3.26	1.74	3.12	1.25	2.92	30.70	42.72	127.66
1981										
% of total Area	53.72	2.93	1.22	2.35	2.88	1.41	1.45	13.37	20.69	100.00
Area in km^2	75.64	4.13	1.72	3.31	4.05	1.99	2.04	18.83	29.11	140.82
Changein % 1971-81	107.46	-24.77	-47.24	90.23	29.81	59.20	-30.14	-38.66	-31.86	10.31

Notation for categories:

1. Residential
2. Business
3. Public Services
4. Educational
5. Administrative
6. Industrial
7. Recreational
8. Open/Arable
9. Miscellaneous

(Based upon planemetric measurements on maps R.F. 1:29,800)

FIG. 4.1

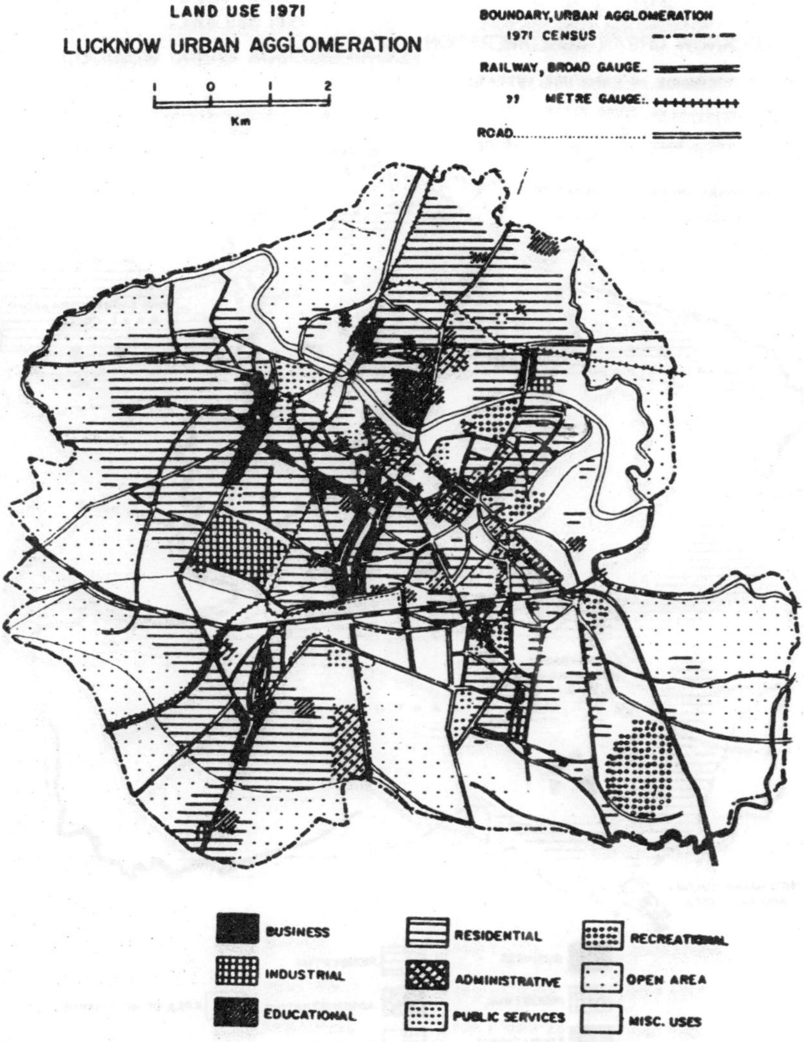
LAND USE 1971
LUCKNOW URBAN AGGLOMERATION
1 0 1 2
Km
BOUNDARY, URBAN AGGLOMERATION 1971 CENSUS
RAILWAY, BROAD GAUGE
" METRE GAUGE
ROAD
BUSINESS
INDUSTRIAL
EDUCATIONAL
RESIDENTIAL
ADMINISTRATIVE
PUBLIC SERVICES
RECREATIONAL
OPEN AREA
MISC. USES

FIG. 4.2

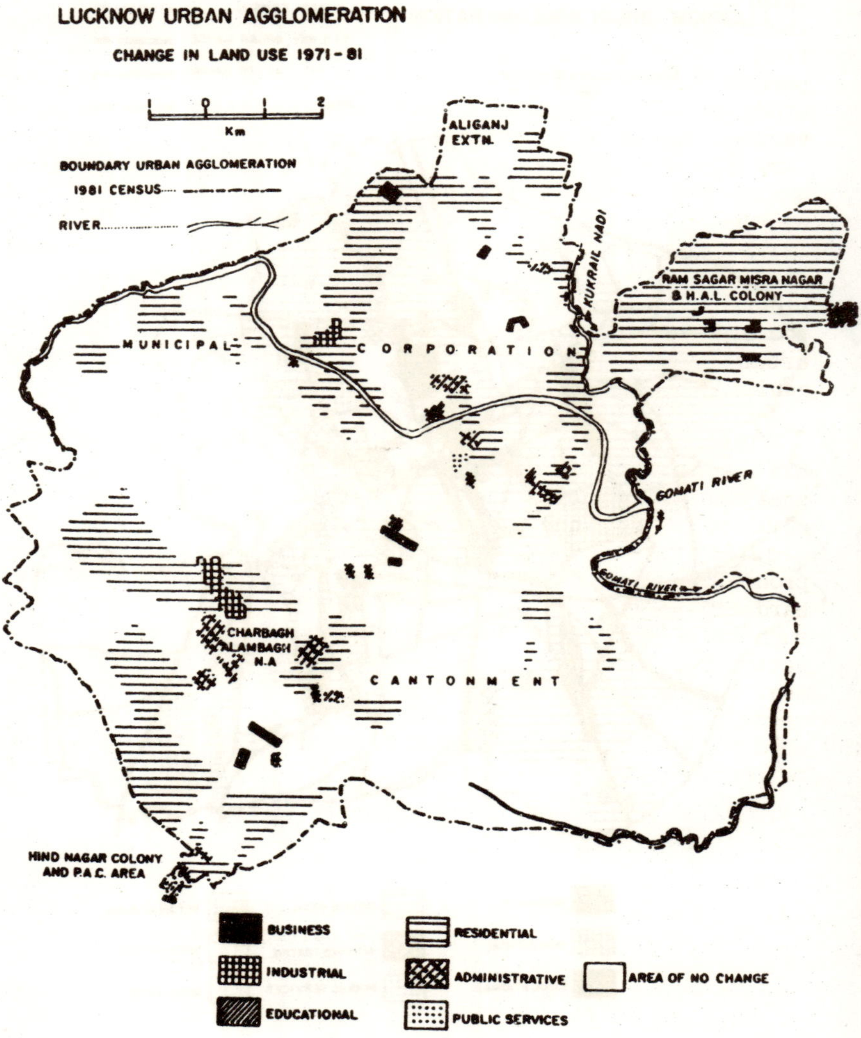
LUCKNOW URBAN AGGLOMERATION
CHANGE IN LAND USE 1971-81
1 0 1 2
Km
BOUNDARY URBAN AGGLOMERATION
1981 CENSUS
RIVER
ALIGANJ EXTN.
KUKRAIL NADI
RAM SAGAR MISRA NAGAR & H.A.L. COLONY
MUNICIPAL
CORPORATION
GOMATI RIVER
CHARBAGH ALAMBAGH N.A
CANTONMENT
HIND NAGAR COLONY AND P.A.C. AREA
BUSINESS
INDUSTRIAL
EDUCATIONAL
RESIDENTIAL
ADMINISTRATIVE
PUBLIC SERVICES
AREA OF NO CHANGE

CONCLUDING OBSERVATIONS

The central theme of presentation of the study focuses certain elements by comparative carto-spatial analysis of internal structure of land uses adjusting the boundaries of the urban agglomeration of Lucknow. The analysis as derived from census materials demonstrates how the differential phenomena are contingent upon projected set up. This case study to a considerable extent indicates the development of various nuclei of activities causing proportional shares in land use. One of the aims in projecting the paper is to acquaint researchers involving to prepare for the orientation so that they may use census materials to find trends of large number of towns in the country to apply rigorous statistical analysis like 'Markov Chains'[8] for which considerable census data and maps can be accepted to determine the process[9] study and give result to weave out the trend of urban land uses in the country which may benefit in reorganising needs of large human settlements.

This may also provide a basis for comparability of social sectors requirements for different urban areas. Such analysis of materials for large number of towns may provide clue to the planners to stop emerging underdeveloped outgrowths in many cases for which redevelopment cost is prohibitive and time taking to streamline the areas causing hardship to the inhabitants in the long run. The findings on such lines would call for strengthening town planning legislation and effective enforcement mechanism in urban development and management. Even this system of study may render certain guidelines to think for a new urban periphery and core city relationship to establish a local government for better habitat and planning.

NOTES

1. U.N. Conference of human settlements, **Habitat 76**, Vancouver May 31-June 11, 1976, Department of Science & Technology, Govt. of India - Country Report, p.16.
2. B.K.Roy, "Urban Land use maps for towns & urban agglomerations in Census of India", **Nat. Geog. Jl.Ind.**, Vol. XXIII (3&4), 1977, pp. 160-165.
3. B.K.Roy, "Internal migration in India's Manpower resources", **Nat. Geog. Jl. Ind.**, Vol. XXV (1), 1979, pp. 8-21.
4. B.K.Roy, "Typograms of service zones of selected cities and distribution of potential population", **Dec.**

Geog. Vol. XV (2), 1977, pp. 281-296.

5. B.K.Roy, "Certain demographic rationales in the small vis-a-vis large urban agglomerations in India and their impact in rural-urban space", **in** Place of Small Towns in India, **NGSI Res.** Pub.21 and ICRHS-3, 1979, pp. 68-78.
6. U.N. Conference on Human Settlements, op. cit, p. 42.
7. Land uses in miscellaneous category are considered mostly belonging to religious, historical and other undefined areas. These areas are more or less showing static dimension.
8. D.R. Cox & H.D. Miller, **The Theory of Stochastic Processes,** John Willey, New York, 1968. "Even more detailed studies of land use sectoral arrangements in city or rural areas overcoming the difficulties associated with a suitable frame can be taken up. Further extension of studies can be undertaken for obtaining estimates from sampling for interesting social sectors of city/cities. Considerable materials are available for research orientation. In this connection, consult D.B. Lahiri, "Technical paper on some aspects of the Development of the sample design", National Sample Survey - No. 5. Govt. of India, Ministry of Finance, March 1954; chapter on land utilisation survey, pp. 30-34.
9. Census of India, State level Town Directories for 1971 Census, various series and years; the forthcoming 1981 equivalent publication would be marked part XA (various series).

FIVE

A.S. Morris

Mendoza
Land Use in the Adobe City

INTRODUCTION

Most cities experience expansion problems in the transition areas between their different functional zones, the best-known examples being the areas of transition between Central Business Districts (CBD) and remainder of city, the so-called CBD fringe, and between the urbanized and rural areas. These transition problems may be the economic and administrative ones of mixed and incompatible land uses, speculative land holding, or derelict land, or the social problems associated with a rootless, unhomogeneous, poor population, unadopted to the problems of inner city life. Inter-group tensions are also created between long-established residents in old houses and newer residents seeking cheap rental housing, or between residential land users and advancing commercial or industrial users. On the urban-rural fringe, the problems are often between farmers and expanding towns, whether in the form of residences or industries and commerce. In some cities, the area of transition is linked to or even areally defined by what may be termed structural maladjustment, old mansions unsuited for high-density cheap housing, but used for it, housing unsuccessfully converted to commercial or industrial use, inadequate public services for domestic or industrial demands. This structural maladjustment may be emplified by speculation on the part of landowners, holding into old properties in the hope of converting them when a sufficiently high value is set on the site.

The purpose of this paper is to define and examine what may be termed a transition area, but one of such size that its problems are distinctive both in quantity and quality from those of the traditional transitional area. In Mendoza, an Argentine city of half a million inhabitants, it is contended here that the problem affects a major section, perhaps one third of the city, because this city, like others of the dry Northwest, was built in adobe, up to some 30-40 years ago. Since that time, adobe or any other construction which is not anti-seismic has been prohibited in Mendoza and San Juan provinces, and this has had the effect of creating a huge area "in transition". Three structural elements may now be discerned; a centre of modern reinforced concrete, a ring of adobe in process of replacement, and a new outer post-1940 ring of anti-seismic construction (Fig. 5.1). The size of the adobe area, the presence of the new outer ring, and the lack of planning control, have created patterns which are distinctive, such as the diversity of land use in the old city, the peculiar geography of urban expansion, and a low density of residential land use.

STAGES OF STRUCTURAL DEVELOPMENT

Virtually all of Mendoza was destroyed by the 1861 earthquake, so that the present buildings all date from the last 120 years, but the colonial tradition of adobe single floor houses was retained in the later building. Reinforced concrete was introduced in the early 20th century, but first employed on a large scale only from 1926, when the first "skyscraper" of five stories was built, overcoming through its commercial success (as shops with flats in upper storeys) an instinctive fear of high buildings among the populace of an earthquake-prone city. From that time much of the commercial centre was converted to reinforced concrete, leaving the rest as adobe with a modest infusion of brick and a fairly common incidence of remodelled houses where remodelling extended only to a brick or concrete facade, leaving the rest adobe.

Outside the adobe city, in a trickle from 1950-72, but in a massive expansion from 1973-77, under the second Peron regime, there has arisen a new residential ring of one storey single family houses. The laws of August 1944[1] forbidding remodelling of adobe houses and permitting new construction only in anti-seismic materials, gives the starting date for a first sub-stage of modest expansion into the outer ring, the advent of the second Peron government in 1973 is the starting impulse for the second substage of massive growth.

 Mendoza : land use in the Adobe city

FIG. 5.1

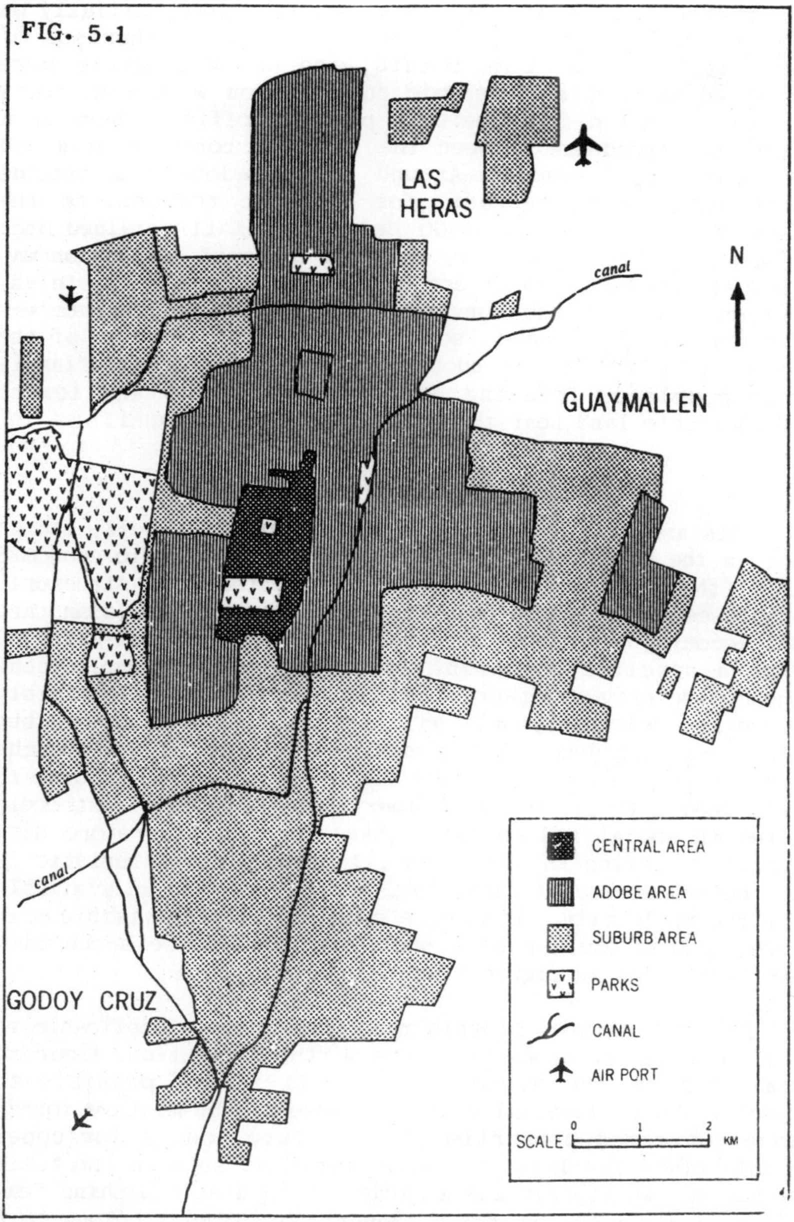

Figure 5.1 shows the three zones, mapped partially on the basis of ground survey, partially on a comparison of maps at different time points, and checked against more detailed maps of anti-seismic construction within the city proper, obtained from the city planning office. There is a fair correspondence between the interior concrete area and the commercial centre. Around it the adobe ring extends preferentially to the east, for historic reasons. On the east side was the pre-1860 centre, and it retained much population through inertia, while to the west, expansion was limited by lack of water and by the San Martin Park. In addition, much of the conversion from adobe to concrete was carried out in the west, so that here little remains of the adobe city. Outside the adobe city, the new concrete ring is near complete, invading both park territory and lower, flood-liable land near the Cacique Guaymallen canal.

THE ADOBE CITY

This area may be thought of as a transition belt, though not in the usual sense of an area defined by socio-economic ills (though these are present) but in terms of structural obsolescence or indeed obsoleteness, since the buildings are not becoming out-dated; they have been declared out-dated as from a specific point in time. Indices of crime, delinquency, poverty or other social disorders would probably correlate reasonably well with the incidence of adobe, but close correspondence is not expected or looked for as the zone is large enough to house all kinds of social groups. It is indeed a thesis of this paper that the zone is extremely mixed in social and economic character, and therefore difficult to define in such terms. A primary characteristic is the heterogeneity of land uses. No land use map is available for the whole city, so to give some idea of the visible mixture, a land use map of a small portion of the adobe city has been made, in figure 5.2.

Several features of this map, more or less applicable to the whole of the adobe city, are worthy of mention. Residential uses are predominant, though it is not possible to specify the residential class, because of the mixture found. Some converted properties are de luxe houses for upper middle class families, and were mapped as such on the basis of having two storeys and a garage, both distinguishing features of the more expensive properties.[2] Others belong to a more modest group, with single storey construction and usually without garages. But many residential units are still adobe, either entire or with the brick or concrete

65 Mendoza : land use in the Adobe city

FIG. 5.2

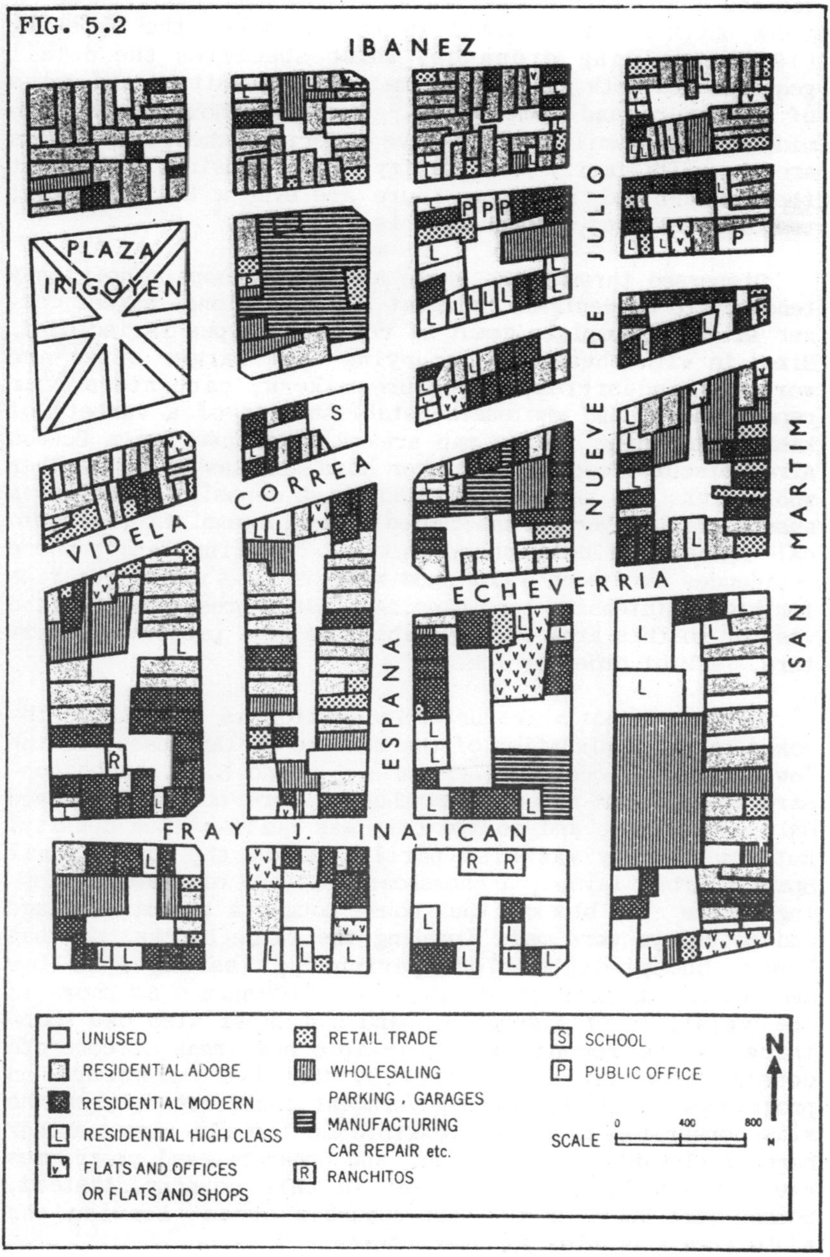

facades that were popular in the 1920s and 1930s. None of these units is anti-seismic in the sense of the existing (1970) building ordnance, which specifies the detail requirements both in terms of materials permitted and types of structure and dimensions.[3] These old houses may house middle class families which have inherited them, but others are now multi-family poor quality rented housing. To exhaust the residential spectrum there are even a few ranchitos, temporary housing, though this is a typical.

Dispersed through the whole are small shops, their only tendency to concentrate being at the traditional street corner sites. A complete gamut of retailing types is included. Mixed in with these and occupying some larger sites are workshop industries, furniture makers, carpenters, car repair shops, and wholesale establishments of a variety of kinds, including in the map area a warehouse for a Buenos Aires biscuit company, a timber yard and saw mill, leather wholesalers and several food and drink deposits. Finally, a substantial number of unoccupied spaces exemplify the typical transition belt phenomenon of "waiting land", where residences have been demolished but the time is not yet ripe for higher intensity land uses. A first impression given the visitor to this area is inevitably one of a patternless mixture, lack of order or logic.

Another aspect which deserves mention as it will be invoked in the explanation of the mixture of land uses, is the low density of occupance (Figures 5.3 and 5.4). Adobe constructions after the 1861 earthquake were normally allowed only one storey, and so the city was built at low density. But low density was also partly due to the traditional Spanish urban layout, a chessboard pattern of roads enclosing square city blocks. Each house sought a street frontage and no alleys were made dividing the large blocks, so that houses occupied the block periphery, leaving a hollow centre. Low density or at least its continuance as shown in the comparison of Figures 5.3 and 5.4, must also owe something to the recent expansion into new areas of concrete construction during the 1970s. Massive construction programmes under the Peron government could not rely on the slow conversion processes possible in the old city, either here or elsewhere in Argentina, and urban renewal programmes are few and limited in extent in this country. Instead, houses were built on the open suburban areas, leaving the adobe area a problem for the future.

Mendoza : land use in the Adobe city

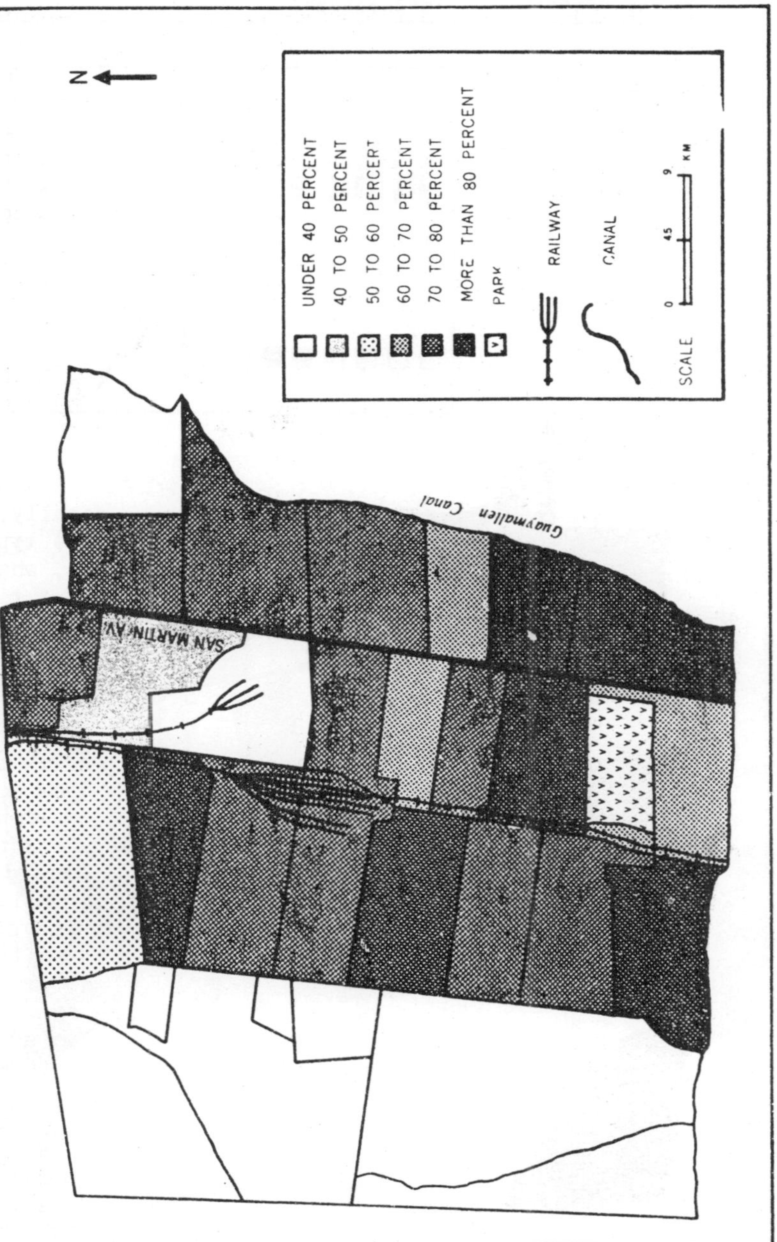

FIG. 5.3

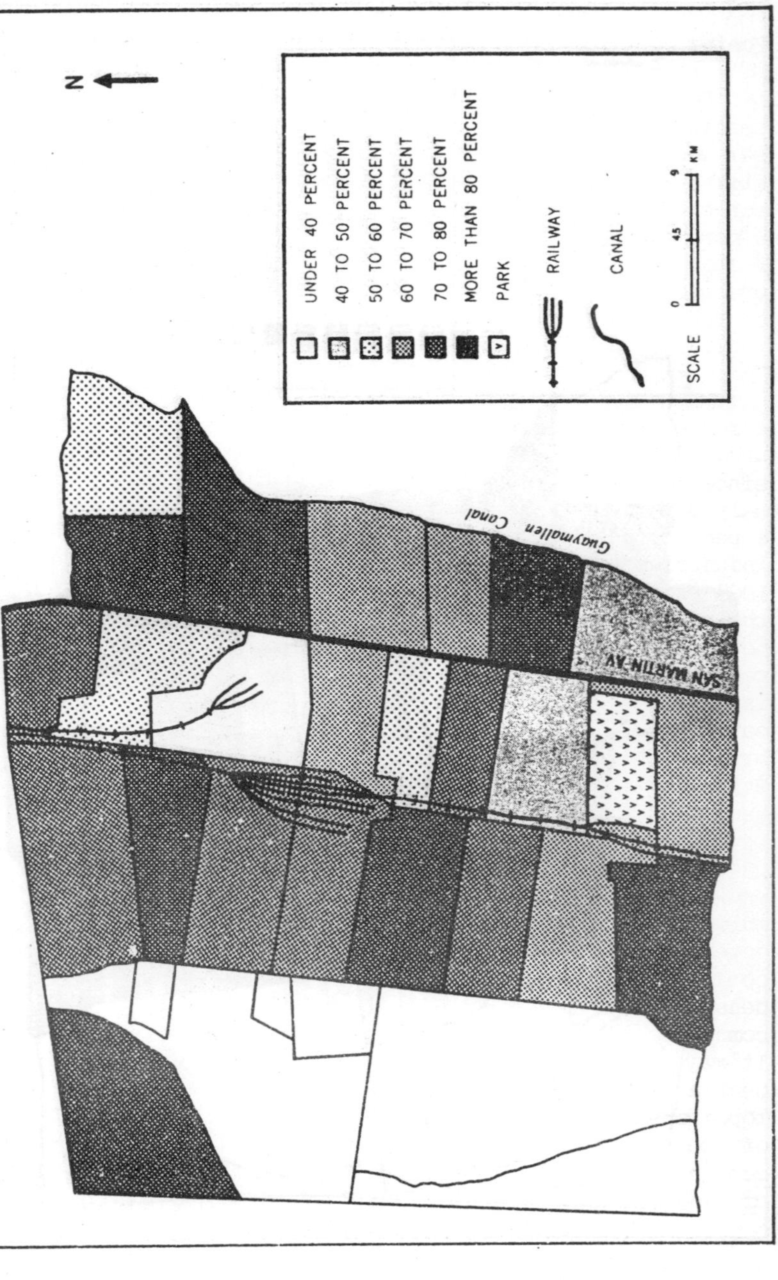

N
UNDER 40 PERCENT
40 TO 50 PERCENT
50 TO 60 PERCENT
60 TO 70 PERCENT
70 TO 80 PERCENT
MORE THAN 80 PERCENT
PARK
RAILWAY
CANAL
SCALE
0
4.5
9
KM
Guaymallen Canal
SAN MARTIN AV

FIG. 5.4

SOME PROCESSES

Zoning controls

Having described the land use scheme as apparently patternless in the adobe city, it may seem presumptuous to offer an explanation of the processes responsible. Order is always much easier to explain than disorder, which may be interpreted as the operation of chance or of a whole host of minor factors which will be difficult to disentangle. Some factors may be indicated here without any pretensions to precise analysis, and it will be seen that the very nature of the factors precludes a quantitative study of their effect.

It is possible to consider as a permissive factor, the absence of zoning and in general of planning control over urban land use. Plans have been made at irregular intervals since 1941,[4] but without reaching implementation stage, and only a desultory planning control has been exerted over any aspect of land use, principally in the banning of noxious industries from residential areas. Zoning maps from 1947 and 1968 exist in the Municipal Planning Office of the city but their provisions seem to have been followed more in areas of new expansion than within the old city. For a variety of reasons, there has been no continuity in either planning or land use zoning, and if we add the fact that Mendoza has outgrown its traditional city limits without managing to co-ordinate legislation among its component parts, there is evidently room for disorder or lack of structure in the land use patterns.

Lack of positive direction by zoning controls means an environment for decision-making with few contours on it, few guidelines as to better or worse locations for this or that enterprise, especially when economic, social and physical contours are not strong. As shall be explained below, low density land use reduces the economic controls, and lack of community identity seems to have reduced the social control. It may be added here that physical guidelines for development are weak, too, because of the smooth piedmont slope topography, and because the chessboard colonial urban layout of houses and streets gives few natural points or lines of concentration or convergence, where the more intensive types of land use would be expected to concentrate.

The decision-makers

In the absence of municipal controls, the decision as to what to do with old adobe or brick properties after 1944[5] lay primarily in the hands of the individual owner. It is important to stress the way the owner was pushed into a position of basic and unlimited decision-making concerning land use (thought not generally concerning location, since the decision was about the property he already held). On the one hand he was forced to make a substantial decision because the law forbade facelifting operations to update adobe property. On the other hand, lack of zoning allowed free choice as to type of new land use.

Changes in the adobe ring have been left in the hands of its multitude of small owners, in a diffusion of decision-making power unusual in an urban environment. In the European or North American city, decision-making might be expected to reside principally in the hands of large landowners, estate agents, private firms, in the event that zoning controls or other institutional powers do not specify the nature of development. In Latin America, a complicating factor is the extreme sub-division of property, which makes it difficult to undertake any large scale development since several properties must be acquired simultaneously to form a reasonably large unit. Subdivision of property has of course frequently been commented on in studies of Latin American agriculture, but its urban counterpart has received little treatment.

As a rough indicator of the diffusion of decision-making, the municipal records have been used, and show the decision-makers in land use changes of the adobe zone to have been very largely the existing owners. As the anti-seismic code is strictly enforced, the Public Works Department keeps a record of all changes and of ownership of the properties concerned, before and after the change.[7] Over 90 per cent, 1973 out of 2154 changes registered in 1968-76, inclusive, were effected by the original owners. In the central commercial area, no comparable data are available, because the area is already all concrete, and there is no necessity for checking construction types when changes in owner or use are made.

Low density land use

This itself has been a contributory factor in the mixture of land use. Lack of any existing high buildings, which would represent a substantial commitment to one or another type of land use, allow an easy change to other low density uses. The land itself retains a high value, but the built structures on it are relatively inexpensive, whether new or old.

In part this low density has been explained as a historical consequence of colonial town layouts, and in part as a function of the siphoning off of residential land demand into the outer ring. Mendoza's rapid growth in the last 20 years could have been accommodated entirely in the adobe city by conversion to three and four storey flats, but in the event only modest use was made of the area, and growth came to the outer ring of Gran Mendoza. The explosive growth of this ring may appear remarkable in an oasis environment, where agriculture is intensive and could presumably compete for land with urban users. In fact, land for urban uses commands much higher prices than any kind of agricultural land, and some of the land used, that to west of the old city, lies above the irrigation canals and therefore has no agricultural value.

In 1973-77, as already noted, the expansion into the outer ring achieved boom proportions, with approximately 10,500 new housing units in the area, by January 1977, nearly all in the outer area and over 90 per cent built with National Mortgage Bank (Banco Hipotecario de la Nacion) loans.[8] During the second Peron governmental period, a policy of housing subsidization was implemented with low fixed interest mortgages provided by the bank, the usual procedure being that a trade or employees' association acquired a large area of land on which to build their **barrio** (estate, suburb) and contracted builders to make houses to a few standard designs, making itself responsible for providing a list of purchasers of houses. Low interest at fixed rates was a particular attraction intended to allow most people to buy the houses, but the fixing of the rate was the undoing of the whole scheme, since inflation achieved values of several hundred per cent through 1975 and 1976, making the repayments too small to finance new building and bringing the bank into difficulty, so that no new schemes are now planned. The military government of 1977 pledged that existing schemes with land and lists of purchasers ready shall be completed, though the interest rates are now adjusted to inflation.[9] The net effect of this expansion period has been to bring into being a sprawl of single houses, with very few flats, all round the city, leaving the adobe area intact (Fig. 5.5). There were exceptions, notably the city block occupied by a public hospital, demolished before 1960 and rebuilt as 3-storey flats in 1970 (Fig. 5.6), and a larger area occupied by a railway yard taken over by the city and remodelled in 1970-77 as low cost four-floor flats. These two areas give an idea of what could have been done with the adobe area generally. But generally the adobe area has faced little demand for space and has considerable supply (because of the anti-seismic ordnance). No economic rigour has enforced a particular pattern of new land use.

Community action

Both cause and effect of the heterogeneous land use pattern seem to have been the lack of any effective community resistance to invasion - no local community action groups are active or even in existence within the city. This contrasts with cities such as Caracas, where very rapid growth of commerce and industry into areas of well defined and traditional residential character have produced a transition belt which is perhaps better called a stress belt, and could no doubt be defined in terms of the number and force of public protests against commercial-industrial invasion from the centre. In Mendoza, the invasion has been more quiet and gradual, over a period of thirty years, not provoking any organized reaction, and by now it is so far extended that any solid community feeling for preservation of residential environments must be diluted. In any case, the classification as unserviceable of all adobe buildings means that any residential opposition to invasion must be based on something other than the preservation of interesting or historic buildings, which has been a common rallying point for residential resistance to change.

THE PATTERN OF URBAN DEVELOPMENT

It is possible to trace some consequences of the existence of the adobe city and the outer ring on the overall growth pattern of the city. Perhaps the most useful of the schemes or models of urban areal expansion in Latin America is Peter Amato's model, developed on the basis of a study of several South American cities.[10] This model is of a sectoral-type expansion, though in irregular jumps rather than through constant growth, and the direction of expansion is determined by one group, the upper class or elite, guided towards such features as high ground and views, open countryside, but little influenced by such mundane matters as transport costs and costs of bringing urban services to isolated or hilly areas.

FIG. 5.5

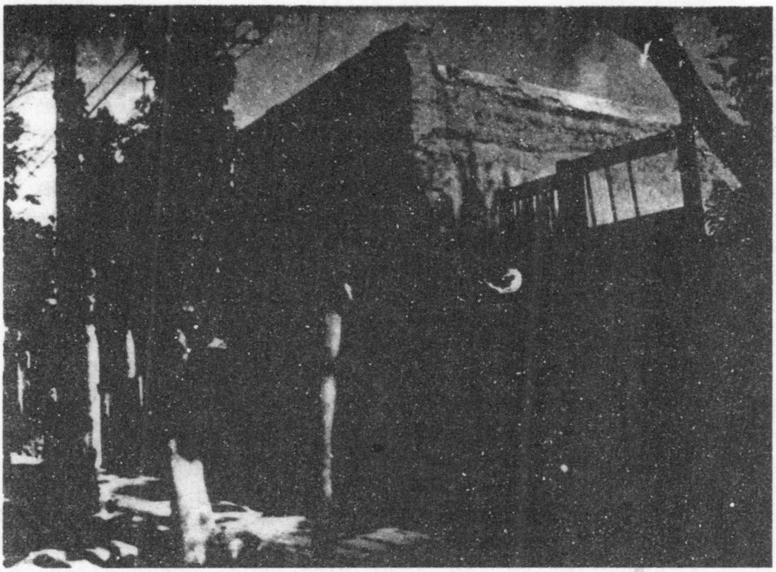

FIG. 5.5

In Mendoza the pattern is different. Over the last few decades a zone of fine housing has emerged around the Avenida Civit access towards San Martin Park and along the park edge. But the force of this elite expansion has been lost, for several reasons. First, the park itself presented an obstacle to further expansion in the same direction, though the barrier was overcome later by the University campus set up to north of the park (Figure 5.1) and then by several recent **barrios**; in both cases, the ability to use the western higher lands, generally thought of as a park reserve and not to be brought into occupation as urban land, has depended on the strength of the agency responsible for new development.

Another factor which slowed any impetus for the elite to move out was the opening of the adobe city to remodelling by the anti-seismic laws, meaning a dissemination of high class housing throughout the area, as some individual owners made the decision to convert old houses to new luxury housing, instead of the alternatives of commercial, high density residential or other use. Finally, the last few years of **barrio** construction in the outer ring have been a disincentive to elite expansion, because the **barrios** are for poorer groups, and because they enclose the city leaving no corridor with a definitely upper class identity. The rapidity and completeness of spread of the outer ring has, as it were, outmanoeuvred the elite group and swamped the tentative outward thrusts of higher class housing in all directions.

These comments do not amount to an alternative model, nor do they destroy the validity of Amato's more general thesis. Rather they demonstrate the difficulty of applying any simple model to a situation where a large land area is suddenly made available for a variety of urban uses. There is an apparent decline in order and neatness of pattern, through time, rather than a reinforcement or extension of existing patterns.

NON-RESIDENTIAL INVASION OF THE ADOBE CITY

In any city a process of outward spread of commerce is natural as the commercial function grows, either in finger like extensions from the centre or in separate subcentres away from the centre. Mendoza had a traditional, highly centralized commercial area up to 1960, with no subcentres and only rudimentary finger extensions. Since then, the adoption of modern styles of shopping involving the car and larger purchases, together with congestion in the centre, have caused commercial spread into the adobe area. But as this growth has been a function of individual decision-making under the peculiar circumstances of the anti-seismic regulations, the commercial pattern is one of considerable scatter through the area. Added to the many traditional corner sites, often maintained in original adobe by owners who are long term residents of the area and provide traditional convenience goods, commerce has often come into the scatter of sites where owners have built a flat-over-shop arrangement, often to rent out the shop area. Other tiny shops are built into former garages or front rooms and operated often as a secondary source of family income by wives or other relatives of the principal breadwinner.

More striking is perhaps the continued industrial presence in the adobe area. In 1961, the industrial structure of the city proper (i.e., very largely the adobe city since few industries were possible in the commercial core) was as indicated in Table 5.1. This pattern, of light consumer industries, was unremarkable for a provincial city. But in 1976 a survey showed a little diminished industrial list and although some specific branches such as carpentries were reduced, at least in numbers, their place was taken by others. Because of some differences in definition of manufacturing industry in specific branches, it seems likely that there were in fact as many manufacturers in 1976 as in 1961, and possibly more land in this use by the later year.[11]

The picture is one of industrial change, but not decline, in the adobe city. In theory all industries are on sufferance in the area and under pressure to move out, but as zoning legislation has been ineffectively enforced, the industries remain. In some cases, as one industry has moved out another has taken its place on the same site, as the map shows; but more frequent are totally new sites for industrial use. One can only speculate on the reason for this changing industrial geography, but one reason suggested by the planning officer for Mendoza is that existing industrial sites are relatively well known, so that when they leave replacements are not easily allowed whereas when residential properties become run down, it is easy for them to be converted clandestinely to industrial use, and possibly later to gain a permit on the basis of their de facto existence for some time on the site.[12] One kind of invasion is notably absent. Shanty towns to house the urban poor are not common in Mendoza, and almost absent from the adobe zone. In 1960 the Shanty population was estimated at only 3500, or 1 per cent of the Gran Mendoza population, and this number has been controlled.[13] Shanty housing has never been common in Mendoza and one good reason is the sheer difficulty of survival in the desert environment, unless the carefully husbanded water distribution network can be tapped.

TABLE 5.1

List of Industries in Mendoza, 1961 and 1976

Type of Industry	1961	1976	
Wineries	1	1	
Olive Oil	9		
Canning	17	46	
Dairies	3		
Metal-working	28	46	
Carpentries & furniture	60	32	
Liquor and bottling	49	9	(under a changed definition; the earlier survey included soda water manufacture)
Construction and mineral working	23	15	(included only mineral working in 1976)
Various	16	23	
Chemicals	2		
Total	**208**	**172**	

Source: 1960: Plan Regulador de la Ciudad, op.cit., (1941)

1976: Censo Industrial en el radio de la Capital, Ref. 2do Informe, 11/10/76

CONCLUSIONS

These are no more than preliminary findings, and it would obviously be interesting to obtain more direct information as to property owners' decision-making processes. Unfortunately, as with any situation where the visible landscape is the result of decisions taken over a considerable period of time, only a limited percentage of the decision-makers can be identified, the rest having died or moved away. Be this as it may, the area is of particular interest as pointing up what happens where decision-makers are operating under conditions of considerable uncertainty, especially uncertainty as to type of land use best suited to their site. On the one hand the whole adobe area is one of mixed character, and it is hard for individual owners to define areas with a purely residential, commercial or manufacturing future in front of them. On the other hand, most of the decisions are as to what to do with the owner's own traditional home site, and preferences may be coloured by long-term associations with the area, wishes to maintain a residence or to combine home and shop or office, etc. To ascertain these points requires a study of the perceptions of the landowners in question, involving the difficulties in identifying these decision-makers which we have mentioned above.

There is another aspect of interest, the general applicability of the findings of unpatterned land use when decision-making is diffused to many individuals, and when the landscape is poorly differentiated, from the decision-makers' point of view. Certainly it would be hard to find elsewhere the Mendoza combination of adobe housing, anti-seismic regulations, and poor planning control, but somewhat analogous situations may be found in many places, the analogy residing in structural obsoleteness or obsolescene. Nineteenth century industrial towns of Northwest Europe such as Glasgow or Liverpool, where bombing has not obliterated large areas, present similar undifferentiated zones, much more than the functionally transitional belts between CBD and rest of city, in which some decision has to be made in respect of land use, as these whole zones have been declared unserviceable. Planning is of course more active in such cities, but it remains to be seen how well new functional zones will be defined in the inner cities, in the process of urban renewal.

In the Third World rapid expansion of many cities with a large old-established residential area, now turned part of the inner city, has led to some of the features noted here, such as a residential-commercial-industrial mix, which relates to the growth of the urban informal sector; a declining level of order in land-use patterning, and a low intensity of present-day land use in the area awaiting expansion from the centre. Concentration of the academic focus on the shanty towns and their socio-economic characteristics has meant the overlooking of important features in these inner mixed zones.

NOTES

1. Mendoza, **Digesto Municipal de la Capital 1961**, ar-

ticulos 600, 682, 683, and 686 (unpaged) Mendoza 1961.

2. This basis for classification is not as arbitrary as it may seem. As lot sizes are fairly even and have small frontages on the street, an owner who wishes a larger house must normally build upwards, and 2-storey anti-seismic houses are more expensive per square foot than the more common single-storey construction. Garages are also still a distinctive feature in a country where the rate of car ownership is only 1 per 8 persons.
3. Municipalidad de la Capital, **Boletin Municipal, 27-7-1976, Codigo de Edificacion de la Ciudad de Mendoza,** Ordenanza 23/8860.
4. **Plan Regulador de la Ciudad de Mendoza; Primera Etapa: Pre-Plan.** F.H. Bereterbide **et al.,** Mendoza, mimeo, 1941.
5. Mendoza, op.cit. 1961.
6. See for example, S. Barraclough and A. Domike, "Agrarian Structure in seven Latin American countries", **Land Economics**, Vol. 42, (1966) pp. 391-442. For Bolivia, some data are available because of the urban land reform attempted in that country; the tiny area actually expropriated, 95 hectares or 2 % of urban land, suggests that the great majority of urban properties are small. See Carlos Calvimontes Rojas, "Urban Land Reform in Bolivia during the Victor Paz Estenssoro administration", pp.179-182 in **Latin American Urban Research,** Volume 2, ed. Francine Rabinovitz and Felicity Trueblood, (Sage Publication, 1972).
7. Municipalidad de Mendoza, Departamento de Obras Publicas, manuscript lists.
8. Estimates given by the regional office of the Banco Hipotecario, Mendoza.
9. **La Nacion,** p.1, Jan. 15, 1977.
10. Peter W. Amato, "Elitism and settlemen patterns in the Latin American city", **Journal, Amer. Inst. of Planners**, March, 1970, pp. 96-105. Amato traces his own model to that of Homer Hoyt, which was also sectoral and based on residential trends alone, but Amato's contribution is distinctive enough to warrant its own designation, more sophisticated and mathematically analytical models such as those by Lowdon Wingo, **Transportation and Urban Land,** (Washington, 1961), or by W. Alonso, **Location and Land Use,** (Cambridge, Mass., 1964), are of even less relevance in Latin America than they are in the

developed world, as a host of special factors, such as skewed income distributions, non-free land markets, topographic effects, and group decision-making, dominate and reduce the relative importance of the distance friction that forms the basis of the classic theories. As much is admitted by Alonso in his paper, "The form of cities in developing countries", delivered at the Regional Science Association meeting in Chicago November, 1963.

11. As the average size of industries has increased, the amount of land used and the general importance of manufacturing is likely to be maintained even if the number of firms has gone down.
12. Information from conversation with Arquitecto Tomas Jose Navarrete, Jefe de Officina Technica Interino, Municipalidad de la Capital, Departmento de Planeamiento Nueve de Julio 500, Mendoza, Argentina.
13. Plan Regulador, op.cit., introduction (unpaged), Mendoza, 1961.

SIX

James B. Kenyon

Land Use Associations *versus* Centrality in the Distribution of Pedestrians in the Urban Core

Atlanta

The city center, variously referred to as the Central Business District (CBD), downtown, and urban core, has recently been of rather sporadic interest to American geographers.[a] Although journal articles appeared occasionally before World War II, it was not until Murphy and his associates produced a practicable method for explicit, and thus comparative, delimitation of the district that this portion of the city became a major concern within the field, in the 1950s and 1960s.[43] This inspired a number of academic and municipal agency delimitations of particular cities in the United States[42], and perhaps even more since 1960 in other countries.[16,31,39,46,53,54] Yet it is only fair to say, in reply to Carter[13, pp.204-247], that nearly all CBD delimiters recognized this objective only as a means to a more remunerative study of the dynamics affecting the development of the district.

Geographic interest has focused primarily upon function—the array of activities present—in terms of form: the stock and arrangement of brick and mortar containment space available. Functional concentrations, again typically as a means to a more elusive end, have been mapped for a number of U. S. cities [5], as well as foreign cities [17,21,25,27,30]. Movement—locational shift—of the central core over time, and identification of zones of assimilation and discard have been a natural adjunct to this line of investigation in the general search for underlying forces and processes[7,10,45,52]. But the structure of the urban core in terms of its functional differentiation into specialized subdistricts, and the nature of linkages among those subdistricts has constituted perhaps the major thrust of recent interest in this portion of urban geography[14,28,51]

All of these studies, and others, recognize the intensity of activity and land usage in the central core, and the consequent importance of maximum population density in giving its special position as the quintessence of urban intensity. A number of studies have considered the matter of intensity of development specifically[12,17,21,45,48,53], while others have approached the question through analysis of the ebb and flow of population to and from the district[11,22]. A few geographical studies show pedestrian density data in the urban core[5,11,12,19].

A growing number of studies has been made by planners and their consultants, in which pedestrians are queried as to their points of origin and destination, purpose of trip, and other aspects of their downtown foot-trave[137,41,47]. Several bibliographies document the growing interest of planners in this aspect of urban development[9,23,29,33,40].

Yet no study in the geographic literature has come to the attention of this worker in which the flow of pedestrial traffic within the district has been used as a direct basis for analysis of functional arrangement of process of development. Nor is this medium envisioned in proposals for new approaches to the study of the city center[3]. In delimiting the CBD, Murphy and Vance find "pedestrian counts .... promising, since movement of people on the streets is essential to the central functions of the CBD" yet reject this approach because of the lack of available data, and because pedestrians may be associated with "non-CBD" activity]43 pp. 196-197[. Since no such distinction is made in this study between CBD and non-CBD activities, for reasons to be outlined below, this objection is obviated.

Here the distribution of persons, specifically pedestrians, is regarded as the basis for CBD development; the structure of the CBD is viewed in correlative relationship with the volume and distribution of pedestrian traffic. The pedestrian is regarded as the mortar which binds the district together, and which provides a basis for clustering, concentrations, linkages and other aspects of land use arrangement.

If there be such an integral relationship between pedestrian distribution and CBD organization (form-function), it should be possible to account statistically for the distribution of pedestrians on the basis of location and development within the district. Conversely, it should be possible to shed light on the differentiation of CBD development: the emergence of nodes, strips and functional subdistricts. On the basis of pedestrian distribution, this research undertakes to measure the roles of position (centrality within the district) on the one hand, and development (improvements on the land) on the other, in structuring the internal form of the CBD.

The central business district of the American city has generally been defined as the zone of the city characterized by highest land values, highest rent and productivity levels, highest daytime population density, and otherwise as the place of greatest intensity of activity, all of which is predicated ultimately upon maximum regional accessibility. The natural zonation of land uses, resulting from competition for the best (most central) location has traditionally been seen as producing a generally conical surface of land use intensity built around the street intersection of highest land value[5,11,13,42].

Yet in some sectors of retail trade, as well as in certain other central land uses, there is symbiotic benefit in clustering by competitive establishments. The tendency of buyers of non-standardized, higher-priced articles to shop—to visit more than one store before buying—encourages clustering, and to a degree accounts for the overall customer attraction of the retail component of the CBD. On the other hand, merchants respond to the repellent forces of competition between stores, leading to more uniform dispersion throughout an area.

Thus among retail stores and personal services catering to the pedestrian passer-by or shopper, the CBD, like the city itself, is characterized by a system of clusters, semi-clusters, and widely dispersed establishments, wherein the degree of concentration depends upon the degree to which buyers tend to shop before buying. The big department store, as a self-contained retail district, encourages "one-stop shopping," and undertakes to minimize inter-store shopping. At the same time, it attracts retail competitors to its vicinity.

But the core is no longer predominantly oriented to retail trade or individualized services. The large American city in the 1970s is centered upon a much more broadly-based set of activities. Among these, administration—office activity—typically exhibits at least as strong competition for prime space as retailing, and also reveals a differential tendency to cluster. Both major categories of downtown land use are sensitive to the general aesthetic attractiveness of the various sections of the district, which underlie its glacial creep-away from the zone of discard towards the zone of assimilation.

Office activity and retail trade are related to each other in ambivalent fashion. Retail trade and personal services, which appeal to the passer-by directly, be he shopper or otherwise, are drawn to the location of high pedestrian density in general, and to concentrations of certain components of that pedestrian flow—namely their prospective clientele-in particular. Office workers are of interest to merchants only to this extent. Office activity involves company linkages with other companies—often other offices—as well as to various personal and business service establishments. Both offices and stores, of course, require easy access to major transport terminals and parking facilities. Since offices generally do not orient themselves to the uninvited passer-by, throngs of pedestrians are not a positive, and indeed may be a negative, factor in office attraction to a given site. Thus the street-level retail-service core with offices above, an arrangement which not only divides the site cost, but also enables office workers to shop during off-hours, is typical, except where the intensity of inter-office linkage is so strong as to preclude generally continuous street-level retail activity. This latter situation occurs only in the financial districts of the largest cities, however. In any case, the interplay of office districts, retail-service districts, and their combinations complicates the land value-land use intensity pattern of the large CBD[6,8,15,17,21,35,50].

But the core is more than a business district. It is the urbane center of a region, one of a family of such centres of the world. It is a place to visit, in which to learn, to be nourished and entertained, to be rested or excited. Thus it is a social and political center as well as a focus of shopping and employment[20,49]. The tourist and convention business of many large American city centres may overshadow its metropolitan shopping function. The location of hotels, restaurants, and evening activity constitutes a strong, if not major, set of associated components of the district, further differentiating it into semi-discrete subdistricts, or nodes.

The nodular structure of the large urban core is universally recognized. Times Square, Grand Central, Columbus Circle, and other major nodes in Midtown Manhattan not only indicate outsized activity concentrations, but also conjure immediate images of differing functional composition. To a considerable degree, these have their counterparts in other American cities, and to a lesser extent in many foreign cities[26,53].

Thus the core needs to be seen in general geographic theory, not simply as a conical surface of land values and correspondent rent-paying abilities with subordinate peaks on its slopes, but rather perhaps as an aggregation of points of concentration, loosely grouped together but differing in functional composition as well as size. It is more the case of a mountain range than a volcanic cone.[35]

The identification, measurement, and functional composition of nodes—and anti-nodes—emerges as a by-product of the main object of the study: to analyze the role of pedestrian traffic in shaping the form and structure of the CBD. To do this, data were developed and analyzed for a particular city – Atlanta – for a particular year – 1973.

Form of the Atlanta Core

Downtown Atlanta seems eminently typical of the center of the large American city.[b] Yet, like other major city centres it does not fully fit the general patterns outlined above. The core, like Atlanta itself, is built around the Zero Mile Post: the terminus of the original rail line from Chattanooga. From this point, rail connections throughout the entire South, from Washington to New Orleans, have developed very much as originally envisioned. The Zero Mile Post lies in a break in a low ridge, an interfluve which forms a sub-continental drainage divide between Atlanta and the Gulf of Mexico. Followed by Peachtree Street, this ridge now serves as the main axis of the core, and indeed of the whole metropolitan area. Characteristically, the district developed adjacent to, but primarily on one side of, the railroad station. The crossing of streets parallel to the rail line (Marietta and Decatur) with Peachtree Street became and remains the focus of the city. The juncture of another street (Edgewood) intensifies the centrality of this intersection and has given it the designation, Five Points (Figure 6.1).

FIG. 6.1

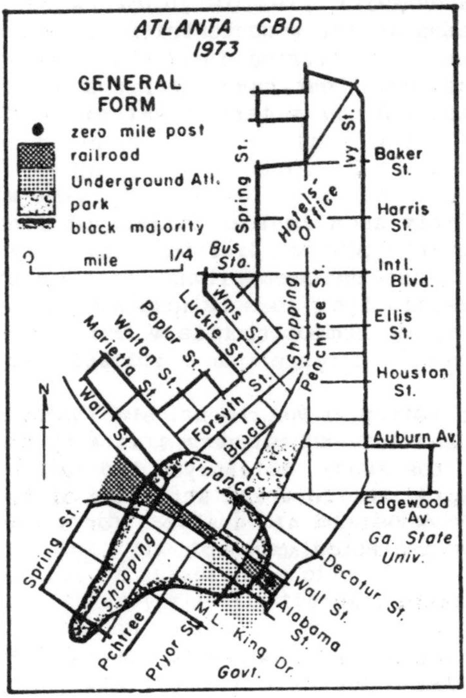

This has become the anchor of Atlanta's financial district, which extends primarily northwestward along Marietta Street, but also eastward across Central City Park. Construction of several major high-rise office buildings in this section affirms its continued function in this role. In Atlanta, office activity plays a dominant role in determining land value and pedestrian patterns.

Atlanta's retail distribution has never fit well into the model in which retail trade is grouped around the point of highest land value. The retail-service function is divided into two semi-detached parts, centering close to, but not at, the two major department stores.[c] Rich's, Atlanta's biggest and best known department store, is located south of Five Points, while Davison's lies northward.

The bi-polar division of the core perhaps reflects Atlanta's Southern history, as a city in a bi-racial, segregated society. Today the portion of the CBD south of Five Points is predominantly black, while that to the north is generally mixed, in racial composition. This dichotomy is reflected in the character of retailing, land value patterns, pedestrian density patterns, and long term locational shift of the core as a whole. There are, of course, exceptions to this general statement. Underground Atlanta, a section of Peachtree Gulch which was bridged over many years ago and which has recently been redeveloped as a center of nightlife primarily for tourists, is one exception. Rich's Department store, which caters more to whites than blacks is another.

The general thrust of the core is towards the north, up Peachtree Street. This is not simply an extension of shop clusters northward, but rather a pattern dominated by office development, and involving a leap-frogging movement far behind the core. To the south, the district deteriorates into the syndrome of low-grade stores, vacancies, dilapidation, and general unattractiveness so characteristic of the zone of discard.

Since 1972, there has been a dramatic shift in the function of downtown Atlanta. Between 1954 and 1972, the Atlanta CBD's share of retail sales dropped from 39.1 to 18.6 per cent within the city, and from 29.9 to 7.4 per cent in the SMSA.[d] Thus the core can no longer be regarded as the prime center for metropolitan shopping]2 (p. 674), 18[. Of the few new stores which have appeared during the past decade, most have been located in new hotels, office centres and convention facilities. Like those in Underground Atlanta, they serve a tourist and convention clientele, rather than the basic home and family needs of Metropolitan Atlantans.

While the Atlanta core declined drastically as a shopping center, its office and hotel capacity have burgeoned. During the decade prior to 1973 four new hotels opened in and immediately outside the CBD, as did half a dozen major skyscraper office buildings. Since that time the Omni International and the Peachtree Plaza Hotel—whose 70 stories make it the world's tallest hotel—have been completed, as have several more high-rise office buildings. Atlanta's historic role as administrative and distribution center of the Southeast has been intensified both within the economic structure of the Southeast, and as a result of the growth in population and economic activity of the Southeast, as a whole in recent years. The city now ranks second nationally as a convention center, as does its airport in air traffic.

It is not surprising that there has been general growth within and adjacent to the CBD, but of a highly selective and differential nature.

Traditional theory of urban development generally considers the land values surface similar to, if not identical with, that of pedestrian density]5, p. 49[. Indeed the "100% intersection", the site of highest land values, is often identified through a pedestrian count. In Atlanta, however, the heaviest pedestrian volume is at Five Points, closely followed by Broad and Marietta, a block away. Yet the highest land value, based upon the fragmentary evidence of several major title transfers, probably lies near the northern end of the core, on Peachtree. The intersection of International Boulevard, or Harris would probably command the highest price today. The modernistic glamour of new hotels and office complexes in this section undoubtedly contributes to its financial value. But implied in the concept of a "zone of assimilation" is the anticipation of future growth, which, of course, underlies financial worth. This implies a physical separation of the point of highest pedestrian traffic from that of highest value, since pedestrian flow measures present intensity while land value embodies also future development.

Land use composition

Prior to analysis of pedestrian generation it is necessary to show more rigorously the character of associations among activities which form the structure of the CBD. To do this, all floor space was measured and classified according to the Standard Land Use Coding Manual, a classification similar to, but not identical with, the Standard Industrial Classification used by the U. S. Census Bureau.[e] Twenty classes were specified, ranging from the 1-digit to the 4-digit level. This was done to show in greater detail street-front activities such as retail trade and personal services, whose locations seem closely related to densities of various sections of the pedestrian population, as well as to one another. These were grouped at essentially the 3-digit level, although cigar stores, by virtue of their abundance, were classed separately as a 4-digit group. Other goods-handling and transport facilities were broadly classed at the 1-digit level. Office activity likewise was classed as a single group. Since banks serve the individual, in depositing and withdrawing money, but also have major office functions, this activity was divided into two parts; the bank floor was classed as a service while its office space was grouped under office activities.

Since pedestrian traffic necessarily peaks at street intersections, as does land use intensity, intersections rather the blocks or block fronts have been taken as units of reference. They constitute areas reaching one half block in all directions (along streets) from the actual intersection. Thus an intersection normally consists of four block-quadrants.

To provide a convenient frame for map presentation, and for consistency with many other city center studies, the district was delineated according to the Murphy-Vance method.[f] Although data were gathered and analyzed for a 104-block area, overlying the formal CBD by a ring several blocks wide, map presentation covers only the 55-block CBD. The intersections around which data are organized include those on the borders of the delimited CBD.[g]

Floor space, grouped by the twenty land use types, was subjected to R-type factor analysis, which produced nine significantly-associated groups, or factors. The nine factors account for 68 per cent of the variance in the locational distribution of the twenty land use categories. This would seem a reasonable level of explanation, since the land use groups contain component activities whose locational requirements are diverse—in other words, there is variance within, as well as between, groups—and because individual establishments are simultaneously drawn to, and repelled by, competitors.

Table 6.1

The main thrusts of the factors, as indicated by their loadings, showed the following patterns of dominance:

Factor	Heaviest loadings
1	hotels, restaurants, cigar stores
2	non-office, non-apparel
3	non-pharmaceutical, non-vacant, non-department store
4	non-furniture, non-vacant, non-storage
5	foods, general merchandise, notions
6	auto dealers, warehousing
7	business service, jobbing, repairs
8	indoor parking, manufacturing
9	transport terminals

Of these factors, three (no's 2, 3 and 4) are expressed negatively, while the others are positive. Although the negative, or reflexive factors, are more difficult to interpret, Factor 2 seems to profile an association of rather nondescript, low-grade activities. Factor 3 suggests a pattern of low intensity, not oriented to shopping. Factor 4, on the other hand, seems to describe a mixture not characterized by low intensity, but rather an area of high intensity, and probably of high land values. Thus Factor 4 seems to augment, though negative alignment, a pattern expressed positively in Factor 1. Overall, the factors identify first the office and business complex, next the two generally opposite types, followed by a negatively-expressed reinforcement of Factor 1, and finally five special districts: shopping, automotive, jobbing, parking and manufacturing, and the bus stations. Factors 3 and 5 seem almost mirror images, identifying shopping clusters. These interpretations are, of course, subjective, but since factor-loadings are given, the reader can form his own.

The locational patterns of the factors, given in figure 6.2, were mapped by interpolation among factor score values by intersection, using the Symap computer package. In general, the locations of the districts identified above could be recognized by any denizen of downtown Atlanta: the financial district, the main shopping sections, parking flanking the Peachtree Ridge, and so on. Yet at the same time, this procedure discerns land use combinations not immediately evident on the ground. Most important, it provides a basic for interpretation of the pattern of pedestrian distribution in the district.

The core is seen here as a broad conglomerate of activities and other elements which individually or collectively attract large numbers of participants—as visitors, shoppers, employees, or for some other purpose. The activities present are those which need to be there, in terms of access to clientele or to other establishments. In addition, attractive elements include points of cultural and social significance. But the ultimate basis is the concentration of people. Location of an establishment is predicated upon the location of other elements, in terms of their accessibility or isolation. Thus the criterion is not simply persons per unit area *per se* but pedestrian traffic: persons in position to participate, who are in motion, or, in fact, in the act of generating the vital land linkages.

Presumably the core as a whole exerts greater attractive force than its component establishments could individually, in the sense that it furnishes the individual establishment better access to clientele than it could garner by itself.

The core could be viewed, in this sense, as the proverbial ant heap, in which the establishments are there because the others are there: each struggling to get to the middle. Similarly, some of the pedestrians at each intersection must be simply passing through, to and from other intersections.

FIG. 6.2

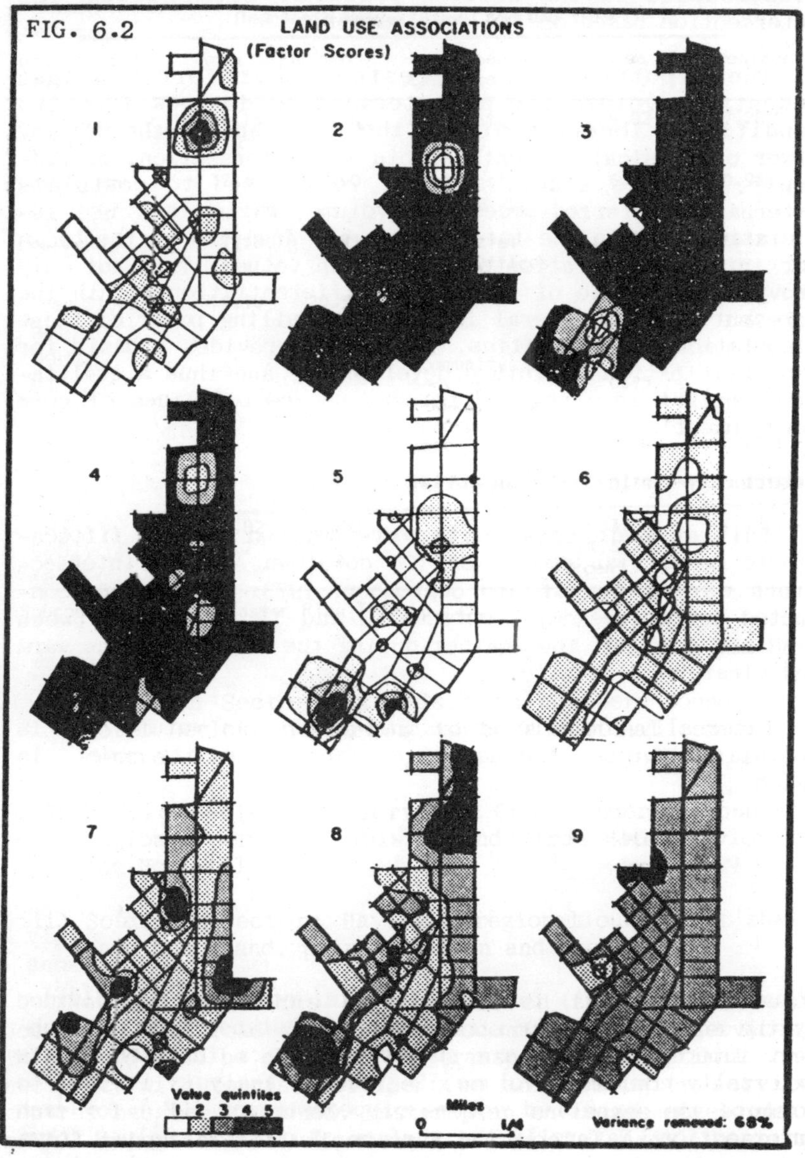

Just as property value is comprised of two parts—land value derived from its location, and improvement derived from investment—so pedestrian density is based upon the flow of persons passing through an intersection—based on its location—and on the drawing power of elements at the intersection—based on its development.

The hypothesis to be tested, therefore, is that pedestrian volume for an intersection derives from two conditions: location within the core, and on the drawing power of physical elements within the intersection. Accordingly, in this study, a model is devised to postulate externally-conferred pedestrian volume, while land use associations within the intersection are analyzed as the basis for internal generation of pedestrian volume. This not only provides a profile of functional differentiation within the core but gives a general idea of the pulling power of these associations of activities. It further provides a basis for the anticipation of future development, and thus a qualitative insight into new and perhaps unexpected lines of core development.

Externally-conferred pedestrian volume

Initial pedestrian data were derived through fifteen-minute pedestrian counts on 104 downtown Atlanta intersections during August and September, 1973. Counts were conducted during weekdays, between 10 and 12 AM, and between 2:30 and 4:30 PM. The weather during the count days was warm and clear.[h]

Externally-conferred-potential-pedestrian volume (PP) is postulated through the use of a standard gravity model, in which

$$PP_i = \sum_{J=1}^{104} \frac{PA_j}{D^2_{ij}}, \qquad j \neq i.$$

Actual volumes (PA) for all other intersections (j) divided by the square of their straight line distance from the subject intersection (i) are summed to give a function of its externally-conferred volume. Regression analysis is used to compute the expected volume of pedestrians (PE_i) for each intersection. Naturally the surface of computed values forms a smoothed-out curve resembling that of the actual volumes

(PA_i) (Figure 6.3). The major pedestrian-attracting intersections—the nodes—stand out even when deflated by removal of the locationally-expected component.

FIG. 6.3

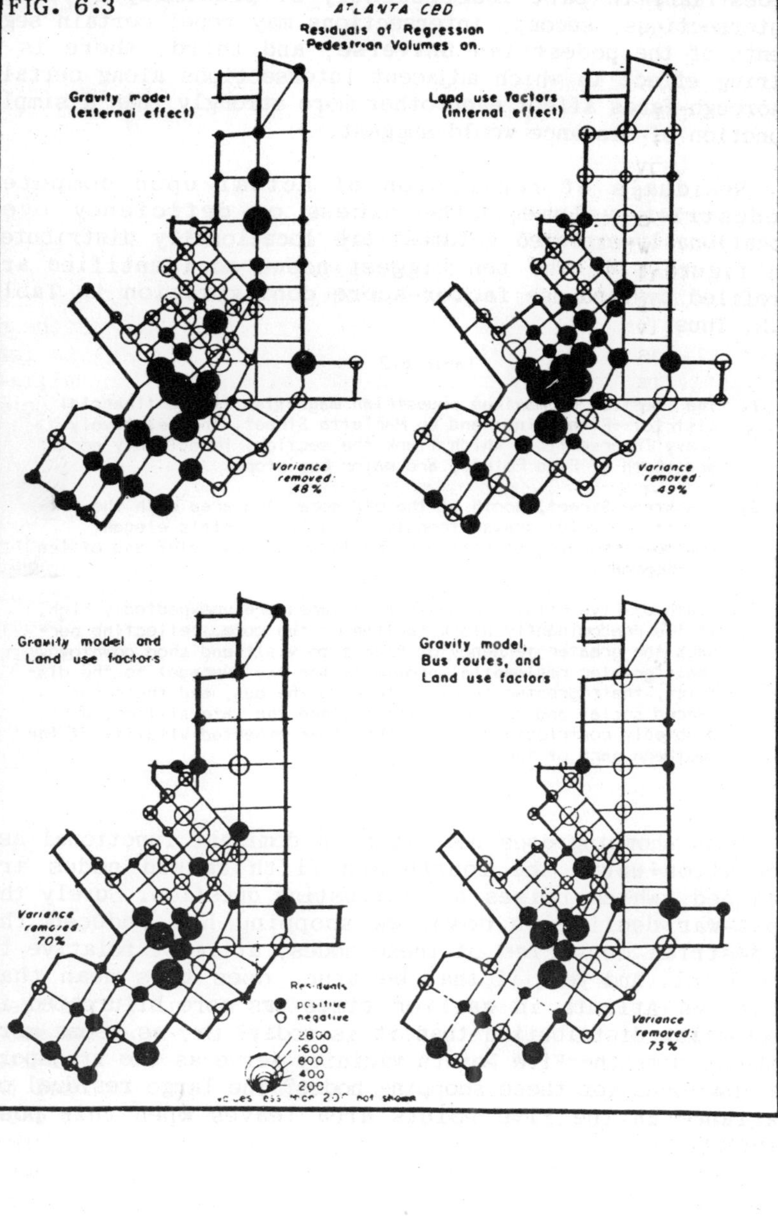

This procedure indicated that the externally-conferred pedestrian volume accounted for 48 per cent of the variance in actual pedestrian volume by intersection, reflecting several rather obvious factors. First, intersections attract pedestrians in part independently of proximity to other intersections; second, intersections may repel certain segments of the pedestrian universe; and third, there is a string effect in which adjacent intersections along certain thorough-fares affect each other more strongly than a simple function of distance would suggest.

Residuals of regression of actual upon computed pedestrian volumes (the excess or deficiency over locationally-expected volumes) are locationally distributed in figure 6.4. The ten biggest nodes so identified are profiled by land-use factor-score configuration in Table 6.2. Thus:

Table 6.2

1. The location of maximum pedestrian magnetism is the financial district--Five Points and up Marietta Street. The relatively heavy intersections which flank the section, immediately north and south of Five Points, are major bus stops.

2. Peachtree Street, north of the old core (the area with the off-set street grid) draws strongly. This is Atlanta's elegant downtown shopping streets and the focus of new hotel and office development.

3. South of Five Points, pedestrian volumes are unexpectedly high, in the predominantly black section of the core, reflecting perhaps the greater tendency of blacks to visit and shop downtown. Their greater residential proximity (on the average) to the district, their greater tendency to ride the bus, and their enhanced social and economic status since the late sixties, undoubtedly contribute to the higher-than-expected vitality of the southern part of the district.

Mass shopping does not become a dominant functional association until the fourth and fifth ranked nodes are reached, which raises an interesting question. Surely the post-war decline in downtown shopping has reduced the pedestrian densities of these nodes, at least relative to the total. And yet, if that be true, does this mean that downtown Atlanta in earlier times was more bifurcated in pedestrian distribution than it is today? Or, as seems more likely, does the Five Points vicinity serve as the transportation focus for these shopping nodes? The large residual of variance in the Five Points area leaves open this possibility.

Although the intersection is taken here as the unit for analysis, it is evident that a good case could be made for the use of the street. Peachtree Street, north of Margaret Mitchell Square (the intersection of Forsyth Street); Marietta Street, west of Five Points; and Peachtree, Broad and Forsyth Streets south of Marietta are all vital magnets for pedestrians.

Yet there are counterbalances, such as Pryor-Park Place between Wall Street and Margaret Mitchell Square, which is characterized by old buildings housing low-grade stores and offices. Much the same could be said of Peachtree Street between Walton and Margaret Mitchell Square. Between these parallel streets lies Central City Park, which in 1973 was being extended northward.

On each side of the park, large office buildings were built shortly before the 1973 analysis: the Equitable Building on Peachtree and the Trust Company of Georgia on Park Place. Together with the park, these would seem major components in the direction of rehabilitation of an otherwise rather run-down flank of the center of the core.

Other strings of low-attraction intersections occur on Williams and Popular Streets, both of which are narrow lanes, serving more as alleys than streets. Parking and loading zones at the backs of major buildings are characteristic of both.

Thus the core may be seen as a combination of nodes, or intersections drawing disproportionate portions of the overall pedestrian volume, and anti-nodes: other intersections, which, while they add to the total CBD size, do not attract their share of the pedestrian load. In this sense, one could look at some intersections as net generators, and others as net beneficiaries. Presumably such surpluses and deficiencies of pedestrian traffic relate to the kinds and combinations of land uses which characterize the various intersections.

Internally-Generated pedestrian volume

In order to test the relationship of pedestrian volume against land use combinations, stepwise regression was used. Overall, the land use factors account statistically for about 49 per cent of the variance in pedestrian volume by intersection.

There is general adherence in the strength of the relationship of pedestrian volume to the extent of grouping of land uses (i.e., there is higher correlation with the higher-ranking land use factors as measured by their eigenvalues). Thus, it seems fair to conclude that the more highly structured (in terms of the factor score) an intersection is, the more strongly it relates to pedestrian volume, either positively or negatively. Analysis of internal and external bases for pedestrian volumes taken together shows this relationship even more clearly. Note, however, that Factor 1, centering on hotels and related services, seems to generate only a moderate density of pedestrian traffic.

Residuals of regression of pedestrian levels against the land use factors are shown in the upper right side of Figure 6.4, where the pattern may be conveniently compared with that of externally-conferred volume. The two patterns are grossly similar; in both charts, the heavy pedestrian surplus centres upon the Five Points-Marietta financial hub and both show, coincidentally, pedestrian surpluses at certain other intersections.

But there are differences in the two patterns. The surplus of pedestrians north of Houston Street on Peachtree Street, based on external forces (i.e., location) are more than accounted for in upper right chart, based on land use associations (i.e., development or improvements). The heavy surplus of pedestrian density south of Five Points is somewhat better (though not fully) explained by internal development.

This analysis suggests that about half the variance in pedestrian volume is explained by external factors and the other half by internal. Yet to the extent that the two upper maps on Figure 6.4 coincide, the pattern is not explained fully by either. Clearly there is a degree of overlap between the two models; in other words, as suggested earlier, there is a relationship in the land use pattern of an intersection with that of the other intersections, related to their location. To explore this, stepwise regression of actual pedestrian volumes against expected (externally-conferred) volumes and the nine land use factors was computed.

Plotting residuals of this regression against the computed values yields a nearly circular, patternless distribution, suggesting that the remaining statistical variance is largely random noise. Yet, as the bottom left map in figure 6.4 shows, some non-random geographic variance is still present.

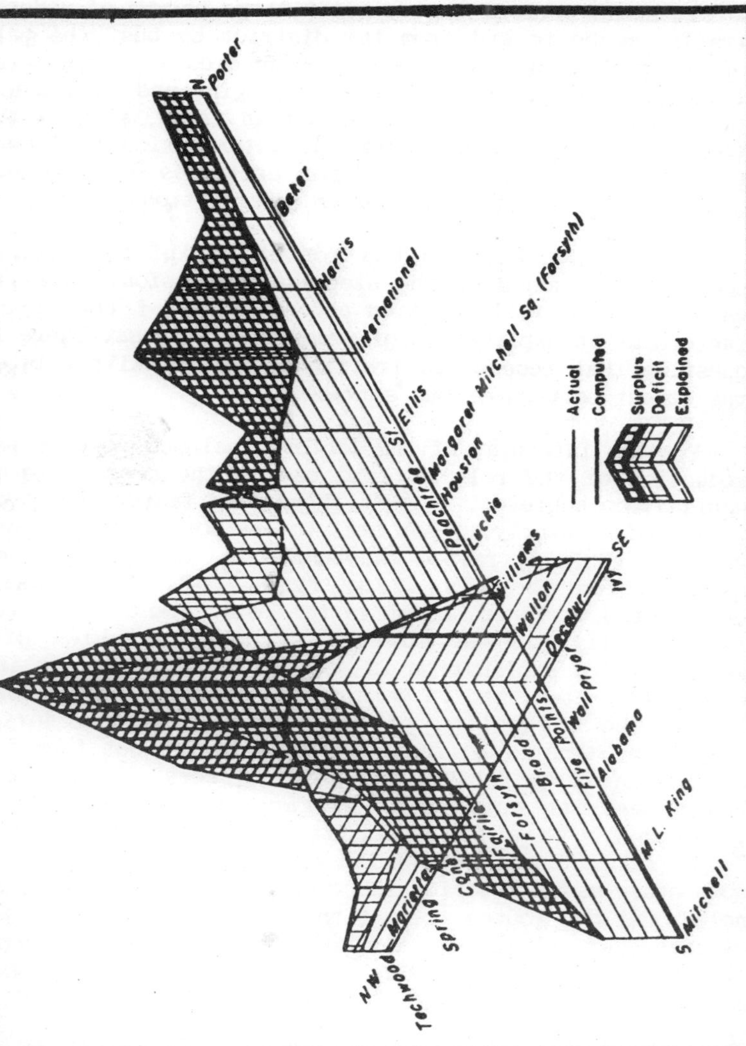
N Porter
Baker
Harris
International
Ellis
St.
Peachtree
Margaret Mitchell Sq. (Forsyth)
Houston
Luckie
Williams
Walton
Decatur
Ivy
SE
Wall pryor
Five Points
Broad
Alabama
Forsyth
Fairlie
Cone
Spring
Marietta
Techwood
NW
M. L. King
S Mitchell
Actual
Computed
Surplus
Deficit
Explained

FIG. 6.4

Bus stops as pedestrian generators

It seems obvious that since a large volume of pedestrian traffic moves to and from the district by bus, the pattern of bus routes and stops cannot be ignored as a generator of local traffic. By looking at bus origins and land use destinations of, say, inbound pedestrian trips, along with estimated volumes moving through an intersection to other intersections, we have bases for estimates of movement to, from, and through the particular intersection.

Accordingly, data on bus routes by intersection were compiled and added to the stepwise regression. This factor entered the overall equation second—ahead of the land use factors—as an explanation of pedestrian volumes. There is no question that pedestrian traffic is meaningfully related to the street pattern of bus service.

Yet the interplay of the factors included results in the reduction of the role of land use in the overall level of explanation achieved. Thus, although the factor, bus routes, itself added nearly 11 per cent to the coefficient of determination (R^2), it raised the composite, or total, level of explanation to only .730, from .703. The remaining unexplained variance, shown in the lower right of figure 6.3 is basically similar to that without inclusion of bus routes. Added explanation is seen to a slight extent in the Five Points area, and on some of the arterial routes leading to it. The channeling of bus routes from the north on Peachtree Street, and their tendency to fan out towards the downtown area on Forsyth and Broad Streets, fully explains the pedestrian volumes at Margaret Mitchell Square, the fulcrum of this bird's-foot pattern. It tends to "overexplain" the pedestrian volume further north, and on some other major arteries where bus routes are heavily channeled. But bus routes are not the same as number of buses or of passenger volume, or traffic origins and destinations by intersection — data which, unfortunately, were not available.

Thus, while the addition of bus route data as a component contributed to overall explanation, it did not produce uniform increases throughout the area. It will be noticed that, in general, pedestrian traffic in the Five Points area is better explained, and yet, still, a sizable unexplained residual remains. This results, at least in part, from the fact that many bus routes terminate a block or so away from Five Points: north, south, and west. Thus, transfer traffic through the city often requires a walk through this area to catch a connecting bus.

Whether or not the heavy bus-oriented pedestrian traffic in fact accounts for the disproportionate volumes in the Five Points vicinity remains moot. Since open space was not included as a factor, the heavy use of Central City Park, adjacent to Peachtree St. at Five Points was ignored, an omission which undoubtedly accounts for some of this excess. Beyond this, the crowd itself may attract additional people – people are, after all, the biggest source of interest and attraction in this type of urban situation. The fact that this is not capitalized upon in the American centrum by provision of outdoor cafes is surprising indeed.

Another factor mentioned above, but not incorporated into rigorous analysis at this juncture is the racial dichotomy of downtown Atlanta. Differences in shopping and transport patterns would seem to underlie some of the still unexplained surplus of pedestrians in the southern part of the CBD. Yet, inclusion of this variable – per cent black by intersection – increases R^2 by .0188, and raises the final level of explanation from .7301 to .7436.

CONCLUSIONS

It is clear that pedestrian traffic volume is significantly related to the functional structure of the core, and that the core is not only organized with reference to relations among land uses but to pedestrian densities as well. The form of the core may be seen as a dynamically balanced system in which land use arrangement is in, or at least tending in the direction of, equilibrium among various forces of attraction and repulsion. Pedestrian distribution serves as the medium within which such organization develops, seemingly through a chicken- and -egg relationship. Its pattern could perhaps be likened to the arrangement of iron filings around interactive magnets, in response to the conditions and relationships which prevailed in 1973.

Thus to a great extent the distribution of pedestrians can be explained in terms of intensity and arrangement of land use. Conversely, the land use composition is seen to be a function of potential optimum pedestrian distribution and stratification. The centrum, then can be viewed as a plastic entity, whose shape, size and location can be changed in response to new cultural and technological demands. It remains to be seen, therefore, how usage of the centrum is differentiated, by time – both cyclical and non-cyclical and within small areas. Furthermore, it is necessary to relate such usage to deliberate efforts by local public and private interests to modify downtown form.

FOOT NOTES

a. For bibliographic coverage of urban geography, see]55, 59[. The currently low interest in the study of the city center in Britain is shown in a recent survey within the IBG]64[. In the United States, the general disenchantment with the district by the increasingly auto-oriented public perhaps underlies the observation by Baerwald that "the use of the CBD is increasingly dominated by people who cannot afford the kind of automobiles that would enable them]to shop elsewhere["]1, p. 308[.

b. For diversified geographic analysis of Atlanta, see Hartshorn, et al]32[, and several bibliographies]56, 57, 58[.

c. Similar disparity in location of the retail cluster and other measures of the center of gravity are shown for six German and six Australian CBDs in]31, 53[.

d. The CBD as defined by the Census Bureau. Although both the city and the SMSA have been enlarged during this period, the decline remains dramatic. U.S. Bureau of Census, **1972 Census of Retail Trade**, Vol. III, **Major Retail Center Statistics**, Part I; and **1954 Census of Business, Central Business District Statistics Summary Report**, Bul. CBD-96 (Washington: Government Printing Office, 1976 and 1958).

e. Urban Renewal Administration and Bureau of Public Roads, **Standard Land Use Coding Manual** (Washington: U.S. Government Printing Office 1965).

f. As a modification of this method, floor space used for commercial parking was not counted either as CBD or non-CBD usage, since it does not represent an ultimate trip destination or origin.

g. The term CBD is used in this study only in reference to the area so delineated and shown on the maps. In other connections, the pedestrian-oriented district seems better reflected in the somewhat smaller "core" as defined by Horwood and Boyce]34[.

h. Distributions of pedestrian densities, as well as some other measures of development of the Atlanta core are shown in Deskins and Nystuen]19[.

i. The fact that straight line distance between intersections rather than street distance is used, contributes to this discrepancy.

REFERENCES

1. Baerwald, Thomas J., "The Emergence of a New Downtown", **The Geographical Review**, Vol. 68, No. 3 July, 1978, pp. 308-318.
2. Beaujeu-Garnier, Jacqueline, "Comparison des centre-villes aux Etats-Unis et en Europe: caracteristiques et possibilities d' evolution,"**Annales de geographie**, 81 annee No. 448 Nov-Dec, 1972, pp. 665-696.
3. Beaujeu-Garnier, Jacqueline, "Methode d'etude pour le centre des villes." **Annales de geographie**, Vol. 74 Nov-Dec, 1965, pp. 695-707.
4. Bell, Gwen, et al., **Urban Environments and Human Behavior, An Annotated Bibliography.** Stroudsbrug, PA.: Dowden, Hutchinson & Ross, 1973.
5. Berry, Brian J. L., **Geography of Market Centers and Retail Distribution**, Englewood Cliffs, N. J.: Prentice-Hall, Inc., 1967.
6. Berry, Brian J. L., "Internal Structure of the city," **Law and Contemporary Problems**, Winter, 1965, pp. 111-119.
7. Bohnert, J. E. and Mattingly, P. F., "Delimitation of the CBD through Time, **Economic Geography**, Vol. 40, 1964, pp. 337-347.
8. Bourne, L. S., **Private Redevelopment of the Central City**, Research Series, No. 112, Department of Geography, University of Chicago, 1967.
9. Bovy, Phillip H., **Pedestrian Planning and Design—A Bibliography**, Exchange Bibliography No. 918 Monticello, Ill.: Council of Planning Librarians, 1975.
10. Bowden, Martyn J., "Downtown through Time: Delimitation, Expansion, and Internal Growth," **Economic Geography** Vol. 47, No. 2 Apr., 1971, pp. 121-135.
11. Breese, Gerald W., **The Daytime Population of the Central Business District of Chicago, with Particular Reference to the Factor of Transportation**, Chicago: University of Chicago Press, 1949.
12. Carol, H., "The Hierarchy of Central Functions Within the City—Principles Developed in a Study of Zurich, Switzerland." **Proceedings of the UGU Symposium on Urban Geography, Lund**, 1960, Knut Norborg (ed.) (Lund, Sweden: Gleerup), 1962, pp. 555-576.
13. Carter, Harold, **The Study of Urban Geography** (2d ed)., New York: John Wiley & Sons, 1976.
14. Davey, Judith A., "Office Location and Mobility in

Wellington," **New Zealand Geographer**, Vol. 29, No 2 Oct., 1973, pp. 120-133.

15. Davey, Judith A., "Wellington's Office Industry," **Pacific Viewpoint**, Vol. 14, No. 1 May, 1973, pp. 45-60.
16. Davies, D. H., "Boundary Study as a Tool in CBD Analysis: An Interpretation of Certain Aspects of the Boundary of Cape Town's Central Business District," **Economic Geography**, Vol. 35, 1959, pp. 322-345.
17. Davies, D. H., "The Hard core of Cape Town's Central Business District," **Economic Geography**, Vol. 34, 1960, pp. 53-69.
18. Dent, Borden D., "Mapping Regional Shopping Center Trade Volumes in Atlanta, Georgia," **Southeastern Geographer**, Vol. 12, No. 2, Nov., 1972, pp. 69-77.
19. Deskins, Donald R., and Nystuen, John D., "Direct Observation as a Learning Strategy in Geography: Pedestrian Density and Functional Areas in Atlanta," **Southeastern Geographer**, Vol. 13, No. 2, Nov., 1973, pp. 105-126.
20. De Vries Reilingh, Hans D., "Tension Between Form and Function in Amsterdam," **Urban core and Inner city**, Leiden: E. J. Brill, 1967, pp. 309-323.
21. Diamond, D. R., "The Central Business District of Glasgow," **Proceedings of the UGU Symposium on Urban Geography, Lund**, 1960, Knut Norborg (ed.), (Lund, Sweden: Gleerup), 1962, pp. 555-576.
22. Foley, D. L., "The Daily Movement of Population into Central Business Districts," in H. M. Mayer and C. F. Cohn, **Readings in Urban Geography**, 1959, pp. 447-453.
23. Garbrecht, Dietrich, **Pedestrian Movement: A Bibliography**, Exchange Bibliography No. 225, Monticello, III.: Council of Planning Librarians, 1971.
24. Garbrecht, "Pedestrian Paths Through a Uniform Environment," **Town Planning Review**, Vol. 42, 1971, pp. 70-84.
25. Gaspar, Jorge, "A dinamica functional do centro de Lisboa,: **Finnisterra**, Vol. XI, 1976, pp. 37-150.
26. Goddard, John B., "Functional Regions within the city Centre," **Institute of British Geographers**, Transaction No. 49, Mar., 1970, pp. 161-182.
27. Goddard, John B., "The Internal Structure of London's Central Area," **Urban Core and Inner City**, Proceedings of the International Studyweek, Amsterdam, Sept. 11-17, 1966 Leiden: E. J. Brill, 1967, pp. 118-140.
28. Goddard, John B., "Multivariate Analysis of Office Location Patterns in the City Centre: A London Example," **Regional Studies**, Vol. 2, No. 1, 1968, pp. 69-

85.
29. Ehrenthall, Frank F., and Cunningham, Michael C., **A Selected Bibliography on Uses of the Urban Street.** Exchange Bibliography No. 266, Monticello, III.: Council of Planning Librarians, 1972.
30. Forrest, James, "Business Trip Activity Patterns," **New Zealand Geographer,** Vol. 33, 1977, pp. 50-59.
31. Hartenstein, W. and Staack, G., "Land Use in the Urban Core," **Proceedings of the International Studyweek,** Amsterdam, Leiden: E. J. Brill, 1967, pp. 35-52.
32. Hartshorn, Truman A., et al, **Atlanta, Metropolis in Georgia,** Cambridge, Mass.: Ballinger Publishing Company, 1976.
33. Hill, Michael R., **Pedestrian Behavior and Facilities Design: A Selected Bibliography, 1970-1975.** Exchange Bibliography No. 1112, Monticello, Ill.: Council of Planning Librarians, 1976.
34. Horwood, Edgar M. and Boyce, Ronald R., **A study of the Effects of Freeways on Central Business Districts,** Seattle: University of Washington Press, 1959.
35. Hoyt, Homer. **One Hundred Years of Land Values in Chicago,** New York: Arno Press, 1970.
36. Klein, H. J., "The Delimitation of the Town-Center in the Image of its Citizens," **Urban Core and Inner City,** Leiden: E. J. Brill, 1967, pp. 286-306.
37. Lewis, David (ed). **The Pedestrian in the City.** Architects' Yearbook XI., London: Elek Books, 1965.
38. Lynch, Kevin, **The Image of the City,** Cambridge: M.I.T. Press and Harvard University Press, 1960.
39. Mabogunge, Akin L., "The Evolution and Analysis of the Retail Structure of Lagos, Nigeria," **Economic Geography,** Vol. 40, 1964, pp. 304-323.
40. Martin, Ann, "The Pedestrian and the city: A Bibliography," **Ekistics,** Vol. 28, 166, Sept., 1969,p. 212.
41. Morris, Robert and Zisman, S. B., "The Pedestrian, Downtown, and the Planner", **Journal of the American Institute of Planners,** Vol. 28 (3), pp. 152-158.
42. Murphy, Raymond, **The Central Business District,** Chicago: Aldine-Atherton, 1972.
43. Murphy Raymond E., and Vance, J. E., Jr., "Delimiting the CBD," **Economic Geography,** Vol. 30, 1954, pp. 189-222
44. Murphy, Raymond E., "A comparative Study of Nine Central Business Districts," **Economic Geography,** Vol. 30, 1954, pp. 301-336.
45. Murphy, Raymond E., Vance, James E., and Epstein, B. J., "Internal Structure of the CBD," **Economic Geography,** Vol. 31, 1955, pp. 21-46.

46. Patel, Ahmed M., "The City Center of Rajshahi," **The Oriental Geographer**, Jan., 1974, pp. 26-47.
47. Petzoldt, Heinrich, **Innenstadt-Fussgangerverkehr**, Nurnberg: Wirtschafts- und Sozialgeographischen Institutes der Friedrich-Alexander-Universitat, 1974, pp. 289-291.
48. Plondke, Donald L., "Parking Rates as Indicators of Land Use Intensity in the Washington, D. C., CBD," **Virginia Geographer**, Vol. XI, 1976, pp. 8-18.
49. Prokop, Dieter, "Image and Function of the City," Urban Core and Inner City, **Proceedings of the International Studyweek**, Amsterdam, Leiden: E. J. Brill, 1967, pp. 22-34.
50. Rannells, John, **The Core of the City**, New York: Columbia University Press, 1956.
51. Schachar, A., "Geostatistical Techniques in Urban Research," **Regional Science Association Papers**, Vol. 18, pp. 197-206.
52. Scholler, Peter, "Center-Shifting and Centre-Mobility in Japanese Cities," **Proceedings of the UGU Symposium on Urban Geography, Lund**, 1960, Knut Norborg (ed.), Lund, Sweden: Gleerup, 1962, pp. 577-593.
53. Scott, P., "The Australian CBD," **Economic Geography**, Vol. 35, 1959, pp. 290-314.
54. Simonsen, Kirsten, and Matthiessen, Christian W., "Bycentres afgraensning," **Geografisk tidsskrift**, 70, 1971, pp. 178-190.
55. Sommer, John W., **Bibliography of Urban Geography, 1940-1960.** Geography Publications at Dartmouth No. 5, Hanover: Dartmouth College, 1966.
56. Starbuck, J. C., **Metropolitan Atlanta to 1930.** Exchange Bibliography No. 606-607., Monticello, Ill.: Council of Planning Librarians, 1974.
57. Starbuck, J. C. **Metropolitan Atlanta Update, 1970-1974.** Exchange Bibliography No. 765-766, Monticello, Ill.: Council o Planning Librarians, 1975.
58. Starbuck, J. C., **Planning Metropolitan Atlanta, 1909-1973.** Exchange Bibliography No. 578-579, Monticello, ILL.: Council of Planning Librarians, 1974.
59. Strand, Sverre, **Urban Geography, 1950-1970**, Exchange Bibliography No. 358-359-360, Monticello, ILL.: Council of Planning Librarians, 1973.

SECTION TWO

COMMERCIAL USE OF URBAN LAND

SEVEN

H. M. Saxena

Morphological Form and Typology of Market Towns in Rajasthan

The morphological pattern of a market town is a complex areal phenomenon consisting of the features of the market places and other infrastructures. It is difficult to establish whether marketing activity determines the man-made geographic structure of the towns or the structure of the town determines the marketing activity. In fact, the market infrastructures are the product of marketing activity and the structure of the town. It is a reflection not of the immediate and current space requirements of the community but rather of the cumulative needs over a period of years. The study of the morphological pattern is not only necessary to understand the present pattern but also to provide a guideline for its better planning.

The objective of the present paper is to study the form and typological pattern of market morphology of the market town in Rajasthan State. In all 80 market towns have been identified in the State and the present study is based on field work done by the author while studying market towns in Rajasthan.

FORMS OF MARKET MORPHOLOGY

Although the form of the market morphology of every town is unique in itself, yet on the basis of their common characteristics the following forms have been identified in the market towns of Rajasthan (Fig. 7.1).

1. Rectangular pattern,
2. Linear pattern,
3. Cross-road pattern, and
4. Complex or irregular pattern.

Fig. 7.1

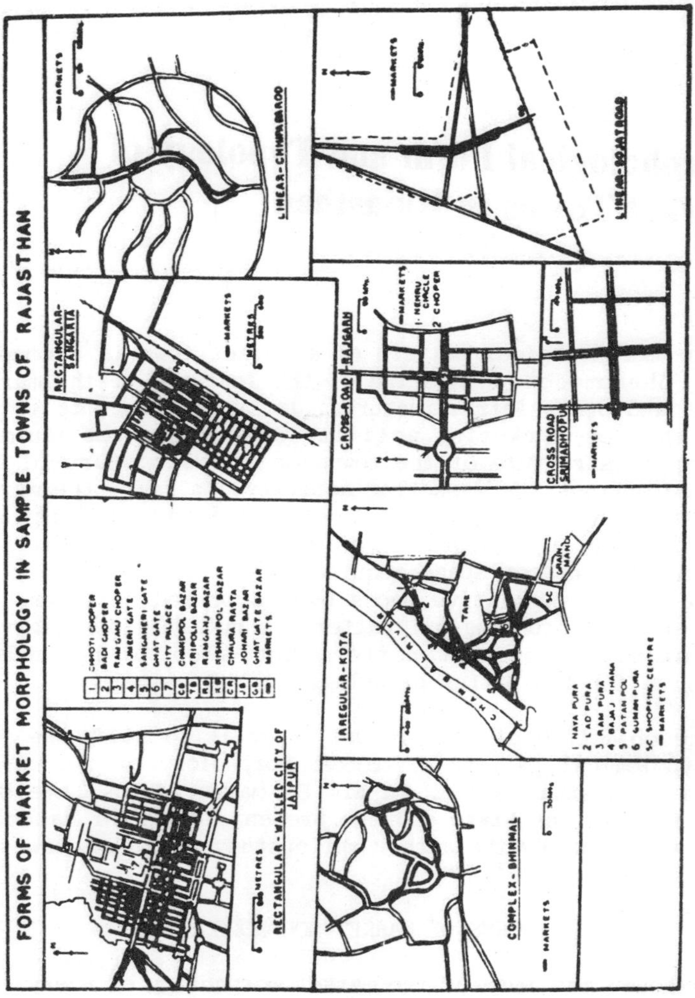
FORMS OF MARKET MORPHOLOGY IN SAMPLE TOWNS OF RAJASTHAN
RECTANGULAR-WALLED CITY OF JAIPUR
IRREGULAR-KOTA
COMPLEX-BHINMAL
CROSS-ROAD-RAJGARH
CROSS ROAD SRIMADHOPUR
LINEAR-SOJAT ROAD

Table 7.1 indicates the names of the market town having particular form of markets.

TABLE 7.1

Morphological forms of market towns in Rajasthan

Form or Pattern	Name of the Market Town
1. Rectangular	Jaipur, Phalodi, Ramganjmandi, Nokha, Ganganagar, Hanumangarh, Sangaria, Raisinghnagar, Sadulshahar, Dungargarh, Jhunjhunu, Sheoganj, Bhawanimandi.
2. Linear	Bandi-kuai, Kotputali, Chhipabarod, Bhimasar, Gangashahar, Bhinder, Salumber, Kherli, Nonar, Karanpur, Gajsinghpur, Padampur, Bhilwara, Neem-ka-thana, Nadbai, Tonk, Newai, Ladnu, Hindaun, Dungarpur, Sagwara, Pirawa, Sojat-road, Sumerpur, Pratapgarh.
3. Cross-Road	Bijainagar, Chhabra, Rajgarh, Lachhmangarh, Ramgarh, Sri Madhopur, Khandela, Bari, Bayania, Sujangarh, Sardarshahar, Bundi, Kushalgarh, Nawalgarh, Chirawa.
4. Complex or Irregular	Jodhpur, Ajmer, Beawar, Kota, Baran Bikaner, Udaipur, Nathdwara, Deogarh, Alwar, Khairthal, Bhadra, Sikar, Bharatpur, Churu, Nagaur, Didwana, Kuchaman, Barmer, Balotra, Gangapur, Banswara, Chittorgarh, Jhalrapatan, Bhinmal, Bari Sadari.

Rectangular pattern

This form of market morphology is a characteristic feature of the planned towns. In these towns street pattern is of 'grid-iron' type, therefore, markets also follow the same pattern. In Rajasthan, 13 market towns are having rectangular form of market morphology. Jaipur, the State capital, is an excellent example of old planned town and all the markets of walled city are typically rectangular in pattern.

Linear pattern

This form of markets located along one or more than one road, is a characteristic of medium-size town, mostly class II or III type of urban centres as classified in census. In the region under study as many as 25 towns are having linear form of markets. Bhilwara town is the largest one in which linear pattern is prevalent, because of its natural growth along a main road.

Cross-road pattern

This form of markets is prevalent in 15 market-towns of

Rajasthan. In these towns markets usually developed along the crossing of the main roads, generally, at the centre of the city.

FIG. 7.2

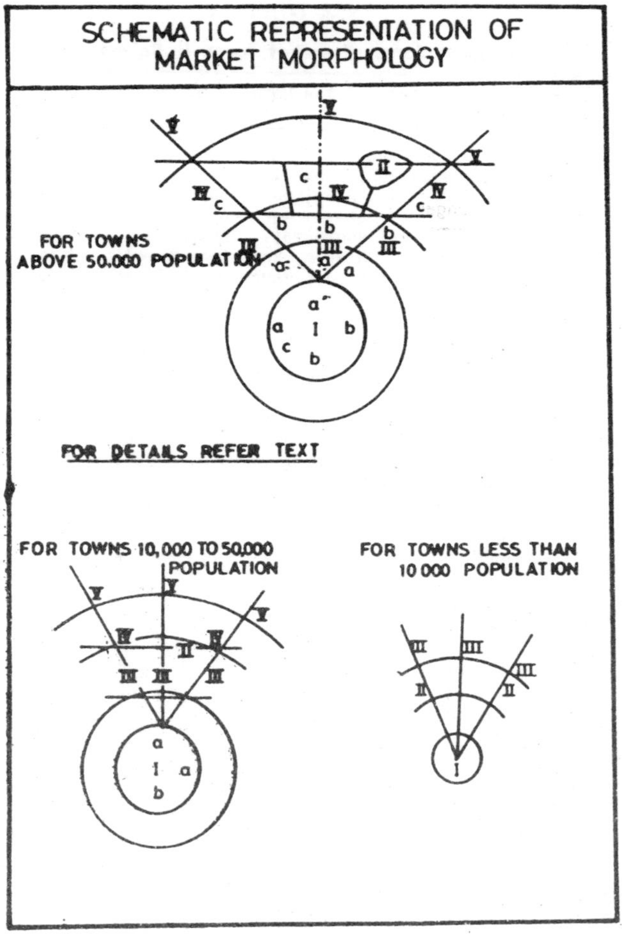

Complex or Irregular pattern

This form is an indication of unplanned or rapid growth of a town. In Rajasthan, big towns like Jodhpur, Ajmer, Kota, Udaipur, Bikaner, Bharatpur, Alwar, etc., are having complex forms of market morphology. In all, 29 market towns possess this type of pattern.

TABLE 7.2

TYPOLOGY OF THE COMPONENTS OF MARKET MORPHOLOGY

For towns having more than 50,000 population

Primary Components		Secondary Components
I	Central Business Area	(a) Mixed retail zone (b) Wholesale zone (c) Regional centres
II	Secondary Business Area	(a) Retail shops (b) Wholesale shops
III	Principal BusinessArteries	(a) Retail strings (b) Service-cum-sale shop (c) Service shops
IV	Connecting BusinessStreets	(a) Grocers shops (b) Furniture row (c) Vegetable and Fruits row (d) Auto-repair shop (e) Drug stores (f) Other specialised rows
V	Isolated Clusters	(a) Commodity stores (b) Service stores (c) Mixed stores

For towns having 10,000 to 50,000 population

Primary Components		Secondary Components
I	Central Business Area	(a) Retail shops (b) Regional centres
II	Secondary Business Area	Retail-cum-wholesale shops
III	Principal Business Artery	Mixed type of shops
IV	Connecting Business street	Grocers, Furniture, Service-cum-sale shops
V	Isolated clusters	Grocers stores and Tea-stalls
VI	Isolated shops	-

For towns having less than 10,000 population

I	Central Business street	Mixed shops
II	Adjoining Business street	M'xed shops
III	Isolated shops	-

MORPHOLOGICAL COMPONENTS AND THEIR TYPCLOGY

Geographers have done considerable work on market structures as a part of urban morphology as well as independent units of city structures. Proudfoot's (1937) work can be considered as a pioneer one and may be considered as classical. The five components of market morphology as described by Proudfoot are (i) the central business district, (ii) the outlying business centre, (iii) the principal business through fare, (iv) the neighbourhood business street, and (v) the isolated store clusters. Other studies in this field have been done by Weimer and Hoyt (1948), Brown and Davidson (1953), Kelley (1955), Berry (1967), etc. All the above mentioned studies are related to highly urbanised market centres of the developed countries and only a few studies have been done to unfold the components of market morphology in India. After intensive study of the market towns in Rajasthan the author has developed following typology of the components of market morphology (Fig. 7.2)and (Table 7.2)

GENERAL CHARACTERISTICS

Central Business Area (CBA)

It is similar to CBD but not having its all characteristics as described by foreign geographers. Therefore, in present context it has been referred to as CBA. It represents the retail heart of the town with facilities of wholesale marketing also. In cities like Jaipur, Ajmer, Udaipur, Jodhpur, Kota, Bikaner, the CBA covers a larger area and consists of inner core, inner-belt and outer belt. There is also a tendency of shift from old congested core to the new core, as in case of Udaipur, where Bapu Bazar and its adjacent street has become a new core of business. In small towns the CBA is either a principal business street or the cross-roads of the main market, while in very small towns there is a tendency of its non-existence.

Secondary business area (SBA)

To fulfill the needs of the growing population SBA has also been developed in big market towns. Merchandise sold in secondary business area are similar to that of CBA with a difference that volume of business is limited. In towns like Jaipur, Udaipur, Ajmer, Jodhpur, Kota, Bikaner, Sriganganagar, and Alwar more than one SBA has developed but in small towns it has no existence.

Principal business arteries

It is a characteristic of all the market towns in Rajasthan, although its size varies according to the size of the town. In small towns this artery has also a function of principal business area. It consists of various types of retail and service-cum-sale shops.

Connecting business streets

These streets are either inter-linked with principal business street or off-shoots of them. These are characterised by the presence of several types of shops such as grocery, vegetables, furniture, automobile goods, service shops, etc.

Isolated clusters and shops

These are characteristically found in all categories of towns. In towns with more than 50,000 population the number is more and widely distributed in several residential areas of the town. These clusters and shops usually comprise mixed types of shops and provide convenient shopping facilities to people residing far-away from markets.

The study reveals that market morphological pattern becomes more and more complex as towns grow in size. The growth of market morphology in Rajasthan is very much related with the growth of settlements. In their initial stage only few shops perform the minimum demands of a small village. When it becomes a town, a series of shops develop along main road or at cross-roads. The growth of population and settlement results in the form of complex market morphological units and other infrastructures. We can conclude that there is a direct relationship between growth of population, urban development and growth of market morphology.

REFERENCES

Berry, B. J. L., **Geography of Market Centres and Retail Distribution**, Prentice-Hall, 1967.

Brown, P. L. & Davidson, W. P., **Retailing Principles and Practices**, Ronald Press, New York, 1953.

Kelley, E. J., Retail Structure of Urban, **Traffic Quarterly**, Vol. 9, 1955, pp. 411-30.

Proudfoot, M. J., City Retail Structure, **Economic Geography** Vol. 13, No.4, 1937.

Weimer, M and Hoyt, H., **Principles of Urban Real Estate**, Ronald Press, New York

EIGHT

Kent A. Robertson

The Downtown Hotel

Evolution and Recent Trends in the Large American City

Throughout American history, the hotel has played a prominent role in the evolving structure of central cities. In physical terms, it has been noted that hotels have consistently been among the grandest buildings in large American cities, while often overshadowing other structures in many medium-sized and smaller cities.[1] Hotels have also been important in cultural terms as they have been traditionally utilized as centres for a variety of social and public affairs, thereby prompting the label "palaces of the public." The historical significance of hotels within American urban culture has been strongly suggested by several historians. For instance, Starrett stated that hotels were "the most distinctively American thing in the world,"[2] and Boorstin maintained "it was not by churches or government buildings but by hotels that cities judged themselves and expected others to judge them."[3] Currently, federal policy is helping to facilitate the development and/or renovation of downtown hotels in the promise of their potential to provide solid anchors of centre city revitalization.

Despite the obvious importance relegated to hotels within the evolution of downtowns, little has been generated in an attempt to descriptively or empirically document the history or current status of this activity. Social science has virtually ignored the subject matter of hotels, with the exception of a few works which examine the type of people who frequent these establishments.[4] A few historical accounts of hotels have been produced;[5] however, these efforts primarily concentrate on the 19th century, and tend to possess an anecdotal quality. The greatest amount of hotel literature can be found in the hospitality and travel journals. Unfortunately, these are principally concerned with issues of management and marketing, and therefore are not particularly useful in an assessment of the historical or contemporary role of the hotel within the structure of the Central Business District (CBD).[6] In sum, it must be concluded that social scientists and historians have conducted infrequent research pertaining to historical, locational, and social aspects of American hotels.

This lack on scholarly attention is somewhat curious in that the hotel has played such a significant role in the historical development of American cities. Moreover, hotels appear to be constituting a major component of many CBD redevelopment plans across the country. It could be asserted, therefore, that a better understanding of the role and magnitude of the downtown hotel, in both the past and present tense, should be acquired in order to facilitate the effectiveness of future policies and plans. Accordingly, the purpose of this article is to (1) briefly describe the evolution of the downtown hotel since the early nineteenth century, and (2) document and analyze some of the trends exhibited by downtown hotels between 1968-1979.

HISTORICAL EVOLUTION

It has been generally acknowledged that the modern first-class hotel, as we think of it today, was born in the United States in the early 19th century. The small-scale inns of Europe emerged as grand hotels in this country. Even the term "hotel" made its first appearance in America in its current context (the word itself was borrowed from a French derivative meaning noble house). Besides their grander scale, American hotels demonstrated many peculiarities which differentiated them from their European counterparts: (1) there was an abundance of permanent residents, (2) they were built for the enjoyment of the masses, not just the wealthy, (3) they became great social centres for the general public, (4) they were frequently utilized because Americans traveled more than did Europeans, and (5) hotels were often built by corporations, thus they were frequently closely tied to railroad and industrial concerns.

It has been reported that the first hotel in this country constructed exclusively for hotel purposes was the City Hotel in New York in 1794.[7] It was located on lower Broadway in what was then the core of the city. The Tremont in Boston (1829) is considered to be the initial modern first-class hotel in terms of its size, structural design, and innovative features. It served as the prototype of first-class city hotels for most of the remainder of the century. New York's first modern hotel was the Astor, which was completed in 1834. Although similar to the Tremont in many regards, it was not as successful because of its location, which was described as "too far uptown".[8] In other words, these early hotels needed a central location to take advantage of traveller's routes and the traffic generated by other core activities. As downtown Manhattan expanded, the Astor's location became more centralized, and thus the hotel became more prominent. New York's rapid growth also facilitated a marked increase in the number of hotels, which grew from 8 in 1818 to 28 in 1836 to 108 by 1846.[9]

Since the inception of the Tremont, hotels in the remainder of the 1800s can best be characterized as (1) increasing in size, (2) increasing in grandeur, and (3) adopting a series of luxury-breeding gadgets, such as elevators, upstairs plumbing and gaslights. Moreover, the building of grand hotels, which had previously been an east coast phenomenon, was becoming common place in other areas of the country in the second half of the century. While many small eastern cities possessed only small hotels or inns, a high percentage of the young growing cities of the midwest were building large fancy hotels: "by 1850, many a booming little city of the plains had at least one hotel nearly...to the standard of those of New York or Boston".[10] In fact, so important were hotels to the viability of midwestern cities that at times a hotel was built in the middle of nowhere in hopes that a city might develop around it. Although usually unsuccessful, such an approach is partially responsible for the growth of Memphis.[11]

As alluded to above, most cities in the midwest would possess at least one New York-like grand hotel which was easily the largest, most expensive and most important building in the city. The typical mid-19th century attitude was that no city amounted to anything unless it contains one or more fine hotels which present the visitor with a favorable image. The belief in this premise underscored the building of the Burnett House in unpretentious Cincinnati, which, at the time of the Civil War, was considered by many to be the finest hotel in the world. Large cities were developing many large hotels, as is evidenced by Chicago's 20 first-class hotels in 1873. Grand downtown hotels were not frequent in the south or west until the last two decades of the century, with notable exceptions being Atlanta, New Orleans and San

Francisco; the downtown of the latter already possessed 26 hotels by 1850.[12]

The early part of the twentieth century witnessed an increase in both the size and number of hotels in downtown areas. In the first decade, several hotels had been constructed which contained in excess of 1000 rooms, including the Waldorf-Astoria and Plaza in New York and the LaSalle, Congress, and Morrison in Chicago. By 1932, the new Waldorf-Astoria in New York and the Stevens (since renamed the Conrad Hilton) in Chicago exceeded 2000 rooms each. An example of the increasing number of hotels is found in San Francisco, where the number of central district hotels steadily increased from 23 to 125 to 140 in 1906, 1915, and 1931, respectively.[13]

Nationwide, a hotel building boom took place in the 1920s for a variety of reasons. First, since the occupancy rates in existing hotels were so high following the First World War, this was a popular industry in which to invest money. Second, as was a key factor in the previous century, hotels were an expression of civic pride and a centre for community activity. Third, as a part of the City Beautiful movement in urban planning, grand hotels were often constructed for the purpose of improving the physical appearance of centralized sections of the city. And fourth, hotels at times facilitated an effort to satisfy individual vanity or to commemorate one's life in the form of a monument. As a result, too many hotels were built which, when combined with the depression and the Second World War, led to a severe decline in number in viable downtown hotels during 1930-1945.[14]

While the lodging industry in general rebounded following World War II, the plight of the CBD hotel continued on a negative note. One reason for this was that downtown hotels were becoming old, and unlike their European counterparts, American hotels usually did not acquire charm with age. Secondly, the growth of Motels in response to the general decentralization of urban activities, the proliferation of automobile travel in part facilitated by the new constructed interstate highway system, and the nature of motel investments which invited speculation,[15] exerted a negative impact on hotels in the CBD; in fact, the number of hotel rooms now exceeds the hotel inventory.[16] Travel mode preference, which changed from the train, for which terminals were usually located in or near the CBD, to the automobile and airplane, also fueled the decline of downtown hotels. Generally, smaller hotels were hurt more so than large ones, and hotels in larger cities (i.e., those over 400,000 population) tended to do better than those in smaller cities. One way in which the large hotel in the large city was able to survive was by catering to the convention business. Although insignificant until the late 1950s, by the mid-1960s conventions accounted for over 40 per cent of the downtown hotel business, with the figure reaching as high as 90 per cent in certain cities (e.g., San Francisco).[17] Another post-war trend is the steady takeover of previously independent hotels by large chains such as Sheraton, Hilton, Howard Johnson, and Holiday Inn. Moreover, almost all new downtown hotels are constructed and operated by these or other large multinational firms, including the airlines.

The potential for this component of the CBD to revitalize in the 1970s and 1980s appears to be mixed. On the one hand, the apparent trend towards office-oriented downtowns has been suggested as a negative factor for hotels because of the absence of activity at night and on weekends, which are prime times for the hotel industry.[18] Further research has indicated that many tourists may actually prefer peripheral hotel locations over downtown locations, particularly if prices are cheaper and transportation is available.[19] However, on the other hand, Lundberg has noted that the 1970s has witnessed a revival of the building of large hotels, especially within large CBDs. Frequently, new hotels are built to replace older hotels which were removed for the construction of new office buildings; if still standing a number of these older downtown hotels have been revived in recent years.[20] Additionally, new hotel corporations such as Hyatt, Marriott, and Radisson have or will build the majority of their hotels in downtown locations, while at the same time, the federal government (i.e., through UDAG), has been providing partial financial support in order to encourage further development of hotels in central cities.

To summarize, hotels have historically been a vital component within the structure of American central business districts, both from a functional perspective (in terms of its actual use) and in terms of perception (based on both external and internal image). However, the extent to which CBD hotels will continue to play an important role is debatable at the present time.

TREND ANALYSIS, 1968-1979

As already suggested, there has been little research

dedicated to the economic, locational, or social aspects of urban hotels, and what little has been produced has come from the field of hotel and tourism management, not from the social sciences. Moreover, the works which have appeared have been descriptive in nature, indicating that empirical studies of urban hotels, downtown or otherwise, have been virtually ignored. Using data published by the American Hotel and Motel Association, the purpose of this section is to present an examination of trends based on the number of CBD hotel rooms in existence between 1968-1979. This will constitute an initial effort in the attempt to fill the void pertaining to empirical research on the downtown hotel.

Research method

The data to be used in the study of CBD hotel trends were obtained from an annual listing of hotels published by the American Hotel and Motel Association (AHMA) entitled the **Hotel and Motel Red Book.**[21] For several decades, the Red Book has listed a series of information on each member establishment on a city-by-city basis, the most important of which being the number of hotel rooms. This data source became considerably more applicable to the needs of this analysis, however, when a locational indicator system was initiated in 1968. Ever since, hotels have been classified as being situated at one of the following sites: airport, downtown, suburb, expressway, or resort. Therefore, for each of the sample cities, the total number of hotels and the total number of hotel rooms were tabulated on the basis of hotels designated as being located downtown. These data were collected for the years 1968, 1972, 1975 and 1979.

Once the individual city figures were calculated and transcribed, they were subject to several further tabulations. First, the number of rooms and hotels were summed so as to determine national, regional, and population size totals. Second, the categorical totals were analyzed on an absolute basis and in terms of the rate of change exhibited over various periods of time. Finally, the rates of change for individual city hotel rooms were determined for 1968-1979. Based on these calculations, a series of interesting research findings were uncovered which should add to the current knowledge base on CBD hotels.

Several criteria were utilized in order to arrive at the final number of 89 CBDs which will constitute the total sample for the trend analysis. First, since the focus of this research is on CBDs of large American cities, only those central cities with populations of over 100,000 people, as determined by the United States Census, are included. Second, of this initial number, only those cities which exceeded the 100,000 figure in both 1954 and 1970 were embodied in the sample. The second criterion is necessary in that a number of municipalities (i.e., Virginia Beach, Virginia; Garden Grove, California; Hollywood, Florida) have experienced substantial growth since the early 1950s to where their population exceed 100,000; however, since many of these are no more than "bedroom communities" with no centralized business district in the conventional sense, they are not deemed as salient to this research. Third, cities that are dwarfed by larger cities in the same SMSA are excluded. Examples of cities which were eliminated from the sample for this reason include Camden, Yonkers, Berkeley and Pasadena. Finally, cities such as Gary, Paterson and Scranton were not included because their CBDs contained no member hotels in any of the survey years. Once the sample was selected, the CBDs were classified into six geographic regions and four population size groupings. The final sample of 89 CBDs, categorized by region and population size, can be observed in Table 8.1.

Limitations

Unfortunately, the AHMA data, which to this author's knowledge have heretofore not been utilized in any social science research, are subject to several limitations which may reduce their analytical value. The first limiting factor centres on the lack of a precise definition of "downtown". There is no indication in the Red Book as to the area encompassed, either generally or specifically for each city, by the label downtown. In other words, the non-articulation of a definition implies that the locational indicator could be highly variable from city to city. However, an examination of several cities of which this author is personally familiar indicates that virtually all hotels labelled as downtown are indeed located within the census-defined CBD,[22] while other hotels found in peripheral areas of the city tended to be labelled as expressway. Hopefully, this relationship also characterizes the locational determination in the remainder of sample cities.

Secondly, the period of time covered in the hotel research is not as extensive as one would like. The primary reason for the limited timespan of the present study is that there was no indication as to location prior to the 1968 listing. Moreover, the locational indicator system was

TABLE 8.1
CBD Classifications

Region/ Population	North East	South Atlantic	South Central	North Central	Midwest	West
1 million + (6)	New York Philadelphia		Houston	Chicago Detroit		Los Angeles
500,000 - 1 million (20)	Baltimore Boston Pittsburgh Washington	Jacksonville Memphis	Dallas New Orleans San Antonio	Cleveland Columbus Indianapolis Milwaukee	Denver Kansas City (MO) St. Louis	Phoenix San Diego San Francisco Seattle
200,000 - 500,000 (37)	Buffalo Jersey City Newark Rochester	Atlanta Birmingham Charlotte Louisville Miami Nashville Norfolk Richmond St. Petersburg Tampa	Austin Corpus Christi El Paso Ft. Worth Oklahoma City Tulsa	Akron Cincinnati Dayton Toledo	Des Moines minnepolis Omaha St. Paul Witchita	Albuquerque Honolulu Long Beach Oakland Portland Sacramento San Jose Tucson
100,000 - 200,000 (26)	Albany Allentown Erie New Bedford New Haven Providence Syracuse Trenton Waterbury Worcester	Chatanooga Mobile Montgomery Savannah	Little Rock Shreveport	Evansville Flint Ft. Wayne Grand Rapids Rockford Youngstown	Kansas City (KA) Salt Lake city	Fresno Spokane
89	(20)	(16)	(12)	(16)	(10)	(15)

Note: Population based on 1970 census categories.

incomplete in 1968 since it was just being incorporated into the directory. Therefore, through the use of addresses and locational determinations in subsequent years, the 1968 data represent a combination of information sources. The end result should be a fairly accurate portrayal of CBD hotels in 1968, although the numbers may lack some of the precision found in the 1972, 1975 and 1979 statistics.

Finally, the study of downtown hotels alone only measures changes in absolute, not relative, terms. No intra-city comparative examination is possible because the AHMA reports on hotels on the basis of the town or city to which they are most closely situated. As a result, it is extremely difficult to examine the data in terms of the SMSA since the information is not assembled on a county-by-county (or other large political units) basis. Consequently, the hotel analysis will not include a comparative CBD-SMSA component which would have greatly enhanced our level of understanding. Although the several inherent limitations cannot be dismissed, the AHMA data can be justified in that, not only are they a relatively good indicator of hotel trends, they also are the only data source uncovered that approaches an adequate level of comprehensiveness on this subject area.

Analysis of hotel data

An overview of national hotel figures for CBDs reveals that this function has been declining in stature from 1968-1979. This trend is most clearly manifested in the total number of CBD hotel rooms, which have steadily decreased in number from 255, 330 in 1968 to 233,867 in 1979; this represents a decrease of 8.41 per cent. The most dramatic change took place between 1975-1979, when over 15,000 downtown rooms were lost (-6.09%); this figure compares to decline rates of only 1.21 and 1.27 for 1968-1972 and 1972-1975, respectively (or just over 3,000 rooms per period). The total number of CBD hotels also displayed a downward trend from 1968-1979, although showing a healthy increase between 1968 (804 hotels) and 1972 (832 hotels). Reflecting the tremendous reduction of downtown rooms between 1975-1979, the number of hotels also rapidly declined from 822 to 771, a percentage decrease of 6.2. Finally, the average hotel size, determined by dividing hotel rooms by hotels, shows an overall decrease from 318 rooms in 1968 to 303 rooms in 1979. However, the average number of rooms which initially fell to 303 in 1972, has since stabilized.

The various geographic regions into which the 89 sample

cities were categorized exhibited several distinct and contrasting trends, as can be observed in Tables 8.2 and 8.3. The cities of the North East and Midwest reflect a trend for number of hotels closely resembling the national pattern, showing an increase from 1968-1972 followed by a steady decline in subsequent years. The North Central and South Atlantic cities also had a diminishing number of hotels, the former steadily decreasing each year while all of the latter's decline took place between 1975-1979. On the other hand, the so-called "sunbelt" regions (South Central and West) both displayed continual increases for each survey period, with both areas having overall increases of approximately twenty-five per cent.

TABLE 8.2
CBD Hotel Rooms Categorical Totals

	1968	1972	1975	1979
Nation	255,530 (804)	252,240 (832)	249,033 (822)	233,867 (771)
Region				
North East	97,436 (220)	98,469 (226)	86,652 (201)	74,104 (184)
South Atlantic	27,206 (140)	23,548 (140)	30,571 (140)	27,113 (114)
North Central	46,609 (116)	40,467 (104)	37,074 (110)	37,184 (95)
South Central	27,398 (98)	27,510 (100)	29,188 (114)	30,965 (121)
Midwest	25,795 (95)	25,611 (101)	24,901 (96)	22,054 (85)
West	30,886 (135)	36,635 (162)	40,647 (170)	42,447 (172)
Population Size				
1 million +	106,860 (207)	106,831 (206)	92,501 (192)	84,082 (182)
500,000-1 million	79,972 (275)	86,405 (304)	90,578 (318)	88,323 (311)
200,000-500,000	52,258 (239)	44,927 (243)	51,365 (234)	47,931 (207)
100,000-200,000	16,240 (83)	14,077 (79)	14,589 (78)	13,531 (71)

Note: Number of hotels represented in parentheses.

An examination of the number of CBD hotel rooms reveals two distinct regional patterns. On the one hand, regions which include a majority of older industrial cities all sharply dropped between 1968-1979. The North East declined by over 23,000 rooms (-23.94%), while the North Central (-20.22) and the Midwest (-14.50) also suffered substantial losses. Conversely, the regions with the newer and more service-oriented cities exhibited healthy increases of 13.02 per cent (South Central) and 37.43 per cent (West). Interestingly, the South Central's upswing was primarily manifested between 1972-1979, while over one-half of the increase in cities of the West occurred between 1968-1972. The South Atlantic was the only region not conforming to one of these patterns, as it showed an inconsistent trend line ranging from decreases of 13.44 per cent and 11.31 per cent to an amazing increase of 29.82 per cent (1972-1975). The trends from 1975-1979 fairly well reflect the overall tendencies as the South Central and West increased somewhat, and the North East, South Atlantic, and Midwest all significantly declined; notably, the North Central deviated from its normal downward trend with a modest gain of 0.30 per cent (see Table 8.3).

TABLE 8.3

CBD hotel rooms: rates of change

	1968-1979	1968-1972	1972-1975	1975-1979
Nation	-8.41	-1.21	-1.27	-6.09
Region				
North East	-23.94	+1.06	-11.97	-14.48
South Atlantic	-0.34	-13.44	+29.82	-11.31
North Central	-20.22	-13.18	-8.38	+0.30
South Central	+13.02	+0.41	+6.10	+6.09
Midwest	-14.50	-0.71	-2.77	-11.43
West	+37.43	+18.61	+10.95	+4.43
Population Size				
1 million +	-21.31	-0.03	-13.41	-9.10
500,000-1 million	+10.44	+8.04	+4.83	-2.49
200,000-500,000	-8.28	-14.01	+14.21	-6.61
100,000-200,000	-16.68	-13.32	+3.64	-7.25

Based on city population size, a trend emerges in three of the four categories which points to considerable decline, both in terms of number of hotels and hotel rooms in the CBD. In every classification except the 500,000-1 million range, substantial decreases were recorded. In the grouping of largest cities, hotel rooms declined by 21.31 per cent while the decline rates for cities of 200,000-500,000 and 100,000-200,000 were 8.28 per cent and 16.68 per cent respectively. Likewise, the number of hotels in each of these size categories diminished between 12.1 per cent and 14.5 per cent from 1968-79. At the same time, cities with populations ranging from 500,000-1 million exhibited a marked upswing in both hotel rooms (+10.44%) and hotels (+13.09%) overall, declining only in the 1975-1979 time period. The category with the most volatile results is the 200,000-500,000 grouping, which had change rates ranging from a 14.01 per cent decrease to a 14.21 per cent increase. One final observation is that the 1972-1975 period was the most prosperous in terms of individual categorical gains, as three of the four groups increased during these years, the one exception being the largest cities (-13.41%).

TABLE 8.4

Individual CBD Hotel Trends
Rates of Change 1968-1979

Population Size	Cities Exhibiting Greatest Rates of Increase		Cities Exhibiting Greatest Rates of Decrease	
500,000 +	1. Phoenix (W)	+121.7	1. Jacksonville (SA)	-45.0
	2. Seattle (W)	+76.6	2. Philadelphia (NE)	-43.1
	3. New Orleans (SC)	+60.2	3. St. Louis (MW)	-40.9
	4. San Francisco (W)	+38.7	4. Cleveland (NC)	-40.2
	5. Pittsburgh (NE)	+35.7	5. Milwaukee (NC)	-35.7
	6. Dallas (SC)	+33.6	6. New York (NE)	-31.2
	7. San Antonio (SC)	+18.9	7. Baltimore (NE)	-29.4
	8. Indianapolis (NC)	+17.0	8. Detroit (NC)	-23.2
200,000 - 500,000	1. Long Beach (W)	+307.5	1. Akron (NC)	-93.7
	2. Tucson (W)	+163.9	2. Newark (NE)	-70.9
	3. Fort Worth (SC)	+140.7	3. Charlotte (SA)	-68.0
	4. Tampa (SA)	+116.6	4. Toledo (NC)	-66.8
	5. Albuquerque (W)	+110.4	5. Tulsa (SC)	-64.9
	6. Nashville (SA)	+78.6	6. Buffalo (NE)	-60.3
	7. Atlanta (SA)	+69.2	7. Jersey City (NE)	-56.8
	8. Honolulu (W)	+44.7	8. Omaha (MW)	-54.9
	9. Corpus Christi (SC)	+39.3	9. Oklahoma City (SC)	-47.8
	10. Des Moines (MW)	+28.7	10. St. Paul (MW)	-46.6
100,000 - 200,000	1. Erie (NE)	+186.7	1. Ft. Wayne (NC)	-100.0
	2. Mobile (SA)	+76.6	2. Allentown (NE)	-100.0
	3. New Haven (NE)	+75.0	3. Flint (NC)	-100.0
	4. Worcester (NE)	+67.7	4. New Bedford (NE)	-100.0
	5. Salt Lake City (MW)	+31.2	5. Rockford (NC)	-100.0
	6. Spokane (W)	+30.2	6. Trenton (NE)	-100.0
	7. Chatanooga (SA)	+19.3	7. Youngstown (NC)	-100.0
			8. Shreveport (SC)	-85.7
			9. Evansville (NC)	-74.9
			10. Albany (NE)	-67.0

Note: Region indicated in parentheses

An analysis of individual CBD change rates for 1968-1979 yields several interesting observations which lends support to a hypothesized relationship between hotel viability and regional location. Looking at cities with populations in excess of 500,000 initially, Table 8.4 shows that, of the seven cities displaying the highest percentage increases, six are in sunbelt regions, including the top four (Phoenix, Seattle, New Orleans, and San Francisco). At the same time, none of the eight cities experiencing the greatest decline was classified as sunbelt. Secondly, an examination of cities in the 200,000-500,000 population range reveals that the ten highest growth rates were registered by cities in the South Atlantic, South Central, or West regions, the top three being Long Beach (+307.%), Tucson (+163.9%), and Fort Worth (+140.7%). Conversely, eight of the ten cities with the highest decline rates were situated in the North Central, North East, and Midwest, with the other two cities (Tulsa, Oklahoma City) possibly resembling cities of the Midwest more so than the South Central in which they are classified. This regional pattern is less apparent in the smaller size sample cities, as the individual cities with high growth rates are geographically dispersed. The list of greatest declines, however, clearly indicates that frostbelt cities dominate, as nine of the ten (the exception being Shreveport) cities are either in the North East or North Central. Moreover, all seven cities (Allentown, Fort Wayne, Flint, New Bedford, Rockford, Trenton, and Youngstown) that experienced a 100 per cent decline rate are located in these two regions.

TABLE 8.5

Individual CBD Hotel Figures (1979)

Population Size	CBDs with the Most Rooms		CBDs with the Least Rooms	
500,000 +	1. New York (NE)	42458	1. Jacksonvilles (SA)	822
	2. Chicago (NC)	20441	2. Baltimore (NE)	1382
	3. San Francisco (W)	15126	3. Columbus (NC)	1491
	4. Washington (NE)	12644	4. San Diego (W)	1609
	5. New Orleans (SC)	9063	5. Memphis (SA)	1807
	6. Los Angeles (W)	8127		
	7. Houston (SC)	6280		
	8. Boston (NE)	6160		
	9. Dallas (SC)	5624		
	10. Denver (MW)	4819		
200,000-500,000	1. Atlanta (SA)	9711	1. Akron (NC)	41
	2. Minneapolis (MW)	3650	2. Jersey City (NE)	82
	3. Portland (W)	2539	3. San Jose (W)	240
	4. Cincinnati (NC)	2365	4. Newark (NE)	288
	5. Miami (SA)	2261	5. Oakland (W)	367
100,000-200,000	1. Salt Lake City (MW)	2865	The following reported zero rooms:	
	2. Spokane (W)	1461	Allentown (NE)	Youngstown (NC)
	3. Chatanooga (SA)	1309	Flint (NC)	Rockford (NC)
	4. Savanah (SA)	937	Fort Wayne (NC)	
	5. Mobile (SA)	814	Trenton (NE)	
			New Bedford (NE)	

Note: Region indicated in parentheses

OTHER CONSIDERATIONS

To better understand the reasons underscoring the CBD hotel trends just presented, factors other than city population size and regional location must be taken into consideration. Four factors are examined in this section: economic functions of cities, governmental activities in cities, the prevalence of some special tourist-related quality of a city, and trends exhibited in downtown retail activity.

A basic way to investigate the question of economic function is by determining downtown hotel performance in cities dominated by manufacturing activity as opposed to those which are considered distribution centres (i.e., dominated by service and retail industries).[23] Regionally, a fairly straight forward relationship is observed whereby areas that primarily consist of manufacturing cities displayed the highest decline in CBD hotel rooms. The regions that experienced the highest rates of hotel decline (North East, North Central, and Midwest) each contained at least seventy per cent manufacturing cities, while the South Atlantic, South Central and West, each of which possessed approximately fifty per cent manufacturing cities, showed stability or growth in their downtown hotel sector (see Table 8.6). This trend also emerges when individual cities are examined. In the 31 sample cities in which manufacturing was the predominant economic activity, only five avoided decline in downtown hotels. The hotel trends were evenly mixed (16 increases, 16 declines) in the 32 cities where manufacturing was the prime activity but where distribution was also an important component of the economy. This suggests that an urban economic base that is diversified and less dependent on manufacturing may provide some opportunity for hotel growth. Furthermore, if manufacturing plays a less than dominant role in the city's economy, the chances for CBD hotel growth increases considerably; of the 25 sample cities classified as being oriented towards distributional activities, 16 showed increases in downtown hotel rooms. Therefore, it is apparent that the role of the CBD hotel is much less significant in manufacturing oriented cities. This is partially attributable to the general decline in the manufacturing sector across the country, and also to the fact that manufacturing firms do not require the hotel capacity for business purposes as compared to other sectors of the business world. Since the majority of manufacturing cities are located in frostbelt regions, it is clear that considerations of economic function must at least partially explain the regional trends in CBD hotel growth.

TABLE 8.6

Regional Distribution of Manufacturing-oriented Cities

Region	Total Cities in Region	Manufacturing Based Cities	Percentage of Cities Manufacturing	Hotel Growth Rank-Order (Table 3)
NC	16	16	100%	5
NE	20	18	90	6
MW	10	7	70	4
SA	16	9	56	3
SC	12	6	50	2
W	15	7	47	1

Note: Manufacturing classifications based on International City Manager's Association Municipal Yearbook, Chicago (1967), pp. 30-65.

A second consideration concerns hotel performance in those cities that are heavily involved with government-related activities (i.e., state capitals, the national capital, military concentrations). The evidence in this study suggests that a city possessing an economy that is oriented towards the public sector is more likely to experience downtown hotel growth. Of the 23 sample cities which fall into this governmental category (19 capitols, 4 military), fifteen exhibited hotel gains between 1968-1979. One explanation for this finding is that most state government facilities are situated in the downtown, and local hotels should be able to attract a steady amount of business from the politicians, lobbyists, constituents, media people, and visitors who frequently travel to capital cities. This consideration, however, fails to shed any light on the regional differences previously demonstrated, as a relatively balanced combination of frostbelt and sunbelt government cities showed both increases and decreases in CBD hotel rooms.

Another consideration which might help to explain downtown hotel trends takes into account special features of a city that would attract a large amount of annual visitors. In other words, one would expect that cities with extensive resort facilitates or historical and cultural attractions should produce many tourists throughout the year who would require hotel accommodations. This line of reasoning can be supported by this study to a degree. Resort cities within the sample, all of which are located in sunbelt states such as Florida, Arizona, California, and Hawaii, for the most part exhibited growth in their CBD hotel sector. One could argue, however, that resorts would exert little influence upon downtown hotels because the actual resort areas (i.e., beaches) are not situated in the downtown and visitors would most likely stay at hotels located at the resort itself, not in the CBD (an exception might be convention business, for which downtown hotels may be more suitable in resort cities). Tourist cities, those with special historical and cultural attractions, also perform fairly well in terms of CBD hotel growth. Of the nine cities classified as tourist,[24] six registered an increase in hotel rooms between 1968-1979; since these attractions are often found in or near the downtown, it would logically follow that many tourists would utilize the nearby hotel facilities. In that more tourist and resort cities are situated in the sunbelt than the frostbelt, this variable may also help to explain the regional differences.

A final consideration involves the extent to which a relationship exists between downtown hotel trends and trends exhibited by other core activities. While comparable data for other activities are difficult to acquire, a recent study by this author which examined retail trends for the same sample cities during a similar time period (1967-1977) can be utilized to determine if hotel growth or decline can be correlated with downtown retail activity.[25] Based on regional performance, the retail/hotel relationship is inconclusive. For instance, the North East suffered the highest decline in hotel rooms but performed relatively well in retailing; the South Central and West displayed high growth rates in hotel rooms but exhibited only mixed results in the various indicators of core retail activity; and the North Central did poorly in both downtown activities. Obviously, no clear-cut pattern of regional performance emerged. Similarly, an examination of individual cities yielded little correlation as cities experiencing the greatest CBD hotel growth showed both strong and weak retail trends. However, it should be noted that most of the cities with high rates of hotel decline performed relatively poorly in retail activity as well. Overall, since the retail and hotel sectors appear to operate independently of one another in most cities, the lack of any straightforward relationship between their growth trends should not be surprising. What would prove interesting would be the degree of interrelationships that exist between CBD hotels and the office or entertainment sectors of the downtown, both of which are much more important to the welfare of the CBD hotel in terms of creating demand.

CONCLUDING REMARKS

The overriding findings of this study point to the following conclusion: CBD hotel growth is considerably more prosperous in the newer cities of the sunbelt regions than in the older industrial cities of the frostbelt. In other words, cities of the South Central and West regions, which closely coincide with common perceptions of the sunbelt, consistently exhibited growth in their CBD hotel sector, while cities of the frostbelt, which generally include the North East and North Central regions, tended to possess lower and/or decreasing figures throughout the analysis. These results reflect the widely discussed and documented population and economic regional shifts prevalent in the United States in recent decades. Moreover, these trends can be partially explained by the nature of sunbelt cities when compared to their northern counterparts. The sunbelt contains more cities that have an economy based upon distributional, retail, and service activities, thereby requiring more centrally located hotel facilities for the many business people travelling to these concerns. The sunbelt also possesses more cities that would be attractive to tourists and vacationers, thus stimulating this aspect of the hotel business. Other factors have undoubtedly shaped these trends as well. The milder climate, cleaner and newer image, and active recruiting efforts attributed to sunbelt cities have unquestionably attracted business, conventions, and tourism. At the same time, sunbelt cities have become more desirable and accessible to a greater portion of the population due to the increasing amount of leisure time and improvements in long-distance air travel.

Despite the growth experienced by sunbelt cities, the overall trend for CBD hotels is downward, with the most substantial decreases occurring during the late 1970s. This decline does not necessarily imply that the role of the hotel within the structure of present-day and future downtowns be insignificant. On the contrary, the direction of contemporary CBD redevelopment policy suggests that the hotel may once again constitute an integral element within our core, thereby re-establishing its prominent position of a bygone era.[26] It is difficult, however, to accurately assess the potential status of hotels in a vacuum because of their direct relationship to the degree of stability demonstrated by other downtown functions (e.g., retailing, office/financial, entertainment) which are more independent in their revitalization patterns. As suggested earlier, a vital entertainment and/or office sector within the CBD has the potential to dramatically increase the demand for nearby hotel rooms. To conclude, when confronted with the question of the future of American hotels, Williamson stated in 1930 that "it would be risky to predict the fate of today's hotels fifty years from now."[27] The essence of this quote is quite appropriate for the 1980s when applied to the question of the future viability of the downtown hotel.

NOTES

1. Boorstin, Daniel J., **The Americans: The National Experience**, New York: Random House, 1965, Chapter 18.
2. Starrett, W.A., quoted in Jefferson Williamson, **The American Hotel**, New York: Alfred Knopf, 1930, p. 49.
3. Boorstin, p. 135.
4. For example, see N. Hayner, **Hotel Life**, College Park, Maryland: McGrath Publishing, 1969.
5. Most notably, Jefferson Williamson, **The American Hotel**, New York: Alfred Knopf, 1930; and Daniel J. Boorstin, **The Americans: The National Experience**, New York: Random House, 1965, Chapter 18.
6. A notable exception is Donald E. Lundberg, **The Hotel and Restaurant Business**, Boston: Cahners Books, 1974, which contains some helpful background material on the development of the hotel industry.
7. Williamson, p. 11.
8. Williamson, p. 35.
9. Lundberg, p. 21.
10. Williamson, p. 73.
11. Boorstin, p. 142.
12. Martyn J. Bowden, "The Dynamics of City Growth: An Historical Geography of the San Francisco Central District, 1850-1931" (unpublished dissertation, University of California at Berkeley, 1967), p. 160.
13. Bowden, p. 473.
14. Lundberg, pp. 47-48.
15. According to John Jakle ("Model by the Roadside: America's Room for the Night", **Journal of Cultural Geography** 1 (Fall 1980, pp. 34-49): "The motel business was characterized by a higher cash flow than most other types of real estate investment. Thus interest and principal on loans could be easily amortized. New motel properties in growth

areas appreciated rapidly producing substantial capital gains when sold, thus inviting speculation" (p. 43).

16. Based on figures supplied by the firm of Harris, Kerr, Forster, and Co., and reported in Truman A. Hartshorn, **Interpreting the City**, New York: John Wiley and Sons, 1980, p. 380.
17. Lundberg, pp. 53-56.
18. Stephen Brener, "What's Happened to the CBD Hotel?" Hospitality (June 1975), pp. 26-28.
19. Avner Arbel and Abraham Pizam, "Some Determinants of Urban Hotel Location: The Tourist's Inclinations," **Journal of Travel Research**, Winter 1977, pp. 18-22.
20. According to A. Brook's "Historic Hotels Ride Revival Wave", **New York Times**, July 19, 1981, Section 8, some of these hotels include the Plaza in New York, the Menger in San Antonio, and the Hotel Washington in Washington, D.C.
21. This annual directory includes only member establishments which, according to Lundberg, takes into account about 75 percent of American hostelries, including almost all major urban hotels.
22. Detailed delimitations of CBD boundaries can be found in the **U.S. Census of Retail Trade: Major Retail Centers**, Washington, D.C.: Department of Commerce, 1977.
23. Determination of economic functions are based on classifications found in Richard L. Forstall's "Economic Classification of Places over 10,000", **Municipal Year-book**, Chicago: International City Manager's Association (1967), pp. 30-65. Classifications salient to this study are as follows:
-Manufacturing (Mm): manufacturing accounts for at least 50 per cent of total employment while retail trade accounts for less than 30 per cent,
-Diversified Manufacturing (Mr): manufacturing is dominant employer but constitutes less than 50 per cent of total employment,
-Diversified Retailing (Rm): retail trade is dominant employer and manufacturing constitutes at least 20 per cent of total employment,
-Retailing (Rr): retail trade is dominant employer and manufacturing constitutes less than 20 per cent of total employment.
The sample used in the present study includes 31 Mm cities, 32 Mr cities, 19 Rm cities, 6 Rr cities, and once city dominated by government-related

employment (Washington, D.C.).

24. Since no listing of tourist-oriented cities based on historical and cultural activities could be uncovered, the author was forced to create his own list which others may disagree with. The cities include New York, Philadelphia, Boston, Washington, Savannah, New Orleans, San Antonio, Salt Lake City, and San Francisco.

25. A detailed analysis of CBD retail activity was conducted by Kent Robertson, "The Redevelopment of the American Central Business District: An Examination of the State of Knowledge, Policy Dilemmas, and Recent Retail Trends," unpublished dissertation, University of Delaware (1981). A condensed version of the retail findings will appear in a forthcoming issue of **Urban Studies** (1983). A summary of the regional results is provided below:

Region	CBD Sales Decline 1967-1977 (Absolute Dollars)	CBD Sales Per City Resident 1977	% SMSA Sales Conducted in CBD 1977
NE	-41.9 %	$520	4.6 %
SA	-42.7	410	4.9
NC	-49.8	310	3.5
SC	-36.1	330	5.1
MW	-37.9	470	4.6
W	-28.6	330	3.8

26. The **Downtown Development Handbook** (Washington, D.C.: Urban Land Institute, 1980) frequently notes that hotels have been integrated with other core functions for the purpose of establishing large mixed-use projects in the CBD.

27. Williamson, p. 55.

NINE

Francoise Brun

Old and New Restaurants in French Towns

Eating-out in french towns is a fact just as old as the town itself and meets basic needs. The need to eat outside your home is what I shall call "necessary meal". The "festive meal" is an intended breack from routine, either that "sociable meal" gathers several guests around a table, or a meal meant for pleasure individuals and more often families in a restaurant during their vacation or their leisure time, this being sometimes the very goal of their outing. How can we resist all those tempting institutions and the new styles which, since the beginning of the seventies and even more of the eighties, play a great part in changing the outside appearance of towns? Attractive to the customers, this multiplicity is in fact the visible part of a deep reorganizing process which we shall try to analyze.

PRESENT UPHEAVAL

An Expanding Market

Sudden growth

Eating-out is a mass-market. It provides since the beginning of the 80s an average of 4.654 to 5 thousand million meals every working day (14 per cent of the whole) to 27 per cent of the population over 4 years old. This represents 36 per cent of the domestic food expense.

89,000 social eating-out places (called in French "restauration sociale"), (firms, hospitals, collectivities, schools) prevail with 65 per cent of the total. The French eat there an average of 1 meal of 10. This "restauration sociale" comes first in Europe. But its turnover does not reach the same level as what is called "restauration commerciale" (44.45 versus 55.55%). The latter, present in all towns, according to statistics, takes place in 76 to 89,000 restaurants. It provides one out of 20 meals.

For about 20 years there is a sharp increase in this way of eating-out which is hard to determine for lack of reliable information before 1970. Within 10 years, according to GIRA (Gordon Institute Research Associates) there has been a 28.6 per cent increase regarding collective eating-out and a 72.2 per cent regarding commercial eating-out.

Causes of such growth: the mutation in society since the sixties

It's due to four major changes. In the background, a strong demographic and economic outburst and furthermore a fast expansion of urban population. In a society whose urbanization has reached over 73 per cent a higher standard of living and new working conditions provide restaurants with custom both mass one and a "captive" one. The spreading non-stop day work, which is in Lyon concerning 60.3 per cent of the companies (of over 49 salaried men) makes necessary to eat-out. Consequently this "necessary meal" represents about 55 per cent of the whole. The quick and massive growth of the tertiary which switched from 60.4 to 67.8 per cent between 1978 and 1981 brought out a general increase in wages. The following creation of restaurant-tickets leads a great number of workers to commercial dining. With new demands: concern about healthier and lighter food generally for aesthetic purposes among the growing number of female workers helps promoting a new low-calorie diet which differs from the country-like way of eating.

The woman's new role in society causes "festive meal" to develop a fact which used to be the prerogative of men going out "as bachelors" or middle-class people with appropriate incomes. Meals for social gathering purpose ("repas-sociabilite") reach 15 to 20 per cent of the whole whereas the ones leisure ("repas-loisir") 20 to 25 per cent. Salaried women become more and more independent. When they do not go back home for lunch they get into the habit of eating outside and even, in the reverse case, they tend to take along to the restaurant other members of their family during the week-end for they feel more and more reluctant to waste their own leisure time by cooking and washing up. In this they enforce upon their family an attitude totally different from that of their own mothers who accepted as going without saying doing both paid-work and house-work.

The new role played by the child inside the family influences the choice of the restaurant since he has become like in the United States (but 20 years later) responsible for the selection of a place to eat out for the whole family. Knowing that the child has played a part in the success of "family restaurants", the cafeteria managers have lately relied on these customers with suggesting special menus. We must not forget either that since the beginning of the seventies, contraception as well as money difficulties play a part in swelling the category of childless couples or of couples with one child who thereby eat out more easily than those suffering from the high cost of life.

At last, the fact that a more and more important part of the population can enjoy hours of rest away from their work causes the market to become wider and undergo some changes. The 5 working day week secured in large and middle-sized cities tends to be extended to smaller ones as well. The rate of holiday-going switched from 43.6 to 56.2 per cent from 1964 to 1979. Eating out in a restaurant is representative of a festive break from daily routine. When travelling, it becomes necessary. This, on the outskirts and along main roads, has generated the growth of quick-food restaurants, grill-rooms and cafeterias, a modern version of horse relays. A journey to an unknown region of France, or the more so, a journey abroad, farther and farther away by now owing to package tours and charters, is an opportunity to make culinary experiments one will try to repeat when back home. This partly explains the success and the late proliferation of restaurants specialized in ethnic cooking, from Swiss "raclette" to Indonesian cooking.

Old and new forms

Contradictory movements:

Collective eating, after growing very quickly between 1950 and 1970 is now progressing at a slower rate. Within 5 years from 1970 to 75, the average annual increase has only been 1.3 per cent instead of an expected 4.3 per cent. This standstill comes from the slowing down of the demographic increase which affects school and university food services and from the economic crisis which sets limits to the social investments of firms. It seems to be even more the consequence of the disaffection of wage-earners for restaurants deemed too impersonal compared with the new ones.

Commercial food is obviously characterized by a great upheaval, particularly since the beginning of the eighties. By lack of general data, which would in fact never be up to date, this situation always being evanescent, remarks are obvious even to the poorest observer. Even though bankruptcies aren't always noticed, ownership changes announced in big letters on the front, opening and closing down for the same institution and chiefly the proliferation of creations are striking by their number, by an often new aggressive-looking window, in the case of fast-food restaurants. An inquiry about Clermont-Ferrand (250,000 inhabitants) shows sensible change occurred in 2 years (1978-80). An increase of 3.4 per cent in the number of restaurants (i.e. 206 instead of 199) and of 20 per cent of the number of meals (17,700 instead of 13,900) comes from complex movements. The average restaurants and higher standard ones from wealthy areas remain unaffected. But the closing down of 50 shops, about one fourth of the potential, related to hostelqries (20 per cent of the whole against 25 per cent) and mostly average restaurants and lower-rate restaurants of the downtown areas and of the outskirts are being largely compensated by the middle-rate built mostly downtown and in the outskirts by cafeterias. They provide 60 per cent of meals under 30 FF.

In the seventies, new restaurants essentially appear in the outskirts. They are mostly restaurants of an average level (inns and mainly grills), generally large cafeterias with a self-service counter. They belong to some new shopping areas of which they are extension. Such places have been designed, according to the growing number of private cars which allow consumers to go out for the week-end or the vacation, but also facilitates concentrated shopping in new shopping centres implanted by powerful commercial chains, the latter being supported by great trusts. Cafeteria represents the first intervention of the great capital in the restaurant business which had been up to now the concern of individual artisans. But toward the end of the seventies, most restaurants are centered in downtown areas, with tiny places often artificially enlarged by mirrors or whenever possible by adding a few terrace tables, especially by night. They belong to two different kinds: the ethnic cooking, growing from 1975/78 (of which the manager is not always a native man and the restaurant not necessarily concerned with the relevant ethnic minority) and the Fast-Food from 1980/81.

Every city, large or small, has the same tendency to rush toward novelty. This is probably a direct consequence from the rather quick urbanization which leads to a kind of love for false country-life, expressed in suburban village-like constructions made up of private houses, in furniture avoiding modern-shape, pretending to be going back to real wood and really being "falsy" truer. Cooking too is expected to be more traditional than ever superior to the kind which is being served in collective restaurants. At the same time an easy switch to foreign exotic food is taking place. The customers seem to have lost the feeling that they are bound to a specific shop. Instead, they are much more interested in finding a new kind of excitement providing what they afford. This explains the successful implantation of the second generation cafeterias in downtown, knowing how to offer a new more welcoming sitting, and that of tiny restaurants, real "wholes in the wall", selling french fries, tunisian sandwiches and pizzas, which can be eaten in the street any time, and the successful implantation of fast-food restaurants, the last on the market.

Such restaurants are working most of the day and until late at night. They offer to be eaten or carried a very limited choice of warm food and drinks having very little unitary value. The meal is served in disposable boxes and generally without forks or knives. It is taken standing up or eventually sitting down but for only 20 minutes: "less than 20 minutes for less than 20 FF". Waiting time limited to 2 to 3 minutes. From the flourishing seventies, Reims and Paris have only kept the McDonald, franchised from the famous American chain and Chicken Shop, a branch of Goulet Turpin. Technical reasons, poorly adapted supplies (precut chickens, buns, bread crumbs and milk shakes) partly explain such failure. This was in fact a premature experiment. Such food didn't match yet the consumer's desire. He wasn't expecting typical American hamburgers, sweet and sour sauce and "buns", too far from "baguette" of French sandwich. Instead,cafeteria, new style which matches the masses is a success: it enables a low price more desired than a fast eating.

The real fast-food start dates from 1981. It is characterized by its amazing diffusion and diversification. It takes place in Paris first and its surroundings. Then it reaches other big cities. In 1981, for instance, in the very middle of Lille, four hamburger fast-food restaurants open eight "viennoiseries" (bakery-like restaurants). Other plans are nearing completion. This expansion reaches "middle cities", particularly those with students and even small cities. But never, the country. Fast-food is a city event. It's spreading at such speed that quantification efforts would fail. One half of the 181 shops have been implanted in 1981. Cities other than Paris represent 51.4 per cent of the whole. Nevertheless Fast-Food in France reaches a level of 0.2 per cent of the market whereas Great Britain is leading in Europe with 3.3 per cent.

Two typical products share the market

Hamburgers and "viennoiserie". The first one imported without any change from the States often develops under the shape of franchised chains of big trusts. Even "broilers" which are originally French, and are quickly spreading, decide to adopt techniques and often signs which, in order to match the market, sound American. "Viennoiserie" is more connected with pastry and thus at once accepted by consumer. Both makers "La croissanterie" are French. The first one started in 1976 in Rennes spreads through franchise and will count toward the end of 1982, 80 shops, 7 of which being implanted abroad (and 150 in 1985). "La Crossanterie" opened in 1977 in Paris counted 20 shops in 81. (Its present expansion is still unknown). From 1980, "Viennoiseries" spread particularly on pedestrian streets where people can't resist the temptation because of the good smelling shops. They serve hot "croissants" at any time of the day : plain, as "breake-hunger" in morning or afternoon and even as meal when filled with ham or various cheeses, omelet, along with puff-pastry desserts or hors-d'oeuvres-like "quiche". Consequently, between "broilers" and "viennoiserie", multi-products" fast-food insert, offering wide range of products, ground meat, fish, eggs, and salads. One can indefinitely improve the variety of choice by calling tart (exceptionally), "crepe" (seldom), pizza and mainly hard bread-sandwiches filled with traditional products and chiefly with "buns"

Fast-Food is amazing successful. As a necessary meal, taken around noon, it matches new city-life situations. The noon-break tends to decrease whereas it's increasing in the States. In New-York and Chicago it changed in 20 years from 29 minutes to 56 and 42 but in Paris from 121 to 51. Unlike in the seventies time is becoming a very important factor in large French cities as well as in smaller ones (about which we don't have any total data). Besides, the crisis reduces the budget meals of salaried men, executives and, what's more, of unemployed, when traditional restaurant prices skyrocket despite their often low prestations. The Fast-Food offers meals 2 or 3 times cheaper. Sure it can't rival with collective eating-out neither in diversity, nutrition nor cost. But collective eating-out is inferior to the theoretical demand and though paradoxically, it suffers disaffection, as already mentioned. Fast-Food seems to imply something positive enough so that it becomes an appropriate setting for parties, specially for youngsters. According to a survey in February 82 concerning towns of more than 100,000 inhabitants, 45 per cent of the customers are under age 25 and 23 per cent between 25 and 34. Not only because of its cheap meal (many are unemployed), Fast-Food helps the youth to feel comfortable. They can eat with their fingers whenever they want to eat far from usual meals. Thus they become freed from their parents, breeding. But what's more, it becomes a sort of meeting place during slack hours in the evening. This socio-cultural problem is characteristic of adolescents. Fast-food somewhat helps them to become acquainted with sociability. Surely it opens to them restaurants which they would have not found out, except much later... or even not at all. But Fast-Food is also in fashion: people who are able to go more elegant restaurants don't seem to disdain such a way of eating. This up-to-date Fast-Food is seen even in Montelimar, a small southern France city, which doesn't follow the non-stop day-work system : most meals are taken in the evening, in the only fast-food restaurant. It remains open until midnight on weekdays and until 1 AM on week-ends. This is rather exceptional, but seems to be what most consumers are looking forward to.

Two other data explain the quick fast-food expansion. First: technological innovations concerning equipment and products. Adequate equipment fosters efficiency, hence profits; "Viennoiserie" consists mostly of frozen ingredients, hamburgers almost completely.

On the other side, ~~the~~ interference big trusts has been decisive in opening the market, and because Fast-Food being generally extremely demanding as far as capital is concerned.

The resulting diversification

Traditional restaurants already offered a wide variety, from the small economical restaurant with only one course, to the great gastronomical restaurant (known outside the hexagon), through the middle level restaurant with its traditional or new cooking.

New restaurants, even more varied, belong to two big categories:

- Ethnic cooking restaurants with a wide range of prices, are increasing in all cities. They are subject to great upheavals.

- The simplified and quickly styles successively appeared: first "creperies" and pizzerias, then snacks, drugstores, grills, cafeterias, and at last, Fast-Food which is nothing but a sandwich-making industry.

HAS THE LOCATION CHANGED ?

Traditional strong points

Downtown is a space of highest density. Strong connections exist between restaurants and transports (railway stations, main roads, entering the cities), and tertiary workplaces and entertainment places (theatres, night-clubs, movies). Scarce in around downtown quarters and suburbs, restaurants reappear in outskirts. They are gathering in favourite places, river's edges, wooded areas and are extremely various (from "guinguettes" (inns), to gastronomical restaurant).

New strong points

Downtown restaurants, the largest number, concentrate :

- in historical area (Petite France, in Strasbourg, Vieux Lyon, Quartier Latin, for instance). Ethnic cooking restaurants prevail with sometimes pioneer aspect.
- in pedestrian streets and around. In the first ones, "Viennoiserie" seem to be more popular. Around : important avenues and squares, having a symbolic value (Cours Mirabeau in Aix-en-Provence, Kleber Square in Strasbourg, Champs-Elysees), showed up, fast-food hamburger shops dominate. In both cases, because of the commercial continuity, restaurant replaces the former shop. In the opposite, in streets and neighbouring alleys, restaurants (especially ethnic cooking) open as pioneer shop, taking advantage of the low rent. The rate varying on a 1 to 4 scale, selects the ap-

plicants. Important avenues belong to the trusts, without commercial past streets, to private owners.

In Shopping Centre Arcades, density is strong. Restaurants are located in far outskirts of town (often close to new big hotels belonging to French or foreign chains), or in the downtown area, right by historical centres in the renewed areas of "directive poles" (Part-Dieu in Lyon, Polygone in Montpellier, Defense in Paris). In both cases fast-food restaurants and quick style restaurants predominate. "Viennoiseries" and "multi-products", "brasseries", grills, "creperies", pizzerias and cafeterias gather, fostering their attraction power more than suffering from competition.

Consequently, locations remain the same as they were in the past (centre and outskirts), but they match less and less the life of the quarter. People move toward downtown which has become only a temporary place for work (rather than living, thus necessary meal), and for shopping, leisure (especially movies), what leads to nibbling and festive eating. People also go out great shopping centre in the outskirts, sometimes just to eat-out, and sometimes to eat-shop-stroll.

In fact, new connections appear. Urban remodelling brings new restaurants because it attracts pedestrians in the case of rehabilitated historical centres, converted into cultural windows, immediately followed by numerous restaurants (Le Marais, in Paris), or in the case of new pedestrian streets. Such streets as well as new shopping centres have something in common: they are used as useful and pleasant areas. Impulsive buying and eating-out too are favoured by density, revival, variety, availability of people.

In such streets or right around, numerous restaurants are neighbouring clothes and interior decorating shops (gadgets, antiques). Each of them helping in making the whole area powerful and attractive.

REVIVAL OF STRUCTURES

New managers

Younger people are interested in this profession. In Clermont-Ferrand, for instance, the under age 45 switches from 67 per cent in 1978 to 72 per cent in 1980. The six great "Chefs" of the "Ecole bourbuignonne" are from 30 to 47 years old. These young are interested in any kind of restaurant, but mainly in Fast-Food.

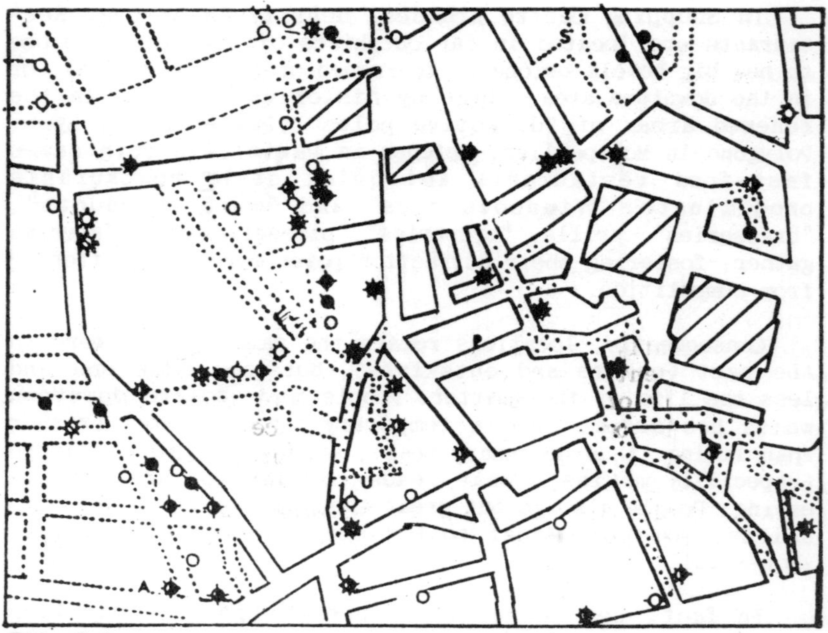

FIG. 9.1

Scale 1/4000

o Traditional

Grill

Snack

Fast-Food

Tea-room

Ethnic cooking restaurant

Asian	Rustic fashion
Greek	Vegetarian
S Swiss	● Nord-african
i Italian	Crêperie
P Spanish	Pizzeria
Q African	A Argentin
Brasserie	U American

Pedestrian street

Street without commercial past

Public building

DENSITY AND DIVERSITY IN THE HISTORICAL CENTER OF AIX-EN-PROVENCE

This profession renews too. Professional people remain the most numerous, but one fact is new: all these outsiders. They are bakers or even dress-makers or teachers. They open a new shop or change the old one into a restaurant. They are young unemployed people looking for a first job or 40 years old middle-class ladies, who have once raised their children hope to find their financial independence. They reduce their investments, settle on streets without many shops and replace their "lack of experience" by a pleasant setting, an easy going, hippie-like atmosphere. It may be a lucrative job for daring people or also a crisis initiated survival experience. Both no doubt!

Interference of trusts is the second big change

The most important ones belong to the profession (big American "broilers"), or to the new style of hostelry, food-processing, distribution. Less powerful ones are created in order to establish their own chain of Fast-Food.

They only aim at one field and generally spread out by franchise. Thus, big or small, fast-food chains get market penetration: Ritter in Alsace or Croissant Chaud, McDonald all over the country. Same policy for Auchan-Flunch cafeterias. These groups mostly have an all directions policy. In a small way, around Montelimar, for example: motel, hotel, grill, Fast-Food. On a large scale: Jacques Borel: hostelry chain, meal-tickets, collective and public eating areas (superhighway), two chains of grills and two Fast-Food chains (its fusion with Novotel-Sofitel is going to bring a new chain of grills).

These groups adopt a most efficient process. They aim at the most profitable fields : collective eating because it only needs light investment, cafeterias and Fast-Food because they are the most industrialized forms. They also invest only in the most favourable locations: shopping centres which have precisely been implanted by great financial groups, and downtown ever since it became again a stake for real-estate developers and for distribution. In each city the density of rival chains restaurants, on narrow spaces, shows where the highly productive locations are.

Eating out is following, a few years later, the same evolution as that of other commercial sectors : local capital is limited to traditional business, which in the case of restaurants isn't necessarily marginal; regional and mainly national and international capital tends to assert itself on most profitable level (styles and locations). Public eating still governed by independent owners, but the aggressive policy of trusts seems very dreadful.

THE FUTURE OF VARIOUS STYLES

Do Data Match Every Case ?

From the viewpoint of technique.

For all kinds of restaurants, it's now necessary to check steadily the prime cost (raw material and work) and to a master most administration problems, Even though there is a 20 year difference compared to other economical areas. This is what Fast-Food requires. This is also the result of the present and even potential threat it implies for many kinds of restaurants. But the management varies with different areas. The importance of know-how in traditional fields justifies the craft-kind approach to the problem. Besides, intricacy increases in the same time as that of supplies, from "grill" to gastronomical restaurant, and for Fast-Food with the bulk of raw material cooked and the quickness of course: if stew improves by simmering on low fire, French fries must be served at once or thrown away.

All kinds of restaurants theoretically benefit by modern techniques. Equipments are more and more efficient but all people can't afford it.

From the social viewpoint

There is no homogeneity like in the States, where, from one coast to the other, people live almost the same way, eat at any time a kind of food which scarcely varies. In France, each group keeps one style of food : frozen-food does not cut out made home preserves. In fact, the progressive equalization of way of life creates a stronger tendency to the difference stressed by means of conspicuous expenses. This is the case in Strasbourg, for example : cafeterias and Fast-Food invades Kleber Square, attracting a lot of young people with low incomes. At the same time, the cathedral area and La Petite France, is devoted to higher level consumers looking for elaborate, inventive and also exotic food. Same thing between la Part-Dieu, its noon restaurants for middle tertiary salaried, and le Vieux Lyon. There seems to be enough room for all kinds of restaurants.

Is each sector affected in the same way by economic crisis situation?

New demands concerning the quality/price ratio act against traditional food as far as during the expansion years, sometimes lower quality was sold at a high price. In this respect Fast-Food sounds much more honest: the consumer who needs security enjoys the stability of quality/price ratio, cleanliness and setting.

Still heavy labour expensive don't weigh the same. Qualification and cost rise according to the level of the restaurant. In the opposite, Fast-Food cuts down the cost of labour by hiring unskilled labour (which doesn't affect strong efficiency since the equipment is very efficient). This mostly temporary labour varies with rush-hours. There really are two ways to face the problem of labour, which are embodied by two styles of food.

Two Different Professions

Fast-Food means a revolution in the field of labour because it's much more "distributor" than "manufacturer". The weakening of added value and of profit margin is compensated by the output which determines high turnover. This mass industry supplying a standardized product breaks away from quality, choice and variety which used to be French cooking's main attribute. The high level of investments of Fast-Food ensues from peculiar demands: location in downtown (such a restaurant cannot be far out of the way) and heavy, peculiar equipment often imported from the States which enables chain-work with standardization of gestures and non-initiative work. At last, a high investment of "manager's brain" because Fast-Food requires previous market analysis to determine the aim and the product, to master the production and steadily check various sectors in order that turnover/investment remains less than one.

Success of each style depends on how opposite factors are mastered: location/prime cost; standardization/know-how, invention; produce/pleasant reception.

Achievement of Various Styles

Moderate expansion of collective restaurants

Growth results from improvement. As already made by some big companies, they need to improve quality, dietetics and setting so it could be possible to compete with public restaurants which is supposed to grow up to 2.3 per cent between 1978 and 1990 compared to 1.3 only.

Expected expansion of Fast-Food

In 1990, its expansion is supposed to reach between 630 (3 per cent of the whole) to 1,000 restaurants. It depends on how well its management can be mastered, but, according to my opinion, on French data. France isn't America which is used as pattern.

Because implanted in downtown for nearly 80 per cent instead of in shopping centres of outskirts as in America, Fast-Food is going to face problems of location. Locations will become more and more rare and expansive, what will balk the independent concern and will perhaps break the general expansion, unless the high density of Fast-Food fosters, feeling of rejection from town council of Lille.

Shouldn't the taste of the French be more taken into consideration? Collective eating having taught people some lessons about a more balanced diet, usually through scientific vulgarization, the consumer might reduce his fast-food consumption. The fear of becoming over-weight by nibbling an unbalanced kind of food too rich in glucides and lipides. This might just have been a fad, and customers might start to ask for a higher quality, a quieter atmosphere and a seat at a table. Typical French demands, opposite to the aim of Fast-Food, made for attracting people but not for keeping them. Profit might still not be quite safe.

Winning cafeterias

Though strongly implanted, competition of Fast-Food on its inferior part, compels cafeterias to spread topwise in order to enlarge its goodwill. After cafeterias in shopping centres and along main roads (highway exits) meant to catch all the vacationers on their way to Italy, Spain, South of France, there also are many of those in downtown. This is where cafeterias attract at noon the middle tertiary and the top tertiary, families at noon and in the evening, at last, just for nibbling : youngsters, housewives, people from the so-called "3d age".

Second generation cafeterias try to find their location in the middle of the ladder. They already start a successful competition with traditional restaurants and also ethnic cooking restaurants (Even though they look fashionable). This achievement results from use of more efficient equipment, (which increases productivity), from larger variety, from altering the space for the customers trying to hide the necessity-aspect and stressing the festive outlook of the place. People try it, come back, stay longer and order more.

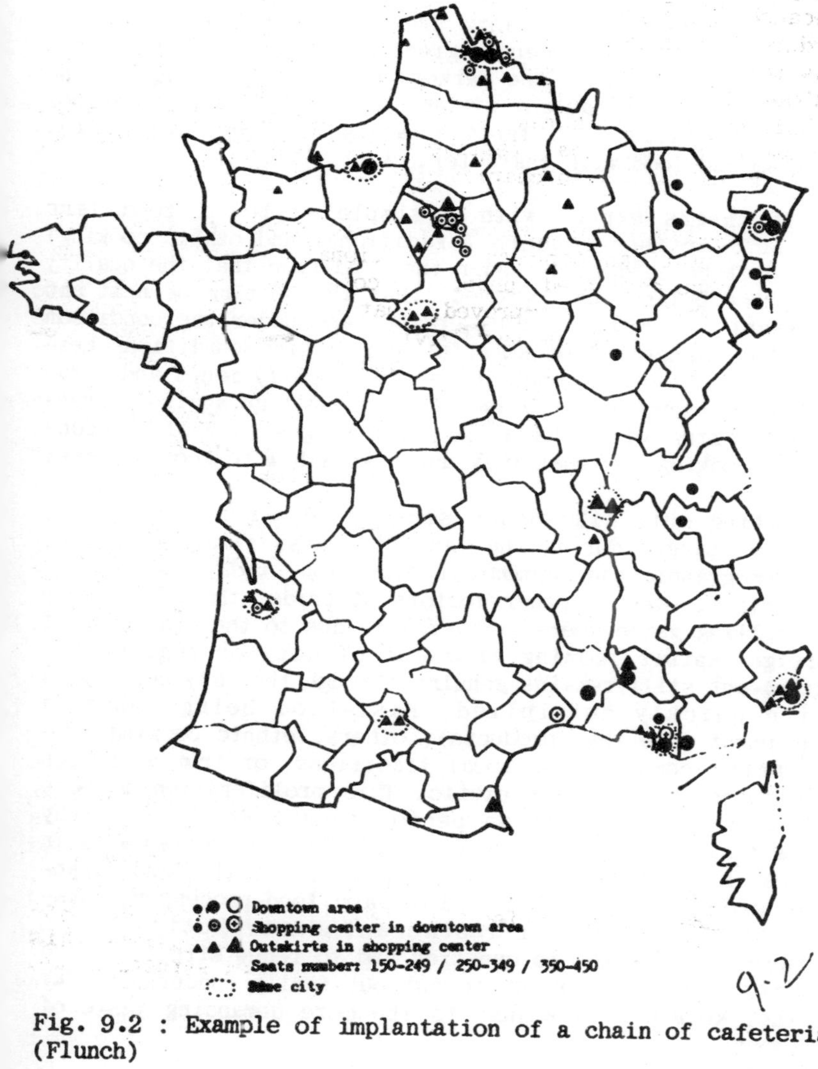

Fig. 9.2 : Example of implantation of a chain of cafeterias (Flunch)

How about other restaurants ?

It's difficult to evaluate the case of the other restaurants because of all the types of food and prices (some of them being 30 FF at their highest, others 250 FF at their lowest). If cafeterias and Fast-Food compete successfully with little restaurants and even endanger their existence, they can't take the richer customers away from the "grill" because they have mastered management, simplifying menus and orders. Business restaurants are suffering from crisis and new tax regulations, whereas great gastronomical restaurants (about 10 per cent of the market) don't really mind it. The ethnic cooking restaurant system is also full of promise because it offers what festive eating requires, atmosphere, exotism and food with character.

If chains expand with a simple style of food like "grill", artisan-concern (traditional and ethnic cooking) shouldn't be condemned, under the condition that the quality and price balance be improved, that the setting be neat and pleasant, as well as the service, and under the condition that the management be skillful and working conditions better. The most clever ones choose to simplify menus and service which improves ratio and still doesn't go against inventive cooking with character, the biggest aim of the consumer, looking for what they don't know how to cook at home.

Eating-out, like other sectors of French economy, quickly changed during the last 20 years, first because of the demographic and economical expansion, today, because of the crisis. Like in other sectors of trade, there is a deep remodelling which seems irreversible due to the crackdown of foreign capital, coming from out of city or region. But eating-out still remains genuine through the many new styles which quickly multiplied: Fast-Food being imported (equipment more than products), others, ethnic cooking restaurants, coming from local traditions, or from a foreign repertoire more or less exotic. This proliferation is more the sign of a transition period than that of a healthy situation. At last, the second originality of restaurants in cities is due to the presence of powerful chains and financial groups mainly oriented toward food-processing, distribution, hostelry or restaurant distribution. This presence contributes to question and to renew structures and methods, but is not ready to cut out family concerns as far as they know how to adjust to the more demanding taste of customer.

SECTION THREE

RECREATION USE OF URBAN LAND

TEN

K.G. Willis

Green Belts

EVOLUTION

Green belts are conceived as rough rings of land, usually several kilometres wide, around a number of developed areas. Within green belts no further urban development is permitted and in this way the expansion of cities and urban conglomerations is to be halted.

The green belt concept has a long history. Elizabeth I in 1580 proclaimed a green belt for a city of great multitudes out of recognition that the inhabitants of London must be provided "of sustenation of victuall, foods and other like necessities" and to prevent crowded housing and great poverty by physical restriction on land available. It is difficult to see how green belts could prevent overcrowding in housing and great poverty rather than adding to these two problems and needless to say the policy failed. While good agricultural land adjacent to cities was regarded as particularly important in the pre-industrial revolution era, with the development of modern transport, the need for a belt of productive farmland adjacent to a city is no longer imperative.

The urban reform movement which developed in the nineteenth century in Britain, took inspiration from and was articulated by, literary and artistic personalities, the core of the intellectual class. While certain writers[1] such as Wordsworth (1803), Dickens (1840-54), and H.G. Wells (1899) were fascinated by the city, others such as Carlyle (1844), Ruskin (1849, 1866), and Morris (1891) were hostile to it. The reform movement comprised three basic strands.

First, the "conservative" element represented by Wakefield (1848), Marshall (1884) and Booth (1887) sought to eliminate poverty and its accompanying social evils by removing the poor from the city either in planned colonies abroad, or in the rural districts around the big city, or by subsidised transport to the suburbs. Second, Robert Owen (1817-1820), the Chartists (1845) and the garden city planner Ebenezer Howard (1898) presented a socialist/co-operative alternative using the capitalist system but advocating public ownership of land. The third element was represented by professional sanitary engineers, medical officers of health, housing managers and the practical efforts of administrative and private philanthropy, who sought by action and precept to guide public policy. The intellectual class's reaction to the cities carried its own answer to the problems it saw in urbanisation. Size, density and social division were considered to be the sources of the social unrest and moral disorganisation the city furthered. So, accordingly, smaller, less densely built, socially mixed communities would solve the urban problem. The answer was planning systematic, deliberate ordering of the environment in such a way as to prevent ill-health, to reduce inconvenience and to promote social harmony. The environmental squalor of the city was not inevitable but could be minimised by rational control over layout and design. The group of people concerned to disseminate these ideas became known as the town planning movement. It included industrial philanthropists such as Lever at Port Sunlight (1889), Cadbury at Bourneville (1895), Rowntree outside York (1901); social missionaries such as Mrs. Barnett at Hampstead Garden Suburb (1905) and Ebenezer Howard at Letchworth (1903) and then Welwyn Garden City (1919); academics such as Geddes; professional men such as Unwin; and social critics such as H.G. Wells and G.B. Shaw.

To bring city dwellers closer to the country, since the image of the countryside and village life was held to be idyllic (Mellor, 1982), Howard proposed a series of garden cities (limited at 32,000 people) each surrounded by a green belt ring (approximately 4 kms wide). It was no Utopia, but a realistic blue print which would integrate all the advantages of town and country life:

> "in which all the advantages of the most energetic and active town life, with all the beauty and delight of the countryside can be secured" (Howard, 1945).

The basis of the entire scheme was the vesting of the

ownership of land in the hands of the community before development started. In this way the return from the appreciation of land values from development, would come back to the community, so financing further development to higher standards than the individual tenant could support.

Two towns, Letchworth and Welwyn, were built, and Howard's ideas later formed the garden city - blue print of the new Towns Act, 1946. But, the English town planning movement in its quest for the romantic idyll of "community in nature" was not the only source of this professionally defined image of the good city. It was supported by the Moder Movement in architecture, particularly the work of Le Corbusier (1964). Although the Radiant-City image has had international effect from Chandigargh to Brasilia, from Paris to New York, as has that of Howard's garden city, yet after the modest successes at Letchworth and Welwyn it is hard to point to any development which can be claimed to satisfy the intentions of Le Corbusier or Howard. In urban design, the Modern Movement and the Garden City concept failed for two reasons. First, although the image of the green city as the good city has sunk deep into popular thinking, into professional training and is accepted in political discussion on town planning and urban design, so deeply entrenched was this image of cities that there was a failure to establish just what individuals, families and children needed and effectively demanded in the market place. Second, given competing demands for resources in the economy, there were just not enough resources to provide and run these new types of cities. Thus although these new towns and cities have been tried in places, they have not been adopted as common practice in urban design. Nevertheless, green belts which were the other half or twin of the new town/city idea have met with more universal acceptance and application to regulate the growth of existing urban areas.

Before 1947, green belt policy could be effectively implemented in England in two ways. First, green belt proposals could be implemented through public purchase. Most proposals centred on London and found fruition in the Green Belt (London and Home Counties) Act, 1938, under which home counties surrounding London were authorised to acquire land for green belt purposes. Contributions up to 50 per cent of the cost of the land could be made by London County Council. Second, local authorities could adopt a restrictive development policy and refuse to grant permission to private developers to build on the edge of existing urban areas. However, this restrictive development policy was affected by the compensation provisions of the principal inter-war planning act in England, the Town and Country Planning Act, 1932. This Act stated that compensation had to be paid at market prices for any loss due to planning restrictions and local authorities were wary of restricting large agricultural areas from residential development for fear that large compensation claims would result.

The Town and Country Planning Act, 1947 gave the State (British Government) property rights in all land development i.e., in effect development rights in land were nationalised. Under the legislation all development throughout the country had to be sanctioned by prior government planning permission. The Act allowed local authorities to acquire land cheaply at existing use value (e.g. agricultural use value) rather than at development value (urban land value). Often acquisition was by compulsory purchase because there was a 100 per cent tax on the difference between developed value and existing use value of land, and this removed the incentive for private property owners to voluntarily sell their land. A change of government led to the repeal of the 100 per cent tax and in 1959 to legislation which made local authorities who acquired land pay the full market price for the land. Although local authorities could have established and extended green belts by public purchase and acquisition of land either by compulsory purchase or free market acquisition under the 1947 system, green belts were eventually established in an alternative way.

Although certain aspects of the 1947 Town and Country Planning Act were repealed, planning permission procedures were maintained i.e., the State retained all development rights in land. It was in this context that green belts became widely established in England and it is still in this context that green belts continued to be maintained and extended. Green belts first became nationally accepted in England as a recognised planning policy with the publication of a government circular (Ministry of Housing and Local Government, 1955), giving local authorities discretionary power to establish green belts around towns to prevent urban sprawl. With green belts there is a strong presumption against all development or change of use, the exceptions being those developments concerned with agriculture or forestry, or other developments which do not substantially detract from the open character of the area. Thus, planning permission for rights to urban development is normally refused within a green belt designated area. Since the individual does not own the right to develop his land (this right being vested now in the State), no compensation is paid by the State to the individual i.e., green belts can be established now without the need for the local authority to buy the land; or if local authority does not buy it, without the need to pay compensation to the individual for restricting the individual's use of the land.

Functions of green belts

The British government circular which established green belts in 1955 stated that they were to be used to check urban sprawl, in particular to:

(a) check the further growth of a large built-up area;
(b) prevent neighbouring towns from merging into one another;
(c) preserve the special character of a town.

The primary function of a green belt is thus one of pure urban containment.

Through the pursuit of this function, green belts also serve other functions. First, green belts serve to preserve agricultural land and serve as a protective cover for the pursuit of farming. The preservation of agriculture is not recognised by central government as one of the reasons for creating a green belt, yet planning permission will ordinarily be given in green belts for residences associated with farms and small holdings. Playing fields, recreational uses, institutional uses, and other "open" uses not out of character with a rural environment will also be permitted. A material consideration in applications for planning permission is the safeguarding of all agricultural land. In this respect many circulars have been published since 1950 (e.g. D.o.E. Circulars 24/73 and 75/76) which give advice to local planning authorities and form the basis for dealing with applications to develop agricultural land. The policy is "that valuable agricultural land (should) not be taken for development when less valuable land can be used instead, and that development which is unnecessarily extravagant in its use of land not be allowed" (Circular 43/58). Second, green belts also serve to preserve amenity. While amenity is not explicitly recognised as a reason for establishing a green belt, it receives indirect recognition in written statements accompanying green belt proposals and amendments which may "include a reference to the special attention which will be paid to visual amenity."

But the functions served by green belts are open to question and analysis and, moreover, comparable attention must be given to the reasoning behind green belts: why should not towns be allowed to merge? Historically many present conurbations exist through the merging of once separate settlements.

The policy of containment of urban England, of which green belts form a significant instrument has arisen through a belief that intervention is required to modify the market system determining urban development (Hall, 1973). The reasons behind intervention are varied. First, it is argued, the price system does not allocate correctly i.e., market prices for urban and agricultural land should not be allowed to determine land transfers. This belief was instrumental in the establishment of Elizabeth I's green belt: that food and animal fodder was an absolute priority. The greatest impetus to containment, and hence green belts, probably came from the Committee on Land Utilisation in Rural Areas (Scott Report 1942). The majority of members did not look with favour on the price system and stated that development on very good agricultural land should not be allowed: only if "it can be clearly shown that it is on balance in the national interest (should) the change be made". Only Professor S.R. Dennison in his famous minority report argued that urban growth is a perfectly proper demand for land if it can outbid other potential users. Second, a more subtle argument, states the price system does not allocate correctly as presently operated, i.e., there are diseconomies of scale in urban areas (congestion etc.) and these are not reflected in the prices charged for local authority services (e.g. road use, local taxes etc.). Therefore, physical policy instruments (green belts) are necessary to prevent greater diseconomies from urban growth. It may be questioned, however, whether green belts are the best policy instrument or whether a more appropriate policy instrument would not be to charge for the full cost of services and raise the level of taxes in congested urban areas relative to non-congested ones. Third, it is suggested that externalities are significant, i.e., the aesthetic qualities of non-urban land around towns is not taken into account in the market forces determining urban expansion. These beneficial externalities include:

(1) amenity from the countryside and open landscape, which the green belt can preserve, and which is valued above dense urban landscapes;

(2) recreation: footpaths etc. and other non-priced outdoor recreational activities which can be found in the rural-urban fringe;

(3) retaining the existing character of the town. Thus the reason behind preventing towns merging is an aesthetic one of preserving the existing town and country landscape. Of course, green belts, while preventing towns merging do not prevent the considerable changes which can take place within an existing urban landscape e.g., the development of high rise buildings, concrete jungles, etc.

These external effects are certainly important and a later section in the paper attempts to enumerate and value them. Finally, green belts have been suggested to deal with the problem of public good[2] provision and cases where jointness in the supply of goods exist. This might arise for example when a population, equally divided between two towns, maximises average benefits; but once this point is left, the marginal benefits from switching to the larger community for an individual will exceed those of staying and the population will redistribute itself until a stable, but inefficient equilibrium is attained. This was the underlying (implicit) theory behind Ebenezer Howard's green belt concept: towns and countryside should be in close proximity to maximise accessibility between them.

The effects of a green belt

Assume initially that the economy of a city is in equilibrium, with rent gradient AA, at which time a green belt is established of width AN, Figure 10.1. Assume that after the green belt is imposed, the city continues to grow because either population or employment expands, so that the rent gradient increases to, say, BB. Because of the green belt, however, no new development can take place in ring AN, and planning authorities may prevent redevelopment at an increased density in ring OA. As a result rents will be bid up until a new rent gradient DD is attained, at which point the increased population will now be accommodated in new developments beyond the green belt. A similar situation will occur if transport becomes relatively cheaper: this will flatten the rent bid curve causing a reduction in rents near the city centre, O, and an increase in rents at the edge of the green belt, at A. Again no new development will be permitted in ring AN which will cause further upward pressure on rents near the green belt. Transport may continue to become relatively cheaper until new development takes place outside the green belt. In both cases some individuals will be willing to put up with the excessively long journey to work because of the high cost of housing inside the green belt ring. Conversely those residing in the old urban area OA and bearing the high cost of housing will do so because the only alternative is a very long journey to work. In either case, because population has continued to grow or because transport has become relatively cheaper, restrictions on development (green belt) have resulted in households being on a higher (less preferred) bid-price curve than they otherwise would be. Moreover, there will be pressure from those owning green belt land, particularly land on its inner edge, for it to be "rezoned" for development since the price of green belt land will now be only a fraction of the price of developable land.

Who gains and loses as a result of a green belt? Those who gain are first, property owners, especially those at the outer edge of the built-up area who either own property when the green belt is imposed or acquire property before the new equilibrium rent (DD) is reached. Such owners benefit because of the increased monetary value of their property, and the amenity value (non-monetary income) they derive from living next to green belt land. Second, property owners elsewhere in the city gain because of the increased value of their property as a result of the green belt. Those who lose are, first, those who rent property in the inner areas of cities because their rents will increase in line with property value, they will not receive capital gain since this will go to the landlord, and since they live so far from the edge of the city, the green belt will be of little amenity value to them. Second, new owner occupiers entering the housing market lose since they either have to pay prices inflated by restrictions on development, or they have to make a very long journey to work.

Green belts can be seen to have a number of consequences. First, they generate pressure to maintain the status quo. Once having paid inflated prices, new owner occupiers have an interest in preserving the status quo, since they would stand to lose all the capital gains received by the previous owners if the green belt were removed. Once a green belt is imposed it also becomes politically difficult to rezone land on its inner edge for development because of the opportunities for land speculation and the vast capital gains which would accrue to landowners. Second, because rents, house prices and land prices in the old built-up area of the city are higher than they would be if the green belt

FIG. 10.1 The rent gradients of a city with a green belt.

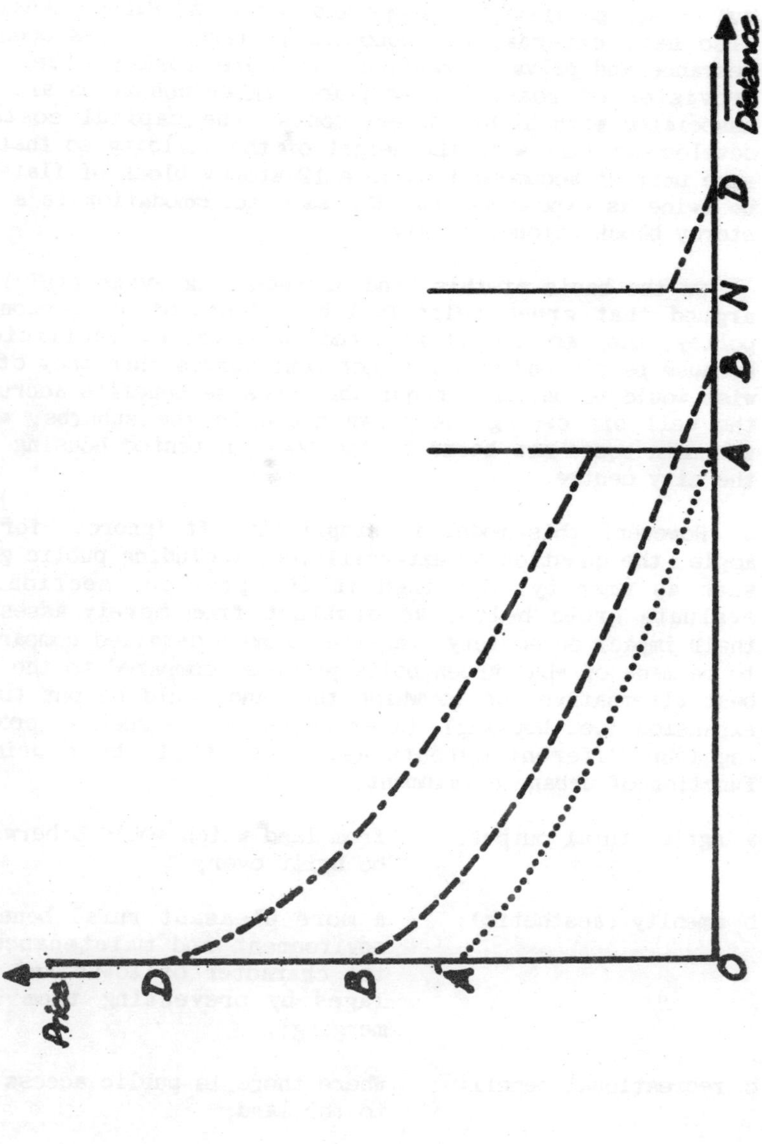

did not exist, it follows that, when sites within this area are redeveloped, they will be redeveloped at densities which are higher than they otherwise would be. Whether this is good or bad is open to discussion. Higher densities have external economies in terms of better public transport systems and closer proximity to shops and services. Higher densities also have external diseconomies in terms of less open appearance and private transport is more costly, i.e., the provision of roads. In addition higher densities are also associated with higher direct costs: the capital costs of development rise with the height of the building so that the same unit of accommodation in a 12-storey block of flats may be twice as expensive than the same accommodation in a two-storey block (Stone, 1959).

On the basis of this kind of reasoning Evans (1973) has argued that green belts fail both tests of micro-economic policy: they are inefficient and inequitable. Inefficient, because people end up on higher rent curves than they otherwise would be on; and inequitable because benefits accrue to the well off owning their own house in the suburbs, while the main costs are borne by the poor in rented housing near the city centre.

However, this model is simplistic. It ignores, for example, the question of externalities, including public goods such as amenity, outlined in the previous section. To evaluate green belts, as distinct from merely assessing their impact on society, requires a more detailed comparison to be made of what green belts produce, compared to the next best alternative use to which the land could be put (urban expansion i.e. housing). Green belts can be seen as producing four different outputs as a result of their primary function of urban containment:

a agricultural output: from land which would otherwise be built over;

b amenity (aesthetic): a more pleasant rural benefits environment and maintenance of the character of towns and villages by preventing them from merging;

c recreational benefits: Where there is public access to the land;

d prevention of diseconomies of scale of urban growth.

The evaluation of green belts

Green belt policy has the effect of causing resources in the economy to be used in a different way from that which would have ensued in its absence. The difference between these two positions (the net social benefit) therefore represents a measure of the value/cost of the policy itself. The NSB comprises the difference between the value of factors of production and consumption under a green belt policy and their social opportunity cost:

$$NSB = \sum_{t=o}^{T} \frac{\sum_{j=1}^{n} Qt_j \, (pt_j - Pt_j^*)}{(1 + i)^t}$$

where Qt = quantity of factor $_j$ used
P_j = value of factor or good $_j$ under green belt policy
P_j^* = social opportunity cost of factor or good $_j$
T = time period of the policy, with t denoting specific years 0 to T
i = discount or time preference rate

Green belts can thus be appraised by enumerating and evaluating the outputs made by them and then comparing these with the alternative use to which the land would have been put in the absence of the green belt. The outputs of a green belt comprise agricultural output, amenity (aesthetic value), recreation, and the prevention of diseconomies of urban size.

What is the value of agricultural output from green belt land? Agricultural land use within the green belt can be determined either by a survey, or as in England, from the government's annual agricultural census. But as Thomson (1981) has pointed out, framing in the rural-urban fringe is subject to problems not found elsewhere, of which four seem particularly relevant. First, trespass and vandalism are more prevalent, though these may be reduced by intelligent farm, stock and crop management. Second, urban service requirements may cause severance and fragmentation of farms, by roads, pipelines, etc., the construction and servicing of which imposes additional costs on farming. Third, the hope of capital gains through development may result in a lack of long term farming objectives. Often much land in the urban-rural fringe is held for speculative purposes by developers who lease the land on short leases to farmers. This can give rise to short term management of the land, almost farming to quit practices. Fourth, against these problems must be set the advantage that a close urban area permits; the marketing of farm produce directly by the farmer himself, and the use of land for non-traditional enterprises such as the keeping of horses for recreational activities by the urban population. This can offer worthwhile outlets for otherwise non-viable agricultural holdings. All of these factors should be reflected in the financial value of farming in the green belt. Agriculture may be valued financially either as:

(1) a capitalised value, in which case the market value of agricultural land/farms would be an appropriate measure;

(2) the annual value of output minus variable (labour plus seed, fertilizer etc. costs) and fixed (e.g. interest on capital tied up in farm buildings and land) costs.

However, the social value of agricultural output can be very different from its financial value. The net social benefit of agricultural output can be defined as:

$$NSB_t = R_t - V_t - F_t - Y_t$$

where

NSB_t = net social benefit in time t
R_t = gross revenue (at free market prices)
V_t = total variable costs (at factor cost)
F_t = total fixed costs (at factor cost)
Y_t = imputed payment for farmer's labour.

The real benefits are the free market value of the relevant agricultural output, and real costs, the unsubsidised costs. In Britain, today, there are few variable input subsidies. Subsidies to agriculture centre on market intervention by the European Economic Commission, and subsidies to fixed costs. For example, it has been calculated that the real benefits of agricultural output are, overall, about 10 per cent than the gross financial revenue the output produces. This is because the E.E.C. buys agricultural output to maintain its price at a higher level than would pertain on the free market. This output is then destroyed, stored, or given to countries in Eastern Europe. Thus, from the financial value of output received by the farmer should be subtracted the payment for output which is destroyed, stored, or otherwise disposed of, since by definition this is of no benefit (has zero value) to people in Britain or the E.E.C. Subsidies are also available for fixed costs. Capital grants cover approximately 30 to 50 per cent of capital expenditure depending upon the type. Thus, to the total financial fixed costs faced by the farmer should be added the amount of capital subsidies, because this combined total is the real resource (factor) cost which must be borne by the economy. There are in addition national aids (subsidies) towards agriculture which include zero local authority rates, much reduced capital transfer tax, and other forms of tax relief.

Assume an average gross margin of E450 per hectare (Nix, 1980). The gross margin is the gross financial revenue to the farmer minus total variable costs (e.g. seeds, fertilizer, hired labour etc.). Then from the ?450 per ha deducting fixed costs (rent or capital tied up in the land), imputed payment for farmer's labour, price support subsidies, capital subsidies and favourable tax treatment, it is difficult to believe that any positive social value would remain. One might reasonably conclude, therefore, that at the margin the agricultural value of green belt land is at best zero and might even be negative in Britain. This is not of course to argue that the agricultural value of all green belt land in the world is zero: differing economic circumstances would lead to differing valuations. Each case needs to be appraised separately.

The case for green belts compared with the alternative use of the land for urban expansion, rests, therefore, in Western Europe, on the value of amenity associated with green belt land, plus any recreational value of the land, with diseconomies of scale in urban service provision somewhat less important. Of course a central problem here is deciding what amenity is and of what it comprises. It may be that an important constituent of amenity is agricultural landscape i.e., amenity is a joint product of agricultural output. This point has been raised and the suggestion made that farmers should be paid to provide landscape amenity e.g., neat hedgerows marking field boundaries etc. (Countryside Commission, 1974). But the alternative amenity value of allowing the land to return to its natural vegetation cover (deciduous woodland in Britain), and what effect this would have on neighbouring house prices and residents' perceptions of amenity, has not been investigated.

The amenity benefits of green belt land can be estimated in two ways, either by a revealed preference approach or through expressed preference.

The revealed preference approach concentrates on information thrown up by the market as a consequence of peoples' effective demand to satisfy this choice. An estimate of the amenity value of green belt land can be made by looking at how much people are prepared to spend to live near the green belt. In the last few years a considerable amount of research has been focussed on ways in which amenities and disamenities affect urban residential property values. In this context the effects upon property values of neighbourhood parks, lakes and reservoirs, air pollution, air craft noise, as well as green belts, have been examined (Weicher and Zerbst, 1973; Hammer, Coughlin and Horn, 1974; Darling, 1973; Knetsch, 1964; Ridker and Henning 1967; Walters, 1975; Correll, Lillydahl and Singell, 1978). In these models the commodity housing is taken to represent a bundle of services offered by the land and structure, which can be classified into three categories:- locational advantages; space (rooms, etc.), structural services; and amenity. A green belt is a public good which confers an amenity benefit. One would expect house prices to reflect the value of the green belt externality given that their consumption is competitive. Therefore, it is possible to test the hypothesis that, holding all other variables constant, residential property values decline with distance from the green belt (assuming that housing markets are competitive and in the long run properties become assigned in accordance with maximum profits and utility conditions).

This hedonic (house) price revealed preference approach has been used to assess the amenity value of London's green belt. On the basis of quite stringent assumption such as :

(a) the amenity value was twice that estimated by the model;

(b) that every house in London attracted an amenity value from the green belt and not only those close to it as predicted by the model;

(assumptions extremely unlikely to be fulfilled in the real world), the amenity value of each hectare was less than half its opportunity cost in terms of house building land (Willis, 1980). Thus, it could be argued that London's green belt is too extensive and should be reduced in size until the amenity (plus any agricultural and recreational value) equals the value of the land to housing.

Hedonic price models to estimate the value of amenity have not been without their critics, notably Pearce and Edwards (1979) who argue that they represent fundamental problems rather than normal discrepancies between the theoretical ideal (individuals as utility maximisers, with homogeneous utility functions, no imperfections in the housing markets etc.) and the practical realities which this sought of empirical research always confronts. There are many aspects in which the actual data diverge from the theoretical ideal. But the question is not whether the model is perfect, but rather does it provide a usable vehicle for increasing our knowledge? Hedonic prices and property values in measuring environmental benefits has been defended by Freeman (1981), who argues for more research into questions of market segmentation and limits on the range of models, model specification and using marginal implicit prices.

The expressed preference approach to evaluating amenity benefits of green belt land makes use of direct inquiry through a questionnaire survey. Such a study of the Tyneside green belt in England used a questionnaire survey of a random sample of 103 houses in two residential districts bordering on to and almost surrounded by green belt land. The expressed evaluation was linked to the scale of rates (taxes) payable to the local authority to provide the respondent with some frame of reference on which to base his judgement, although this did not preclude the respondent from going outside this range (i.e. of the amount of taxes paid). The precise questions were:

1. If the restrictions on development were removed, how much would you want your rates (or rent) reduced to compensate for the loss of the green belt?

2. If, to preserve the green belt (for ever), the local authority had to buy the land, how much extra would you be willing to pay in rates to finance this?

The whole exercise involved the householders in introspection about choices between alternatives. Can the average respondent be expected to do this? While the initial response to this question is typically pessimistic, it is worth recalling that individuals do have to make judgements about the amount of money required to compensate them for losses incurred e.g., as a result of accidents; and more frequently when individuals buy and sell e.g., houses they have to put national monetary values, when comparing alternative properties, on such things as amenity (the view from the house), its accessibility to the city and so on, to compare prices of houses and arrive at a decision. Moreover, individuals also make regular decisions as to whether to subscribe and donate to charitable causes and "worthy" public projects. Thus, in view of the fact that most people have had extensive practice in taking similar decisions to the two questions/problems posed, there is probably less cause for scepticism about the proposed experimental procedure than initially appears to be the case. It would therefore seem rather unreasonable to discount the experiment either on the grounds of the potential untruthfulness of householders or the inherent difficulty of introspecting about the broad category of choices involved.

Table 10.1 shows the results of the small sample survey. Most respondents indicated that some reduction in their rates (taxes) would compensate for the loss of green belt amenity, if urban development were allowed on the site. No-one indicated that no amount of money would compensate him for the loss i.e., no-one suggested that green belt land had infinite amenity or aesthetic value. Nor did any one suggest that a 100 per cent reduction of taxes was required: the maximum reduction expressed or desired was 60 per cent and 26 per cent of respondents said they would not require compensating for the loss of the green belt.

TABLE 10.1

Amenity value of green belt using an expressed preference method of inquiry

	Bruton Park District	Melton Park District	Both Areas
Average rates (taxes) # per year	431	494	471
Average % Decrease in taxes desired	15.1	25.8	22.1
Average % Increase in tax acceptable	5.4	8.5	7.4

The amount that respondents were willing to pay to keep the green belt was significantly less than the compensation required if it was lost. Willingness to sell exceeds willingness to pay to acquire green belt land for aesthetic purposes: willingness to pay for green belt provision is bounded by income, but willingness to sell green belt development rights is not bounded by income and will exceed willingness to pay in the case of a positive income effect (which is a reasonable assumption with regard to amenity/aesthetics). Willingness to pay may also include free rider problems (see Willis, 1980), which would also account for willingness to sell exceeding this valuation.

Table 10.1 indicates that the value of green belt land was greater to some (Melton Park) residents than to others (Brunton Park). Two factors account for this observed difference. First, household income is higher in one area (Melton Park) than the other. Increased demand for amenity and aesthetic quality is likely to depend on income rather than any cultural differences between rich and poor in a community i.e., this assumes at least roughly similar preference functions for rich and poor; or more accurately, it presumes that lower income groups do not possess systematically stronger preferences for environmental quality than the more wealthy. Otherwise the poor, because of their intense preferences for amenity, might, in spite of their lower incomes, still be willing to pay more than the rich for a given level of environmental quality. That amenity and aesthetic value is an income elastic good seems to me a valid assumption. Second, there is a striking contrast between the landscapes surrounding the two areas. Indeed, as Tyne and Wear County Council's (1980) subject plan on the green belt reveals, there is tremendous variation in landscape quality within the green belt and this will affect not only the total amenity value of the green belt but will give rise to considerable differences in the amenity value of different portions of the green belt.

The amenity value of the green belt can be derived from the expressed preference approach by assuming that the amenity value to each household is 22 per cent of local taxes (the average value derived from the survey). The average tax per domestic hereditament in 1980-81 was ?186.54 for Tyne and Wear (County plus Districts) and the number of domestic hereditaments 447,699 (Chartered Institute of Public Finance and Accountancy, 1981). The amenity value of the green belt is then

$$£186.54 \times 0.22 \times 447,699 = £18,373,030$$

Since the existing statutory green belt covers 7,700 ha this gives a value of £2386 per ha. The proposed green belt outlined by Tyne and Wear County Council (1980) in their subject green belt plan to operate in conjunction with their structure plan, covers 24,860 ha, which gives an amenity value of £739 per ha.

These are annual values. The (capitalised) present value of these annual benefits to perpetuity at a 7 per cent discount rate (the rate by the Chief Secretary to the Treasury, Mr. Joel Barnett (Parliamentary Papers, 1978) and more fully discussed by H.M. Treasury (1979) as the appropriate rate of discount for project appraisal in the non-trading public services) are ?34,086 per ha and ?10,557 per ha respectively for the existing and proposed green belt area. Clearly, this averaging has concealed differences in urban social and physical fabric. With outward growth and new development on the periphery (Burgess Model of urban growth) domestic rateable value will be higher near the urban fringe than in inner city areas, so that the figures may under-estimate amenity value. On the other hand, the same amenity (proportionate) value has been ascribed to all hereditaments despite the fact that the hedonic price models show that amenity value of green belt land declines with increasing distance from the green belt.

Additional recreational value of green belt land over and above amenity value will be limited to specific areas depending upon present access arrangements. Green belts often provide the setting for many private recreational facilities such as race courses, golf courses and so on. These are private facilities for which an entrance fee can be charged, but in addition many major open access recreational facilities, e.g., footpaths, bridle paths, areas of particular landscape interest, etc., are to be found in green belts. For these latter recreational facilities no price is charged, nor is it optimal to charge a price since the facilities are by way of a public good. But this does not mean that they have no value to society. Appropriate methods of evaluating such recreational facilities are by way of techniques such as Clawson demand curves (Willis, 1980). Recreational value must be added to amenity value in evaluating green belt benefits.

Also to be taken into account in any evaluation is the expected value of any minerals extracted from green belt land. Clearly mineral working is possible under green belt policy compared with the alternative of urban development and the loss of amenity entailed would be temporary if restoration was made a condition of planning permission. Such an evaluation requires the analysis of timing of investments and development; otherwise another investment (urban development) may pre-empt the site of mineral extraction (Willis, 1980). However, minerals do not have a ubiquitous distribution, and the mineral problem is likely to be confined to localised areas of a green belt.

Lastly, there are diseconomies associated with urban expansion. Diseconomies associated with the size of urban areas are difficult to identify and quantify and there is considerable uncertainty about them. More recognisable are diseconomies of scale in the size of local (including government) services like housing, education, etc. The correct remedy here would be to have smaller agencies or "firms" supplying these goods rather than restricting the size of the urban area as a means of limiting the size of an agency.

The limited set of data assembled for Tyne and Wear suggests that while the present statutory designation of green belt may be economically justified as a whole, the full extension proposed by Tyne and Wear Council is not. The alternative to some of the proposed green belt is new housing, producing benefits of ?56,600 per ha (standard deviation ?9,780) in terms of 1979 land prices (Department of the Environment, 1980). Even allowing for a housing subsidy (tax relief for owner occupiers) the difference in benefits between the two land uses, green belt and housing, is significant. There is room for marginal changes: reductions in the extent of the green belt proposed by Tyne and Wear but also perhaps marginal extensions to the present extent and distribution of statutory green belt land.

CONCLUSIONS

A number of problems still remain in any evaluation of green belts. First, since amenity is income elastic demand for amenity will be much greater in the future, perhaps growing faster than the demand for housing in Western Europe and the U.S.A., although not necessarily so in countries with high rates of population increase. This will have implications for the future size and distribution of green belts. Second, there is the question of who own the rights to amenity in green belt land. In the analysis it has been assumed that amenity rights accrue to householders around the green belt (i.e. householders, willingness to sell amenity in green belts to permit urban development). But amenity rights are not recognised in English planning law. The alternative is to assume that householders would need to buy green belt land to secure amenity rights to it. But willingness to buy is much less than willingness to sell (7.4 per cent of local taxes compared with 22.1 per cent in the survey) and this would imply a very much smaller area of green belt land. It might be argued in Britain that the amenity rights of green belt land are vested with the local authority on behalf of the community: but local authorities in Britain have been all too willing to permit urban development on green belt land (e.g. if sufficient new jobs are provided from the development) without compensating local residents in any way for loss of amenity.

NOTES

1. The writers noted in this section can be found in extracts edited by Coleman (1973).

2. A pure public good is one whose consumption by one person in no way detracts from its availability to others. Private goods, by contrast, are such that consumption of one unit by one person necessarily precludes consumption of the same unit by others. Public agencies can supply both public goods (e.g. clean air by controlling pollution; visual amenity; etc.) and private goods (e.g. housing; water; etc.)

REFERENCES

Chartered Institute of Public Finance and Accountancy, **Finance, General and Rating Statistics** 1981-1982. London: CIPFA, 1981.

Coleman, B., **The Idea of the City in Nineteenth Century Britain.** London: Routledge & Kegan Paul, 1973.

Committee on Land Utilisation in Rural Areas, **Report** Cmnd. 6378. London: H.M.S.O, 1942.

Correll, M.R., Lillydahl, J.H. & Singell, L.D., The Effects of Green Belts on Residential Property Values: Some Findings on the Political Economy of Open Space, **Land Economics 54**, 1978, 207-217.

Countryside Commission, **New Agricultural Landscapes**, Cheltenham: Countryside Commission, 1974.

Darling, A.H., Measuring Benefits Generated by Urban Water Parks, **Land Economics 49**, 1973, 22-34.

Department of the Environment, **Development Involving Agricultural Land. Circular 75/76**, London: H.M.S.O.,

1976.
Department of the Environment, **Development for Agricultural Purposes, Circular 24/73**, London: H.M.S.O.,1973.
Department of the Environment, **Housing and Construction Statistics**, 4th Quarter, Issue 32, London: H.M.S.O., 1980.
Evans, A.W., **The Economics of Residential Location**, London: Macmillian, 1973.
Freeman, A.M., Hedonic Prices, Property Values and Measuring Environmental Benefits: A Survey of the Issues, in S. Strom (ed) **Measurement in Public Choice**, London: Macmillan, 1981.
Hall, P., **The Containment of Urban England**, London: Allen & Unwin, 1973.
Hammer, T.R., Coughlin, R.E. & Horn, E.T., The Effect of a Large Urban Park on Real Estate Value, **Journal of the American Institute of Planners 40**, 1974, 274-277.
H.M. Treasury, **The Test Discount Rate and the Required Rate of Return of Investment**, London: H.M. Treasury, 1979.
Howard, E. **Garden Cities of Tomorrow.** London: Faber & Faber, 1945.
Knetsch, J.L., The Influence of Reservoir Projects on Land Values, **Journal of Farm Economics 46**, 1964, 231-243.
Le Corbusier **The Radiant City**, London: Faber & Faber, 1964.
Mellor, R., Images of the City: their impact on British urban policy in The Open University **Urban Change and Conflict.** Milton Keynes: The Open University, 1982.
Ministry of Housing and Local Government **Green Belts** Circular 42/55, London: H.M.S.O., 1955.
Ministry of Housing and Local Government **Safeguarding of Agricultural Land**, Circular 43/58. London: H.M.S.O., 1958.
Nix, J., **Farm Management Pocketbook**, 11th Ed. University of London: Wye College, 1980.
Parliamentary Debates (Hansard) **House of Commons Official Report, 5th April 1978, Written Answer** by Mr. Joel Barnett on Test Discount Rate.
Pearce, D. & Edwards, R., The Monetary Evaluation of Noise Nuisance: Implications for Noise Abatement Policy, in T. O'Riordan & R.C. D'Arge **Progress in Resource Management and Environment Planning**, Vol. 1, Chichester: J. Wiley, 1979.
Ridker, R.G. & Henning, J.A., Determinants of Residential Property Values with Special Reference to Air Pollution, **Review of Economics and Statistics 49**, 1967, 246-257.
Stone, P.A., Economics of Housing and Urban Development. **Journal of the Royal Statistical Society A 122**, Part 4, 1959, 417-476.

Thomson, K.J., **Farming in the Fringe.** Cheltenham: Countryside Commission, CCP 142, 1981.

Tyne and Wear County Council, **Tyne and Wear Green Belt and Urban Fringe Subject Plan: Draft Proposals.** Newcastle: Tyne and Wear County Council, 1980.

Walters, A.A., **Noise and Prices.** Oxford: Clarendon Press, 1975.

Weicher, J.C., Zerbst, R.H., The Externalities of Neighbourhood Parks: An Empirical Investigation, **Land Economics 49**, 1973, 99-105.

Willis, K.G., **The Economics of Town and Country Planning.** St. Albans: Granada, 1980.

ELEVEN

Antal Lehmann

A Phyto-Geographical Method for the Investigation of Agglomeration

Example of Pecs and its Vicinity

Since it is a basic attribute of society to function in a permanent and close relation to its physical environment; therefore the latter is transformed as required by the society in accordance with the mode of production and the level of development of the productive forces. Consequently, changes in the physical environment within a given area reflect the quantitative and qualitative impacts of the social activity inducing the change. As a result, the processes of urbanization and agglomeration, so characteristic of our days, must be well indicated in the alterations in the physical environment of the area involved. The question remains to be answered which factor of the physical environment is most sensitive to these influences. In my opinion it is the biota since it has the strongest links with all other factors of the physical environment (topography, soils, water, air) as well as with society; thus living organisms immediately indicate changes in any other physical factors. As social interventions affect surface vegetation first, its transformation is a quick indication of environmental changes in forms well visible to the naked eye. Thus surface vegetation 'vascular plants' can be applied to be one of the indicators of environmental changes.

Any kinds of anthropogenic, social activity being examined, the general observation is that it is first the vegetation of the terrain that is influenced more or less intensively by man. 1. He either transforms (often in an unconscious way) the natural vegetation in an area to various extents, e.g. in forests and pastures; or 2. completely exterminates natural vegetation and creates a new type of vegetation in its place constituted of other species; this happens in arable lands, gardens, vineyards and orchards; or 3. similarly to the previous, exterminates natural vegetation and creates or leaves behind a completely barren ground which in turn is populated by a so-called 'ruderal weed association' with low number of species and specimen, spontaneously or by conscious human action as in the case of buildings, yards, industrial establishments, mines, transport routes etc.

The special features of the vegetation type resulting in the area from the above three social influences of different intensity are demonstrated with the following data. The data well present also the botanical, qualitative (floristic) consequences of the social intervention.

The percentage distribution of forest vegetation (1) which most resembles to 'or in places is identical with' the original 'potential' vegetation; the vegetation of agricultural lands (2) and the ruderal weed association (3):

(a) By vertical distribution	1.	2.	3.
Plants occurring everywhere from plains to mountains	70	88	89
Living only in plains	+	1	+
Occurring both in plains and hills	3	9	4
Living only in hills	+	0	0
Occurring both in hills and mountains	15	2	5
Living only in mountains	12	+	2
(b) By floristic elements /area types/			
Plants living all over the Earth's surface: cosmopolite	2	25	16
Immigrated with cultivation: adventive	2	3	6
Living on most of our continent: Eurasian	81	65	70
Overwhelming in inner Eurasia: continental	1	1	1
Spread from evergreen Mediterranean areas	8	5	7
Characteristics of the Atlantic			

coast of Western Europe	3	+	+
Alpine species of high mountains	2	0	+
Plant species characteristic in the Balkan peninsula	1	1	+
Endemic elements of the Hungarian flora	+	+	0

(c) By habitation

Arboraceous plants (trees, shrubs, sub-shrubs: MM, M, N)	28	2	12
Dwarf and creeping shrubs (Ch)	3	3	3
Perennial herbaceous plants (H)	47	40	38
Bulbous and tuberous plants spending winter underground (G)	11	8	11
Plants spending winter under water or swamp (HH)	1	1	1
Biennial plants (TH)	1	7	12
Annual herbaceous plants (Th)	8	40	23
Epiphyte, parasitic plants (E)	1	+	0

(d) By thermal requirements

Cryophyte species (TI)	1	1	+
Cold-tolerant plant species (T2)	22	12	20
Less cold-tolerant (T3) plant species	46	23	34
Thermophilous species sensitive to cold (T4)	20	19	16
Species with high thermal requirement (T5)	1	+	1
Eurythermous (TO) plant species	10	45	29

(e) By water requirements

Highly xerophilous species (F1)	2	5	5
Xerophilous plant species (F2)	28	45	47
Living on soil neither extremely drying out nor wetting (F3)	51	17	19
Species demanding moist soils (F4)	11	10	11
Hydrophyte species (F5)	1	4	1
Euryhygric plant species (FO)	7	19	17

During urbanization and agglomeration which necessarily involve various construction activities (the establishment of residential and industrial buildings, the development of the utility and road network), the third type of vegetation change is most frequent and the ruderal weed association conceived in a broader sense extends over new areas. Therefore, it is possible to use this vegetation type as an indicator of the spatial and temporal extension and intensity of socio-economic processes.

Author outlined the impacts of agglomeration on the living environment (Lehmann, A. 1979, 1981a.). So instead of going into details a brief summary will suffice here.

- Ruderal weed association gains ground at the expense of other vegetation types in direct proportion, while forested areas grow in inverse proportion to the extent of urban growth and agglomeration;

- the extension of the adventive, plain and plain-mountainous, arboraceous as well as of dwarf and creeping shrubs are in direct proportion to the extent of urbanization-agglomeration, while the Atlantic, Alpine and Balkanic flora elements and the hill-mountainous, mountainous, biennial and annual herbaceous species spread in inverse proportion to that;

- similarly, the ratio of thermophilous and xerophilous species show direct proportion, while of those with lesser thermal but higher water requirements are inversely proportional to urbanization-agglomeration;

- changes in the ratio of species sensitive to soil reaction are dependent on the extent of human intervention (i.e. the intensity of urbanization--agglomeration) but also on the chemistry of subsoils in the area;

- as far as species distribution by nitrogen requirement is concerned, the advance of neutral and hydrogen-loving species indicates the extension of agglomeration.

What do we mean by 'ruderal weed association'? It is a collective name for all plant associations, biocenoses growing wild which can be found around human settlements, residential and other buildings, in their yards, near mines, industrial and agricultural plants and their neighbourhood, along roads, railways, at litter and waste disposal sites. In the vicinity of towns and industrial establishments, e.g. associations of kinds of goose-foot, orach, amaranth and sisymbrium are most frequent. Later cabbage-lettuce, hunger-grass, horse-thistle and other thistles, nettle and then black wormwood colonize among them. Along railway beds, in the yards of mines, the association primarily comprises colt's-foot, viper's-bugloss, evening primrose, and melilots. In fallow lands, gardens, along roads, associations of wall barley and kinds of brome-grass occur. It is generally characteristic of these associations and thus of all vegetation type that they include species with the least requirements, tolerant to extreme conditions which spontaneously colonize these sites, in a natural way. It can also be seen from the data above since the shares of species neutral to mountainous conditions 'plain-mountainous', immigrated with agriculture 'adventive', xerophyte (F2) and biennial herbaceous (TH) species are highest, at the same time the least shares are represented by the highly cryophyte (TI), thermophilous (T4) and perennial herbaceous (H) species. The most valuable elements of Hungarian flora as well as the epiphyte and parasitic (E) species are practically absent from these associations.

Even this rather general description makes it clear that the vegetation type in question is a botanically well delineated and defined, typical one the areal extension of which can also be well determined. Practically this is the vegetation type that covers built-up areas, roads, fallow and abandoned lands (free of land taxation) registered in cadastral surveys, thus their area can be delimited and quantified with exactness. This circumstance enables us to apply cadastral statistical data in order to exactly determine the spatial extension and the significance at any selected time of the vegetation type and its quantitative changes in the area.

On this basis a statistical data series was collected to demonstrate at three dates (1865, 1935 and 1975) what percentage of the administrative area of settlements around Pecs was covered with this vegetation on the one hand, i.e., what share it had from area and what was the trend (decreasing or increasing) and the intensity of changes in this ratio within the 1865 to 1935 and the 1935 to 1975 period (on the average of ten years), on the other. Using the same data, Tables 11.1 and 11.2 were compiled which well illustrate the spatial pattern and temporal change in the two periods of ruderal weed association.

Now the question obviously arises what is the relation between ruderal weed association and agglomeration, what is common in these distant concepts or phenomena. Our observations seem to give evidence to a sufficiently close positive correlation between urbanization-agglomeration and the spatial extension of ruderal weed association; as it was previously hinted at when construction always involved by agglomeration or the spreading of built-up areas were mentioned. In fact this process is well illustrated by the three sketch maps in fig 11.1 and the two in Fig. 11.2. interpretable the following way:

In 1865, when could not be traced in the environs of Pecs, only 2 per cent of the investigated area was covered with ruderal weed association and it was chiefly characteristic of lands where the cultivation system was in formation (deforestation and other changes of land use to increase arable land areas, water regulation works, the construction of drainage canals, ditches, characterized the period) with temporarily increased fallow land areas. For instance, the ratio of ruderal weed association from area was 9.06 per cent at Magyarszek, 7.65 per cent at Magyarhertelend, 5.80 per cent at Szoke, 5.78 per cent at Martonfa and 5.72 per cent at Egerag. This vegetation type extended only to 3 per cent of the largest settlement, the town of Pecs. In more than half of the investigated area the ratio of weed-covered surfaces was below 2.5 per cent.

In the seven decades before 1935 the share of weed vegetation from area had doubled but it was a heterogeneous growth in a spatial aspect. The largest percentage figure in 1935 (7.74 per cent) refers to Pecs where certain features of most intensive urbanization-agglomeration were manifest (in the western section of the present town 4 settlements were united under the name of 'Mecsekalja' in 1929). In the case of Pellerd the ratio increased over 13 per cent (!) due to the fish-ponds established in the early 1930s. A certain growth is observed in most settlements as a consequence of large-scale construction activities but in the period between 1865 and 1935 a decreasing trend is also shown in 19 per cent of the area just in case of settlements where owing to the situation with smallholders' economy at that time, cultivated land was extended to its maximal area; in order to gain land any potential terrain was used for the purposes of agricultural production.

It was in the 1950s that urbanization-agglomeration accelerated in the investigated area. In that period the villages of Mecsekalja, Mecsekszabolcs, Somogy and Vasas were united to Pecs and the building of Komlo, our new socialist mining town and the other centre of agglomeration started. Komlo later incorporated the villages of Manfa, Budafa, Mecsekfalu, Mecsekjanosi and Kisbattyan. To the west of Pecs, near Kovagoszolos, the mining of uranium and production at the ore concentration works began; several enterprises and plants have been relocated to Cserkut, a village also lying to the west of the town. Parallel to the establishment of mines and plants a large-scale housing estate building programme commenced in Pecs and Komlo; the same is experienced in the area of Szentlorinc and Pecsvarad (former district seats) which have been transformed to the satellite towns of Pecs. Family homes began to be built on a similarly large scale in the villages of Pellerd and Kozarmisleny near the town. By 1975 the administrative area of Pecs extended over 15 thousand hectares after the villages of Malon, Nagyarpad and Hird had also been united with it and 20 per cent of this area was covered with ruderal weed association. In the area of other urbanizing-agglomerating settlements the ratio of this vegetation type rose everywhere above 10 per cent in 1975.

Hassagy is an exception since, like in Pellerd in 1975, the 11.90 per cent ratio of weeds is due to the establishment of a fish-pond. I consider the above a further argument to support the previous statement that there is close positive relationship between urbanization-agglomeration and the ruderal weed association.

Agglomeration of settlements comes about, apart from and closely connected to large-scale constructions, basically through the concentration, growth in number of population in the area. The share of ruderal weed association from area and population number or its change also present a close positive correlation. Here only Fig. 11.3 is meant to illustrate and prove it since I have treated the problem in detail in another paper (Lehmann, A. 1981b). It is well seen in the figure that changes in the population number of the settlement are always followed with more or less time lag and with identical - either increasing or decreasing - trend with altered ratio of areas covered with ruderal weed association. There are four types indicated in the figure: Pecs is a steadily growing settlement; Komlo stagnated for a while, then suddenly started to grow and lately increased on a moderate scale; Kozarmisleny grew for a time, then decreased and lately started to grow again while Magyaregregy is the type of settlements first growing, then decreasing in population number. On their land surfaces the spatial ratio of ruderal weed association showed identical trends in the period between 1865 and 1975.

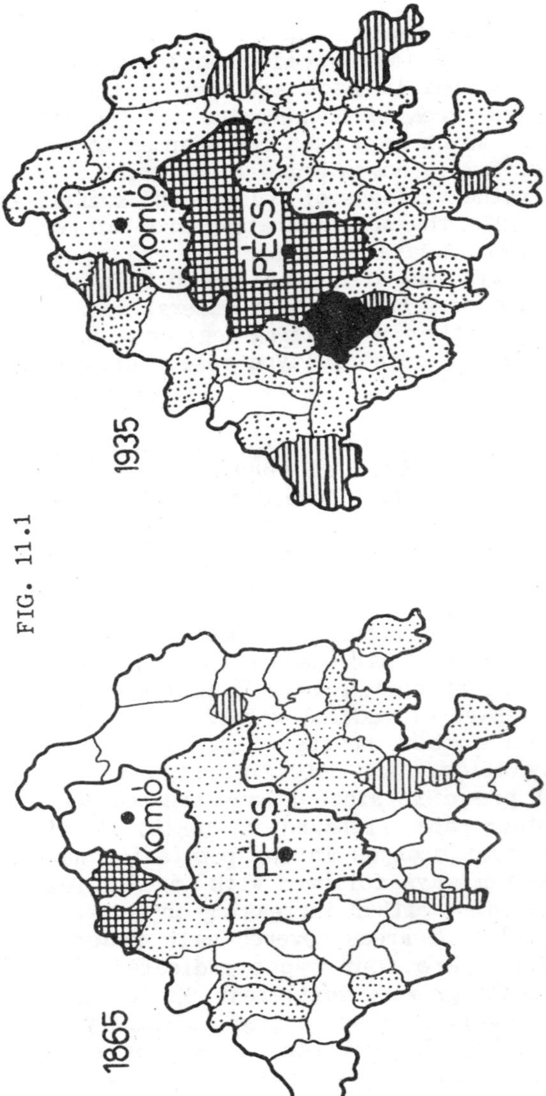

FIG. 11.1

Table 11.1 Contd.

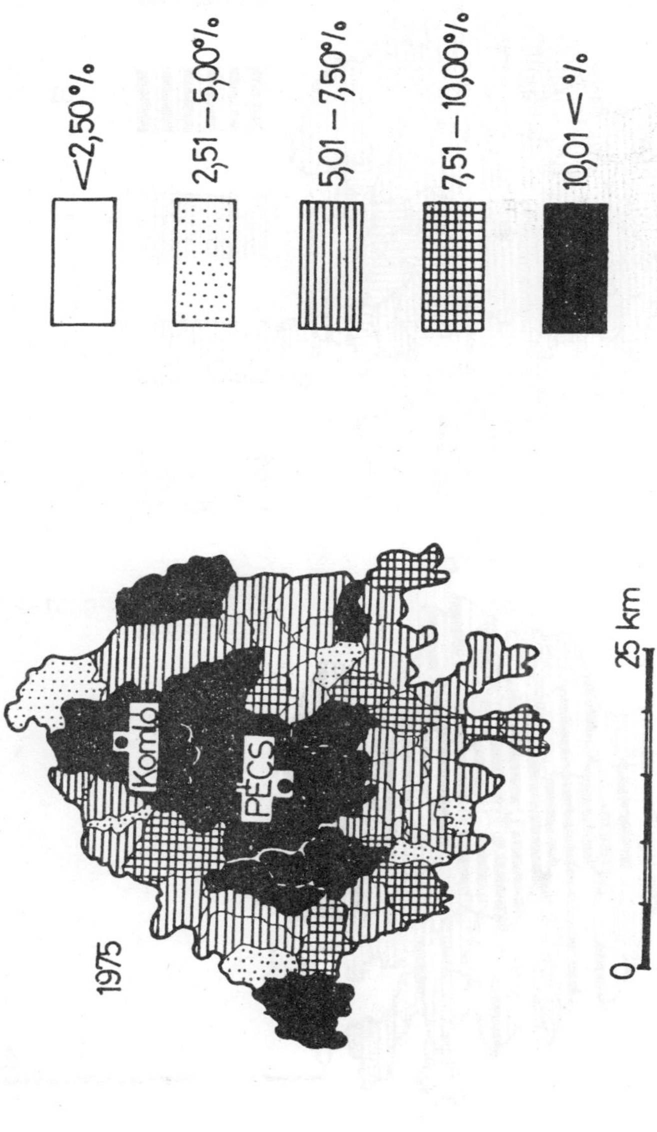

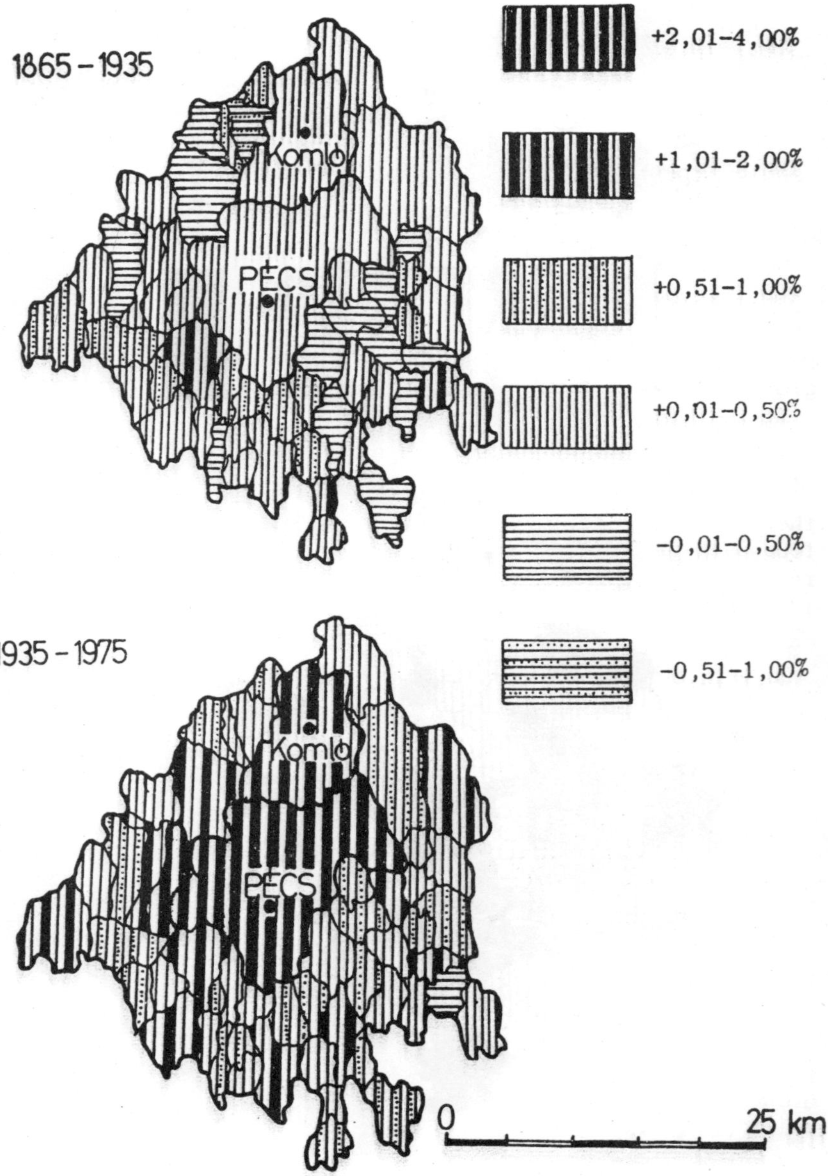
1865 - 1935
Komló
PÉCS
1935 - 1975
Komló
PÉCS
+2,01-4,00%
+1,01-2,00%
+0,51-1,00%
+0,01-0,50%
-0,01-0,50%
-0,51-1,00%
0
25 km

Subsequently I decided to apply the quantitative indicators of ruderal weed association, their spatial ratio and its temporal changes in order to delineate agglomeration or to determine the 'degree of agglomeration', the intensity of relations of individual member settlements to the agglomeration. The Pecs agglomeration serves as an example further on as well.

The method applied was as follows:

1. We have determined the ratio of areas covered with ruderal weed association in the total administrative area of the settlements selected for the investigation (the towns of Pecs and Komlo as the centre and sub-centre of the agglomeration and the 52 villages lying between them) in 1935 - when there was no agglomeration yet in a modern sense - and in 1975.

2. The (rising or falling) trend and rate of changes and the differences between these ratios were calculated for the four decades between 1935 and 1975. In order to make the rate of changes comparable to the previous period between 1865 and 1935 the average change for 10 years was calculated.

3. The arithmetical average of the 10 year average change for the period between 1935 and 1975 and the ratio for 1975 was calculated. Settlements are referred to an 'agglomeration system' by these data on the basis of the following principles:

4. All the settlements where both the ratio of the area of ruderal weed association in 1975 and the change in ratio between 1935 and 1975 (the change of the 10 year average of the latter) were above the average, are assigned to Group 1. This category includes the settlements of the so-called conurbation ring.

5. Settlements where only the magnitude of ratio change (the 10 year average) is higher than the average, belong to Group 2. (This is the category of the so-called 'peripheral villages').

6. Settlements where only the ratio for 1975 is higher than the average, are placed into Group 3. (To this category the so-called connected settlements, belong).

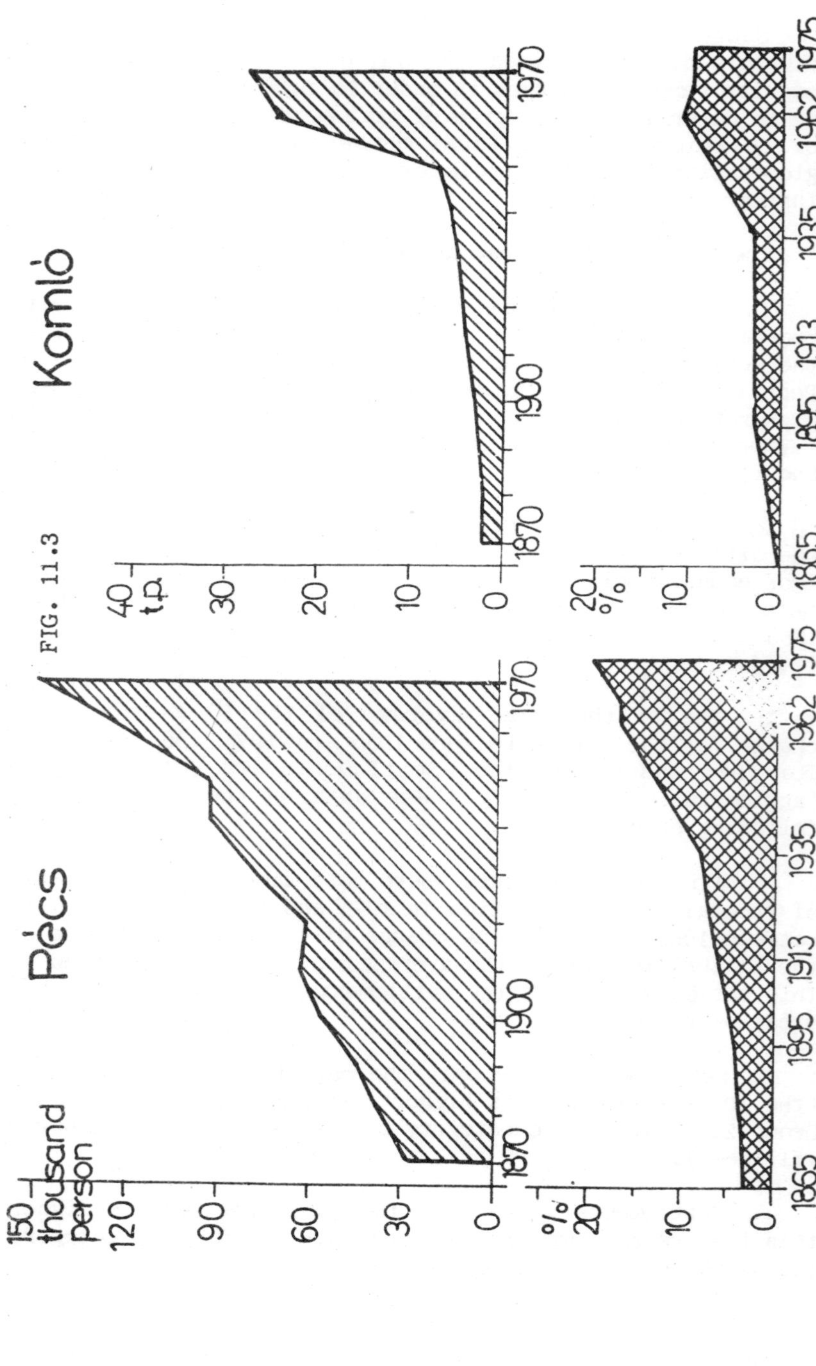

Pécs
Komló
thousand person
150
120
90
60
30
0
%
20
10
0
40
t.p.
30
20
10
0
20
%
10
0
1870
1900
1970
1865
1895
1913
1935
1962
1975

FIG. 11.3

Table 11.3 Contd.

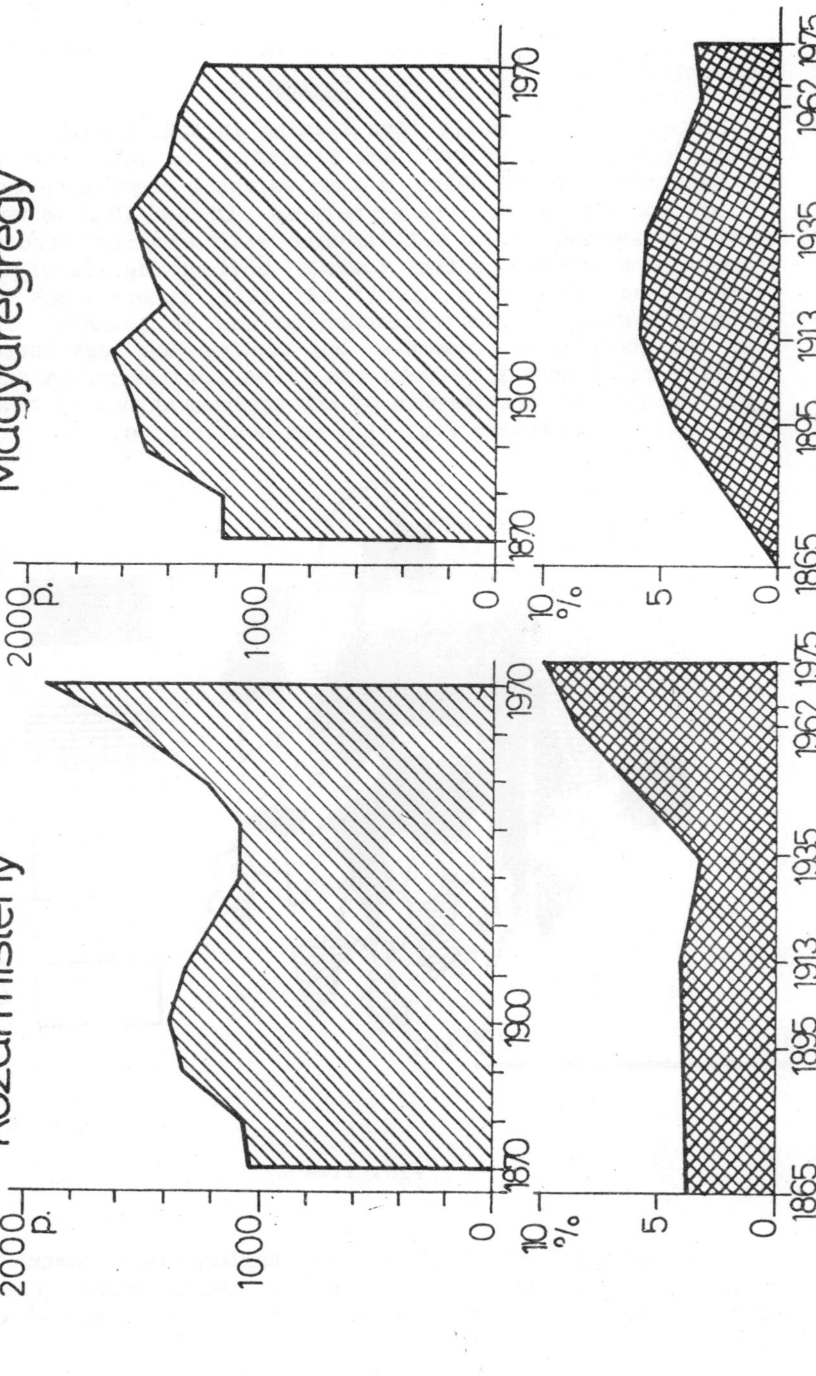

7. All the settlements where both figures are below average are referred to Group 4 (of settlements outside the agglomeration).

Since both in Pecs the town leading in agglomeration and having central functions, and in Komlo, the sub-centre of the agglomeration the share of the indicator vegetation type in 1975 and its rate of change between 1935 and 1975 is well above the average; thus settlements with similar figures resemble most to the central towns of obvious signals of agglomeration, therefore, their affinity, interactions and stronger system of interrelationships can be assumed. The less the above data 'resemble' one another the less intensive the relationship between the given settlement and the core, the central settlements of the agglomeration. By these data and considerations Fig. 11.4 was constructed.

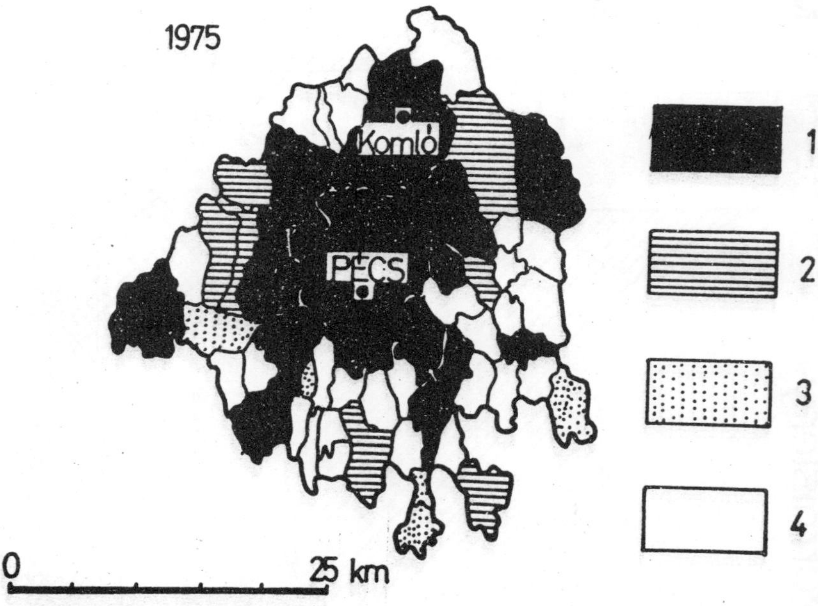

FIG. 11.4

This categorization of the Pecs agglomeration seems to be feasible by a factor of the physical environment, i.e., ruderal weed association as an indicator. As a matter of course, the primary significance of agglomeration studies on the basis of socio-economic factors cannot be debated but as a peculiarity the above outlined method of natural sciences relatively well indicates the socio-economic processes, though with a time lag. It seems to give evidence of a system of interrelationships between the physical environment and society. The applicability of the method but also the phase shift of time is justified by the good agreement observed between the categories of agglomeration identified in the area by various methods of the social sciences (economics, sociology etc), on the one hand and the above categories, settlement groups on the other. Agreement is 67 to 68 per cent in Group 1, 25 to 28 per cent in Groups 2 and 3 and 58 to 64 per cent in Group 4. It is also related to the fact that the economic, sociologic investigation methods usually show 'stronger' relationships between the settlements and the agglomeration centre than the ecological phyto-geographical method.

At last as a curiosity it can be mentioned that the present method can be used in the detection of spatial changes in socio-economic processes. To demonstrate it Fig. 11.5 was drawn in which the settlement system is represented in the investigated area by the above described methods in 1935 and 1975 already treated. Changes in the attraction zone of Pecs can be read from the figure. As a matter of fact, in 1935 it was not through the urbanization-agglomeration process but primarily by the agricultural activity serving vegetable, fruit and poultry supply that the villages of the environs were connected to Pecs and only secondarily by means of residence and workplace. Therefore, rail connections providing communication to markets (long distance road traffic being backward at that time) determined the intensity of the relationship. Ruderal weed association indicates intensive relationships with Pecs in the case of settlements along the Pecs-Szentlorinc, Pecs-Harkany and Pecs-Mohacs railway lines as well as of those which were developed and regulated in the period between 1865 and 1935. The areas with worse physical endowments for vegetable and fruit production and with less favourable position to transport did not link up with the town, even though they lay closer to it (like e.g. Orfu, Abaliget, Kovagoszolos, Kozarmisleny etc.).

This older system of relations was disintegrated in response partly to agricultural transformation and partly to the advent of actual agglomeration and the present situation has resulted. Influenced by this process three types of changes occurred in the settlements of the investigated area:

(1) there was no alternation in the intensity of the relationship between the village and the town (e.g. in case of Szentlorinc and Boda); or
(2) the relationship weakened (e.g. in case of Keszu and Szilvas); or
(3) it strengthened (e.g. in case of Orfu and Kozarmisleny).

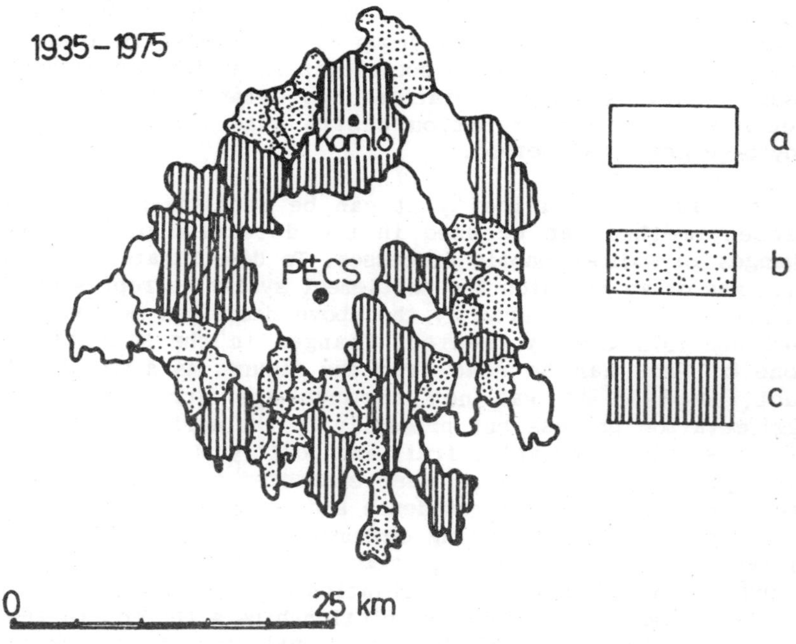

FIG. 11.5

Naturally further development, transformation in the existing system of relationships are to be expected in the future which will be marked by the spatial distribution in the area of ruderal weed association as an indicator.

REFERENCES

Hortobagyi, T. (ed.). Agrobotanika, Agrobotanics, **Mezogazdasagi Kiado**, Budapest, 1974.

Horvath, A., Die Vegetation des Mecsekgebirges und seiner Umgebung, **Akademiai Kiado**, Budapest, 1972.

Jakucs, P., A potencialos vegetacio es taji ertekelese Del-Dunantulon (Potential vegetation and its landscape evaluation in South-Transdenubia), **Foldr. Ert.** Vol. 23. No. 3. 1974, 295-309.

Lehmann, A., Az agglomeralodas hatasa az elo kornyzetre. Az agglomeraciokutatas modszertani kerdesei c. nemzetkozi konferencia eloadasai (The impact of agglomeration on the living environment. Papers of the international conference on 'Methodological problems of the study of agglomeration'). **MTA Dunantuli Tudomanyos Intezete Kozlemenyek** 26. 1979, 105-112.

Lehmann, A., Pecs kornyeki telepulesek novenyzetenek valtozasai 1865-1975 kozott (Changes in the vegetation at settlements near Pecs between 1865 and 1975). Pecsi Tanarkepzo Foiskola Foldrajz Tanazeke, Pecs, 1981 (a) 1938. + 3 tables and 13 figures.

Lehmann, A., Az agglomeralodas hatasa a novenyzetre es a talajokra Pecs tersegeben (The impact of agglomeration on vegetation and soils in the area of Pecs). In: **Vonzaskorzetek-agglomeraciok I. (Attraction zones--Agglomerations)** ed. by Rechnitzer, J. MTA DTI Ertekezesek, 1981(b) Bp. 229--315.

Magyarorszag muvelesiagak szerinti terjedelme es foldjovedelme **(Area and land income of branches of cultivation in Hungary)**, M. Kir. Helytartotanacs, Buda, 1865.

Mezogazdasagi Statisztikai Adatgyujtemeny (Agricultural Statistics) 1870-1970. **Foldterolet** (Land area) III. Kozsegsoros adatok (By villages), KSH, Budapest, without date.

Pecs varos es a pecsi agglomeracio kozep-es hosszutavu fejlesztesi koncepcioja (Intermediate and long-term development plan for the town of Pecs and the Pecs agglomeration), Vol. 1-3, with maps MTA Dunantuli Tud. Intezete, Pecs, 1974.

Soo, R., **A magyar flora es vegetacio rendszertani novenyfoldrajzi kezikonyve** (A taxonomical-phytogeographical handbook of Hungarian flora and

vegetation). Vol. 1-5. Akademiai Kiado 1964-1973, BP.
Ujvarosi, M., Hol, milyen gyomok ellen vedekezzunk? (Where to defend and against what weeds?). Debreceni Mezogazdasagi Kiserleti Intezet Evkonyve, 1950.

TWELVE

Donald A. Fraser

Plants and Parks of Montreal

Montreal is situated on the south-east side of the Island of Montreal, at the confluence of the Ottawa and St. Lawrence rivers, at 45° 30' North latitude and 73° 36' West longitude. It is located at about the same latitude and hence has the same photoperiod as Portland, Oregon, U.S.A, Bordeaux, France, Venice, Italy, and Odessa, U.S.S.R. The photoperiod of the longest day at the summer solstice is 15 hours 45 minutes, when the noon angle of insolation is approximately 70°. The continental humid climate has an annual precipitation of 1000mm and a potential evapotranspiration of 550 mm giving an average water surplus of 270 mm. The summers are hot and often humid. The winters are cold with an unusual abundance of snow that often exceeds 2500 mm.

The City lies in the Great-Lakes St. Lawrence Forest Region. It is characterized by the eastern white pine, **Pinus strobus** L., red pine, **P. resinosa** Ait., eastern hemlock, **Tsuga canadensis** (L.) Carr., and yellow birch, **Betula al-leghaniensis** Britton, together with certain dominant broad-leaved species including sugar maple, **Acer saccharum** March., red maple, **Acer rubrum** L., red oak, **Quercus ruba** L., basswood, **Tilia americana** L., and white elm, **Ulmus americana** L. The latter is fast disappearing from the Canadian landscape, a victim of the ever-spreading Dutch elm disease caused by the fungus **Ceratosystis ulmi.** This fungal disease is transmitted from infected trees to healthy ones by the European elm bark beetle **Scolytus multistriatus.** Other tree species include the eastern white cedar, **Thuja occidentalis** L., aspen poplar, **Populus tremuloides** Michx., large-toothed aspen, **P. grandidentata** Michx., and to a lesser extent beech, **Fagus grandifolia** Ehrh., white oak, **Quercus alba** L.

butternut, **Juglans cinerea** L., and white ash, **Fraxinus americana** L. Boreal species, such as white spruce, **Picea glauca** (Moench) Voss., black spruce, **P. mariana** (Mill.) BSP., balsam fir, **Abies balsamea** (L.) Mill., Jack Pine, **Pinus divaricata** (Ait.) Dumont, and white birch, **Betula papyrifera** Marsh are intermixed. Red spruce, **P. rubens** is abundant in certain eastern areas.

The frost-free period extends from mid-May to mid-September. Some species, either introduced or at the northern limit of their range, are often killed back by freezing temperatures that follow abnormal mid-winter thaws. The most conspicuous of these species are the Catalpa, **Catalpa bignoniodes** Walt and the mangolia, **Magnolia** spp.

The importance of trees in the urban **milieu** was recognized in 1882 by Sir Henry Joly de Lotbiniere who sponsored the first law related to the 'tree festival' in the City. Different propositions have been put forward every year to celebrate this occasion, when trees are planted in front of homes. It is the objective of the City Parks Department to have a tree in front of every house. The choice of the species consists mostly the native hardwoods. American elm, silver maple, **Acer saccharinum** L., sugar maple, ashes, **Fraxinus** spp., the American basswood, poplars, and black locust, **Robinia pseudo-acacia** L. The once very popular native elms are now disappearing as they succumb to the Dutch elm disease and are replaced by other species.

In 1951, an inventory of tree species along Montreal streets showed a presence of some 32,000 trees: 14,000 silver maples, 7,000 elms and 7,000 poplars and 4,000 willows **Salix** spp. There was, at that time, one 'arbre de rue' for every 30 inhabitants.

By 1975 a total of 87,000 'arbre de rue' was counted. Now the ratio is one such tree for every 15 citizens. There has been an extensive distribution of trees along the sides of the asphalt-covered streets in the central core of the City. The planting of silver maples, poplars and willows has recently been limited because roots of these trees interfere with the drain pipes. Susceptibility to fungus or to insect has limited the use of black locust, white birch, mountain ash, **Sorbus aucuparia** L., and the pin cherry, **Prunus pensylvanica** L.

Trial testing of new species for their adaptability to an urban environment is a continuous process. Thus today we can find in parks and street plantations the horse chestnut, **Aesculus hippocastanum** L., honey locust, **Gleditsia triacanthos** L., Tartarian maple, **Acer tataricum** L., white ash, the mulberry, **Morus alba** L., particularly the pendulous type used in parks.

A large park and perhaps the most interesting is La Fontaine Park, east of Mount Royal. It is a former military site that was selected as a training ground by the army in 1845 and rented to the City of Montreal for one dollar per year since 1888. The park reflects the two major cultures in Montreal. The area around the lake is laid out in the style of an English country garden. Another section represents a 'park a la francaise' with straight rows of trees, smooth flat lawns and formal flower arrangements.

Recently several linear parks have been developed. They can be divided into two categories: the first is used by pedestrians and cyclists in the summer and by skiers in the winter. One such park is located along the waterfront on the site of a former railroad. This park is only 18 m wide. The second, regarded by the Montreal Parks Department as a mini-park, is the development of back alleys in high population areas into bright and safe refuges by planting grass, trees, shrubs and flowers and installing special lighting.

Eight regional parks, twelve golf courses, two natural reserves, one bird sanctuary and two airports are included within the Montreal area. Of special interest, not only to the citizens, but to biogeographers, botanists and horticulturists, is the Montreal Botanical Garden that ranks with the best of the world.

The top of Mount Royal in the centre of the City includes a large public park with an artificial lake and a service building with a cafeteria at its centre. The area around its periphery has been left undisturbed and together with the two adjacent cemeteries, it offers a wealth of natural vegetation to study at one's leisure. Poison ivy **Rhus radicans** L. occurs abundantly in some areas. This native plant produces serious dermatitis in susceptible individuals; the allergy causing agent can be carried on clothing.

While remnants of natural vegetation can be found dispersed throughout the Montreal Island, it is slowly becoming a victim of the developers. An example of this is Nun's Island. However, due to public pressure, a portion of the

northwestern Island has been designated a natural area to protect it from further development.

The Agricultural Faculty of McGill University, Macdonald College, is located on the western end of the Island of Montreal. It represents the last sizable working farm where active plant and animal research is conducted. Woodlot management is also studied. An Arboretum was established in 1948 so that both native vegetation and introduced tree species could be studied. Two thirds of the area are woodlands with over 20 km of hiking, skiing and riding trails. A bird sanctuary serves both scientists and naturalists. The native tree collection on 30 hectares includes 170 species indigenous to Canada. Of special interest is the collection of 400 white birch from ecotypes across Canada. They form the 'Canada Birch Trail', a trail made of single tree specimens of white birch obtained from each of the ten provinces and two territories of Canada. Native vegetation of the wetter areas include: rushes, **Scirpus cyperinus** (L.), Kunth., the cattails, **Typha angustifolia** L. and **T. latifolia** L., and **T. latifolia** L., sedges, **Carex** spp., willows, **Salix bebbiana** Sarg., **S. discolor** Muhl., S. **petiolaris** J.E. Smith, and the iris, **Iris versicolor** L.

Several parks were developed for a particular purpose. These include the Montreal Botanical Garden, Angrignon Park and most recently the heritage of Floralies on Ste. Helen's Island. The Botanical Garden is owned by the City of Montreal and integrated into the Public Works and Parks Departments. It is first and foremost a centre of research and popularization of horticultural plant materials. It has a close association with the University of Montreal and Concorida University.

The Garden sponsors the SAJIB (Societe d'Animation du Jardin et de l'Institut Botanique) that is a thriving organization. Public oriented courses in horticulture and guided tours of the greenhouses are offered. The Garden consists of 73 hectares of land with 23,000 species and varieties of plants from all over the world. Frere Marie-Victorin (1855-1944), who was Director of the Botanical Institute of the University of Montreal, founded the Garden in 1931. He is the author of Flore Laurentienne and of many contributions of the vegetation of Eastern North America and Cuba. He was instrumental in bringing Henry Teuscher (1891-1979) to Montreal in 1936 to direct the expansion of the Garden.

The statue of Frere Marie-Victorin looks down on the main path leading into the Garden. This path is bordered by flowers from bulbs or flowering annuals. In May there is a beautiful show of tulips and daffodils that is later replaced by various annuals. Past a pond and fountain we continue towards the main administrative building with its lecture halls, laboratories, herbarium, library and offices that direct the horticultural activity around the City and arrange for seed and plant exchanges around the world. Circling the administration building are numerous specimens of locally rare trees and shrubs.

The outdoor section of the Garden extends one and a half km along both sides of a paved access road, closed to the general traffic. There is a decorative garden of perennials and flowering annuals: chrysanthemums, fuchsias, dahlias, celosias and others, followed by a grape arbor. This section, with a fountain in the background, is a particularly favourite setting for pictures of summer weddings. It is followed by a garden of economic plants, interesting both to the lay person and the botanist. There are representatives of modern crops such as wheat, **Triticum aestivum** L. and **T. durum** Desf., rye, **Secale cereale** L., soya bean, **Soja glycine** var **max** Piper, tobacco, **Nicotiana tobacum** L., **T. spelta** L, and the wild beet of the Mediterranean, **Beta maritima** L., the spcies from which all our different types of beets: common sugar, the Swiss chard and mangels, are believed to have been derived.

We find in this garden the representatives, both of primary, flax, **Linum usitatissimum** L., and secondary importance, broom corn, **Sorghum vulgare** var **technicum** Jav. Culinary herbs and less common vegetables such as a variety of Japanese burdock, **Arctium lappa** L. are also represented together with important forage grasses.

This garden is complemented with the vegetable test garden where vegetables from different seed sources are grown. There is a similar test garden of annual flowers. In the Alpinum, plants are grouped according to their geographical origin: Eastern Canada, the Alps, the Caucasus, the Pyranees, and the mountains of Asia.

The Monastery garden suggests the herbs grown by monks of the Middle Ages. Several plants qualify for a position in both the Medicinal garden and the garden of poisonous plants, for while small quantities might have a beneficial effect, an overdose might kill. A good example of this is the foxglove **Digitalis** sp., a source of an important heart stimulant, but known to be deadly when ingested without proper precautions.

There are many other sections too numerous to mention, including aquatics, insectivorous plants and a children's garden. A large complex of greenhouses includes extensive collections and produces the material used in the exhibition houses accessible to the public. The Central Rotunda changes its theme four times a year with traditional Thanks giving and Christmas themes and others honouring different nationalities.

Montreal can only boast a modest Zoological Garden aimed at the junior visitor. It presents live animals mostly in a storybook setting. Its summertime location is in Lafontaine Park, but in the winter the animals are moved to indoor quarters in Angrignon Park.

The Floralies Floriculture Exhibition dates back to 173 B.C. when it became an annual event in ancient Rome. It lapsed in the Middle Ages and was revived in Holland in 1837. Montreal was the first North American city to host this International Horticultural Exhibition in 1980. Thus Montreal, that in 1967 hosted the Universal Exhibition: Expo 67, and in 1976 the XXIst Olympics, has completed a trilogy of special International Events with an emphasis on Nature. The Island of Ste. Helene was extended for Expo 67. During the 1980 Floralies, a section of the Ste. Helen Island was transformed into a series of gardens sponsored by different countries, provinces, cities and commercial organizations. Of special interest was the true representation of a peat bog from the James Bay region of Northern Quebec. Large sections of a bog were cut out during the winter and transported **en masse** to the Floralies site. Since 1980 hardy plant material has remained **in situ.** Frost sensitive plants such as palms, that form an intrinsic part of the gardens in southern countries, are removed to a special greenhouse to overwinter. The 'Son of Floralies', a scaled-down version of the original display, now represents a new Montreal park with free admission.

Montreal is a dynamic ever-changing urban development of some two million people. One scheme that may alter the face of the city is Project Archipel. It is a multi-billion dollar construction scheme, bigger than such other megarojects as Mirabel Airport or the Olympics. The project could exert human control over all water flowing past metropolitan

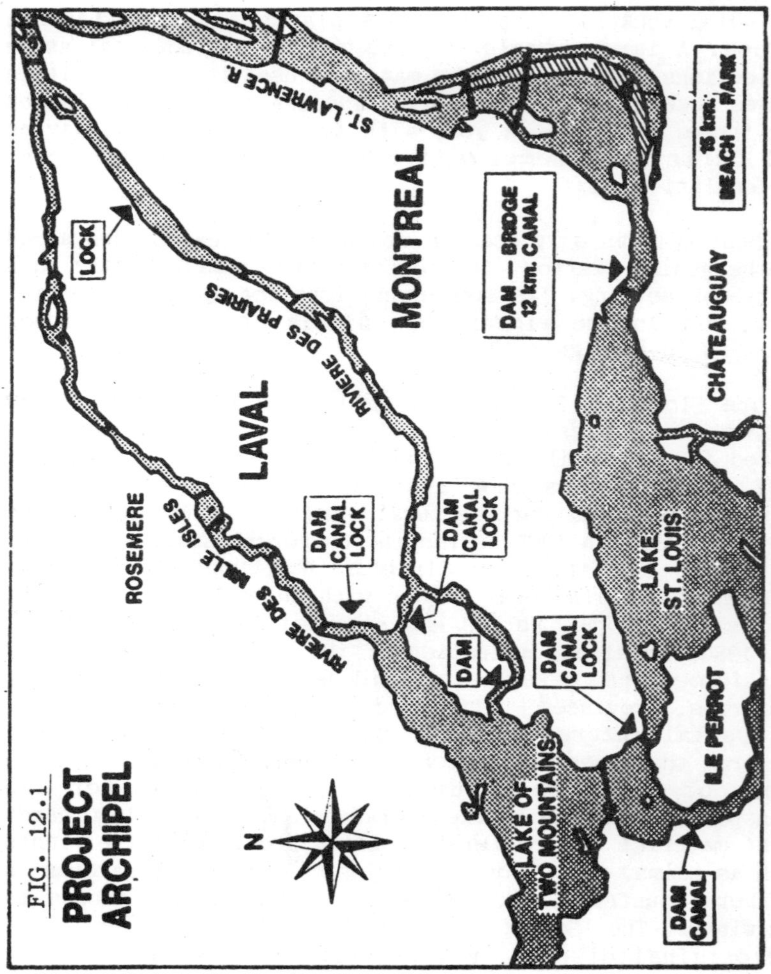

FIG. 12.1 PROJECT ARCHIPEL

Montreal'. Up to six dams, five canals and four locks could be built for the stated purposes: to prevent flooding; to improve water quality; to provide hydroelectric power; and to enable Montrealers to enjoy their now under-utilized waterways.

REFERENCES

Aubin, Henry, Project Archipel, In **The Gazette**, Montreal, Monday, June 21, 1982, p. B-3.

Bailey, L.H., **Manual of Cultivated Plants**, The Macmillan Company, New York, 1949, pp. 1116.

Clark, T.H., Montreal Area Laval and Lachine Map-Areas. Geological Report 46 Department of Mines Quebec Can, 1952, 159 pp.

Clark, T.H., Montreal Area. Geological Report 152 Department of Mines Quebec Can, 1972, pp. 244.

Collard, E.A., **Montreal: The Days that Are No More**, Doubleday Canada, 1976, pp. 240.

Fraser, D.A., Montreal's Green Spaces, in **Occasional Papers in Geography Number 1**, Concordia University, Montreal, pp. 15-24.

Hosie, R.C., **Native Trees of Canada**, Canadian Forestry Service, Queen's Printer, Ottawa, 1969, pp. 380.

Hill, A.F., **Economic Botany**, McGraw-Hill Book Company, Toronto, 1952, pp. 560.

Marie-Victorin, Frere., **Flore Laurentienne**, Les Presses de l'Universite de Montreal, 1964, pp. 925.

Marsan, J.C., **Montreal in Evolution**, McGill-Queen's University Press, Montreal, 1981, pp.456

Percival, W.P., **The Lure of Montreal**, The Ryerson Press, Toronto, 1964, pp.204

Powe, N.N., **Le Climat de Montreal**, Etudes Climatologiques Numero 15, Ministere des Transports, Ottawa, 1969, pp.51

THIRTEEN

J. Donald Hughes

Forests and Cities in the Classical Mediterranean

The great cities of antiquity, creative Athens, imperial Rome and a hundred others such as commercial Corinth and Marseilles, templed Jerusalem, and polyglot Alexandria, were dependent on the forests that were within their reach even more than the modern cities that stand on their ancient sites. Today the casual visitor does not think of the Mediterranean as a particularly forested area, but in ancient times it most certainly was. When the Hebrews first entered Palestine, they were told, "the hill country shall be yours, for though it is a forest, you shall clear it."[1] The process of urbanization in the littoral was accompanied by a process of deforestation and the two stood in direct relation to one another.

How extensive was deforestation in the ancient Mediterranean basin? The classical writers give the impression that it was immense. Examples of vanished forests mentioned by them range from Pliny's region of giant trees in Egypt to the woods of Sicily and Spain whose passing Diodorus chronicled.[2] "In those days," says Livy of fourth-century Italy, "the Ciminian forest was more impassable and appalling than were lately the wooded defiles of Germany."[3] Readers in his own day would have found precious little forest where Fabius' army had marched with such difficulty. These authors knew that human hands were unclothing the earth. The lines of Homer and Virgil resound with axes and falling trees. Strabo complains that the forests around Pisa were being consumed in order to construct the public and private buildings in Rome and ostentatious villas in the countryside.[4]

They could see deforestation that was widespread and severe in Classical times; we are told that it was hard to find timber suitable for shipbuilding, that good forests were generally limited to the mountains and that sources of valuable wood were exhausted. In their pages, modern scholars can find further evidence that the Mediterranean forests were in retreat: away from population centres, up the hillsides and into moister and more isolated retreats. The fact that forests disappeared first near the cities was not an accident; of the many forces acting for the removal of the woodlands, the most important were generated by urbanization.

Fairfield Osborn maintained that environmental history and specifically that of Greece and Rome, "assumes the character of a prologue to modern times. Assuredly there is an affinity between then and now." In the decline of ancient urban societies, he sensed "a contemporaneous deterioration of environment and peoples," of which "the causes were man-made, not natural."[5] Osborn recognized the particular importance of deforestation and resultant erosion, producing a decline in agricultural productivity, in the classical world. "It is apt to be forgotten," he wrote, "that...in some of the desolated countries around the Mediterranean the forests have never reappeared...because the land has been denuded of its soil."[6] Similar statements had been made in the last century by George Perkins Marsh and Henry David Thoreau. Thoreau's graphic statement also deserved to be quoted:

> The civilized nations—Greece, Rome, England—have been sustained by the primitive forests which anciently rotted where they stand. They survive as long as the soil is not exhausted. Alas for human culture! Little is to be expected of a nation, when the vegetable mould is exhausted and it is compelled to make manure of the bones of its fathers.[7]

Osborn's comments gain importance from their immediacy, written as they were when the extent of modern human damage to the worldwide natural environment, and its consequences, were becoming apparent. But the inexorable deforestation of the Mediterranean area did not pass unnoticed by the ancient Greeks and Romans. Speaking of the disappearance of certain trees from Cyrene, Theophrastus says, "there was an abundance of those trees from where now the city stands and people can still recall that some of the roofs in ancient times were made of it."[8] And as the Roman poet Lucretius put it:

>]Men[made the woods climb higher up the mountains,
> Yielding the lowlands to be tilled and tended.[9]

Areas described as forested in ancient times are certainly not so today. The Greek historian Thucydides, describing the siege of the city of Plataea, calls the Boeotian countryside well-wooded, a term which would now be hardly apt and a later writer said that the Sila forest of Calabria was "full of fir as high as heaven, and pine sufficient for the fleets and housing of the whole of Italy."[10] Modern Calabria is not treeless, but has suffered deterioration, to say the least, since the words just quoted were written.

The Mediterranean forest, under the attack of human beings and domestic animals, was degraded from its original state down a scale of ecosystems from timber forest through brushy **maquis** to a denuded rocky state with spiny shrubs, termed **garigue.** The role of grazing animals, chiefly goats, in this process has been often remarked. The preference of goats for wooded country was well known; the Greek comedian Eupolis had his chorus of goats bleat out a list of some of their favorite foods:

> We feed on all manner of shrubs, browsing on the tender shoots of pine, ilex and arbutus, and on spurge, clover and fragrant sage and many-leaved bindweed as well, wild olive and lentisk and ash, fir, sea oak, ivy and heather, willow, thorn, pullein, and asphodel, cistus, oak, thyme, and savory.[11]

This sounds something like a botanist's list of a typical Mediterranean plant community; **maquis**, to be exact, and it should be noted that on the goats' bill of fare, a number of young forest trees are included. The most important effect of pastoralism was not in actually producing deforestation, but in making it permanent when it occurred. For the original removal of the high forests, it is necessary to examine causes directly related to urbanization and that is the major purpose of this essay.

The ancients were quite aware that the city itself stood where forests had once flourished; Ovid said, "Here where now is Rome, the world's capital, were once trees...men lived in huts and there were few to be seen."[12] Place names often preserved the memory of forests that had been encompassed by the growth of cities and towns. Latin writers mention various quarters of Rome named after a laurel grove, an oak forest, beeches, cornel trees and willows. The Caelian Hill, one of the seven on which the city was built, was called **Querquetulanus** "Oak Hill" and the Viminal is named for osier-willows (**vimina**, therefore "Willow Hill"). There was a place in the Campus Martius called Aesculetum after **aesculus**, the winter-oak. And the Aventine Hill was once "covered with trees of every kind...but the whole place is now covered with buildings, including among others, the Temple of Diana," according to Dionysius of Halicarnassus.[13]

In Greece, the old geographies yield traces of vanished trees and timber trade in place names like Elatea "Firtown", Pityoussa "Pine Junction", Castanea "Chestnutville" or Xylopolis "Timber City".[14] The Athenians had a fortress named Peuke "Pine" and their tribute-lists for the payments in 422 B.C. include a northern community called Drys "Oak", located just east of Maroneia on the mainland that faces Samothrace. Of course the effects of urbanization were much more far-reaching than the simple clearing of sites for cities, as the names of some of the timber-ports given above indicate.

But to understand the meaning of deforestation for the ancients, we need first to place it in the context of some of the meanings they found in the forest itself. For example, a persistent idea held by Greeks and Romans was that the forest had been the original home of mankind. The story of men sprung from oaks was ancient in Homer's day, and Vitruvius says,

> "Men, in the old way, were born like animals in forests and caves and woods."[15]

The way of life in that past age was variously described; at times it seemed to have been the Golden Age itself, when trees, the "foster-mothers" of mankind, bestowed gifts of food, shelter, and clothing. It ended, Vergil says, when the acorn crop failed, forcing people to learn how to plow and use saws and wedges to fell trees and split wood. At other times, they stressed the difficulty of forest life. Loss of the forest after the dawn age was seen both as loss of paradise and as a concomitant of the rise to civilization. But in either case it was envisioned as a change from living on nature's bounty, or at her mercy, to living by human labour that altered nature. And writers like Pliny the Elder decried the state of people who were forced by circumstance to live in regions without trees as the most lamentable, primitive and uncomfortable of all.

The polarity of forests and cities was a standard theme in classical literature. Some definitely favoured the healthy and natural life to be found in the forests; as Martial boasted to Juvenal, "You have to put up with the city, while I walk in oak woods."[16] But not all agreed. Socrates speaks out clearly for the city: I'm a lover of learning and trees and open country won't teach me anything, whereas men in the town do.[17] Cicero added a good word for urbanization, saying that it is humans "whose industry...adorns the land...with houses and cities," not allowing it "to become...a barren waste of thickets and brambles."[18]

On the whole, writers who took up the subject tended to side with Martial rather than Socrates and Cicero. The character with the title role in Menander"s **Dyscolus**, for example, fled the market place for the solitude of tree-clad Mt. Parnes, where the nature-god Pan was known to dance. The orator Dion Chrysostom argued the moral superiority of hunters in the Euboean forest to city-dwelling lovers of lawsuits, and the poet Horace told his friends, in effect, "You can have the city; I'll take the country," where he could "live in accordance with nature."[19]

But however nostalgic classical writers may have been about the forest and the ancestral life tradition assigned to it, their own affairs centered in the great cities like Athens, Rome and Alexandria. And city life inevitably laid a heavy tax on the forest resource and there is no doubt that the Greeks and Romans regarded forests as a resource. Wood was a material so commonly used for so many purposes that the Greek word for it, **hyle**, came to mean "substance" or "matter" in general. In Latin, both concepts are also expressed by a single word, **materia**. It will be useful to enumerate some of the major urban-related uses of forest products.

Cities required timber to build houses and public buildings such as temples, theatres and basilicas. Even after most large buildings began to be constructed of stone, beams and rafters were of timber, and scaffolding and ramps were needed. Doors and their frames and hinges were often of wood and roofs at times were covered with shingles—that was the old custom at Rome. Images of the gods were anciently made of wood, as were the frameworks of colossal chryselephantine statues. Plato, perhaps reflecting contemporary usage, advised carving public notices on cypress wood.[20]

Cabinetwork and furniture like tables, chairs and beds were the work of skilled carpenters, who knew techniques like inlaying and veneering. Even bedding could be provided by trees. All sorts of tools and utensils were made of wood, or even if of metal, often needed wooden handles. So the forests provided cups, jars, combs, barrels, the handles of daggers, etc. Basketry of flexible trees like willows was widely used. Musical instruments like the lyre and aulos were often of wood. Agricultural and industrial machines, including those used in irrigation and construction, were usually built sturdily of timber. All vehicles of transport were wooden: wagons and carts and of course ships, whose building is perhaps the use of wood mentioned most often in ancient literature. Almost everything on a ship, from keel to mast, spars and oars, came from trees, and even the pitch used to caulk the vessel was a forest product.

It is important to remember that wood was not the only forest product; the ancients also exploited cork, pitch and tar, dyes from bark and forest insects, cedar oil, resins for varnishes and preservatives, spices, medicines and drugs from forest trees and shrubs, not to mention beeswax, honey and nuts. Wine was flavored with pine resin as a preservative.

The single most important use of wood and its carbonized product, charcoal, was as fuel. As in many Third World countries today, probably close to 90 per cent of all wood used was consumed for this purpose. Although coal and petroleum were known to the ancients, they were not used to a great extent in any area. The forest, therefore, made its contribution in home, public affairs and industry. Every householder might have said with Virgil:

> My hearth is piled with branches of pitch-pine
> Free burns my faithful fire and every hour
> My walls are black with smoke,[21]

although rooms in the city were more often heated by glowing charcoal in braziers. And those who set out on foot into the night in those years before there were flashlight might well have remembered that "the loftier forest gives our torches."[22]

Wood and charcoal fired the kilns that hardened Greek and Roman Ceramics, including pottery, bricks and tiles;

melted the metal for statues, utensils and weapons; forced pitch out of pinewood; reduced limestone to fertilizer, and their ashes afterwards also served to enrich the soil. These fuels heated the water and the floors in the huge and numerous Roman bathing establishments, cooked the meals and warmed the drinks. So numerous were fires in ancient cities that air pollution was actually a problem on which ancient authors commented.

The mines and smelters used prodigious amounts of fuel, primarily for reducing ores to metals. Reasonable estimates hold that a single major ancient metallurgical centre would have required as much as 1,000,000 acres of coppice forest to supply this need, even allowing for regeneration and regrowth. This has been correctly identified as a major cause of deforestation. In addition, miners used timbers for supports and extended their tunnels by setting fires underground to crack the resistant rocks. Excavations for mines also destroyed forests directly. It is interesting in this regard that ancient writers attributed the original discovery of mining to the natural melting of ore pockets by forest fires.

With so many essential uses for products derived from trees, a city well-supplied with forests obviously was rich in a necessary commodity and item of commerce. Plato and Aristotle agreed that an ideal city ought to have its own forests, near enough for easy transportation, so that it could be self-sufficient, although Plato, who disliked the political influence of sailors, thought there ought not to be too much shipbuilding timber around. But the ancients knew that not all cities could expect to have an adequate domestic timber supply and the timber trade, which hastened the deforestation of the Mediterranean area, was the result.

There is much information on the timber trade and on the activities associated with it. Tree cutting was a specialized task, and loggers took pride in their work. "I never saw a better **hylotomon** "woodcutter" than myself," says one epitaph.[23] Columella advises a landowner who wants good use from his forests to have his overseer instructed by "a good forester" who would not "refuse to impart to one desirous of learning them the principles of his art."[24] Woodcutters were kept busy on the hills to supply the need for fuel wood and they made good money by packing it into the cities on mules and donkeys. Phaenippus of Athens was reported to have made 12 drachmas a day in this way, and Hybreas supported himself as a student on the income from his firewood-laden mule.

Since much wood was reduced to charcoal before being used as fuel, charcoal-burning was an occupation for thousands of men like the Acharnians of Aristophanes.

The removal of forests began near the cities and then invaded progressively more remote areas. When Plato described the deforested state of Athens' nearby mountains, he gave evidence from his observations.[25] In buildings, he had seen large beams from trees cut on hillsides where only shrubs grew in his own day. And the process was still going on. In his own time, Strabo complains, the forests of Pisa were being consumed to construct buildings in Rome and Villas "of Persian magnificence" in the countryside.[26] As abundant sources near the centres of consumption disappeared, wood became rarer as a commodity and had to be imported over longer distances. The result was a rise in price, particularly noticeable in the case of fine woods, but affecting all kinds of timber and fuel as well. Ancient prices of wood are recorded only in a few scattered cases, but these can be interpreted to show a pattern of rising prices. People caught in areas of short supply might well have found, as did later Mediterranean travellers, that the wood for a supper fire cost as much as the meat in the pot. Pay in kind for Athenian jurors included fuel wood, recognized as the third necessity along with bread and **opson** (fish, fruit, etc.). Later evidence for the rising price of wood is contained in the **Lives of the Sophists** by Philostratus, who remarks that the timbers used to support the roof of the music hall or **odeon** built in Athens by Herodes Atticus were of imported cedar wood, although cedar was considered expensive even when it was to be used for sculpture. The shortage and high costs of building timber due to deforestation may well be reflected in the observable shift from wood construction to stone in both Greece and Rome, or even to marble from brick, since the latter required forest fuels for firing. Cremation of human remains also required firewood, of which the rising price might explain the change to inhumation (burial) as the dominant means of disposal of bodies from the first century A.D. onward.

As more distant forests were developed, especially in the mountains, the problems of transportation and supply to the cities had to be solved. Often logs were floated down rivers or canals to ports on the coasts. Rome brought much timber down the Tiber directly to the city. The Po was a major artery for Alpine timber, including larch and alder. Some of the trees thus transported were very large; one of the logs brought to Rome for the construction of the naval arena of the Emperor Tiberius was over 120 feet long. A typical lumber port might be at the mouth of a river with a mountainous, forested area in its watershed: like Luna, Ravenna, or even far-away Colchis. Those without major rivers usually had the mountains at their backs, like Genoa or Antandros.

From such ports timber was shipped to populated centres; we hear of businessmen involved in the import trade, and are told that long sea voyages were sometimes involved. Rome's timber entered the city through the Porta Trigemina on the downriver side of the city, indicating that major supplies were brought up the Tiber through Ostia on the coast. From the landing place, lines of carts carrying long logs of pine or fir made the streets shake, according to Seneca and Juvenal says the innocent stroller in the streets of Rome at night ran the risk of being maimed by the wide-swinging tree trunks.[27] These carts were steered from behind, where the person responsible may not have had a very clear view ahead. In order to avert the danger of a breakdown in the supply of firewood for the Roman baths, the city placed the import of wood from North Africa in the hands of the salt-contractors, who brought that cargo also up the Tiber River and assigned them a wood-market in the **porticus inter lignarios.**[28]

Transportation costs increased due to the greater distances merchants had to go to find wood. Meidias, a fourth-century Greek merchant, for example, used a ship for his own profit to bring wood, presumably from Macedonia, for his mining concessions. But good ship-building timber was especially rare, above all that for masts, and warships had priority over merchant vessels in the competition for essentials. Siltation constantly clogged harbors, and herculean labours were needed to keep them usable. The repetitive efforts of the Romans to keep open Ostia, Rome's major port at the mouth of the Tiber River, are described in ancient written sources and are apparent in archaeological studies of the site, including aerial photographs showing the successively constructed and abandoned basins for the use of shipping. In some places overland transport was necessary; Meiggs reports that the great building inscription of Darius' palace far inland at Susa records Ionia and Carian Greeks "engaged in the transport of timber and in skilled labour on the building."[29]

It is clear from what has just been said that city governments understandably considered the fostering of the timber trade, the control of the use of timber, the provision of an adequate supply of wood particularly for shipbuilding, and the mitigation of the negative effects of deforestation, to be important matters within their concern. Ownership of unoccupied forest land by the sovereign power was universally assumed, and that implied either the local city government or the paramount administration of a more distant metropolis.

Supervision of forests and waters was relatively constant, involving regulation of trade in forest products, of the timber harvest, and of land use, as well as the construction of works to provide and control the water supply and drainage. Responsibility for these matters was delegated to certain government officials; for example, in some cities the timber trade was under the **agoranomoi** "Overseers of Commerce", while forest land in the countryside was supervised by **hyloroi** "Custodians of Forests," who, Aristotle says, had "guard-posts and mess-rooms for patrol duty."[30] Shepherds taking sheep from one pasture to another in the forested Italian hills in the first century B.C., and no doubt during most of the Roman period, could expect to run into government "checkers" because the land they were using was public forest land belonging to the "Senate and the Roman People."

It was in the interests of the governments in large population centres to encourage shipbuilding and the import trade in timber. Colonies were founded with this in mind. Many Roman emperors customarily offered financial and legal incentives to shipbuilders. While taxes were usually assessed on imports, timber importers received special privileges like those granted in the Code of Theodosius.[31]

It was a recurrent policy of Greek and Roman city governments to encourage the private exploitation of forests through leasing the right to cut trees on public land, probably a lucrative source of revenue, or through outright sale or grant of forest land to private individuals or consortiums. Some local authorities, says Eratosthenes, thought the land was too thickly overgrown with forests, so "they permitted anyone who wished, or was able, to cut out the timber and to keep the land thus cleared as his own property, and exempt from taxes."[32] Rome sponsored the clearing of land and the cultivation waste land by granting title to it. Forest land in the City of Rome was turned into a residential subdivision for the Plebeians by the tribune Icilius. It was Roman practice to rent huge tracts of woodland to syndicates of **equites**, citizens of the second highest rank who were usually businessmen, for development. There is evidence from the late Empire that forest land belonging to the emperor was regularly sold to private owners who would pay the taxes on it. In addition to the duties of clearing land and paying taxes on it, private landowners had to provide other services, either as regular obligations, or as liturgies, supposed "free gifts". These could include payments in kind of lumber, charcoal, burnt lime for concrete and fertilizer, and wood for weapons. Subsidies for the construction of public buildings were exacted from the well-to-do. All the governmental measures mentioned thus far seem designed to accelerate the process of deforestation. An earlier example of this occurred during the land reforms of the second century B.C., when large areas around Rome were cleared and developed into small farms. During this period the rate of erosion increased to between seven and twenty times what it had been.[33]

But urban governments were not unaware of the danger of a diminishing supply of wood, and a few of the enactments affecting private land were such as to encourage conservation. Plato's recommendation that landowners be fined if fire spreads from their property to the timber of a neighbour's land doubtless represented actual law.[34] Published decrees of Ptolemy II Euergetes in Alexandria prohibited the unauthorized cutting of wood by private individuals on their own land, and required the planting of trees.[35] Land leases elsewhere also contained restrictions on timber cutting and stipulations for replanting.

Government ownership, whether by a monarch or by the sovereign people, not only of all forest land within the city's local territory, but also the forests of conquered provinces, was universally assumed. Although such lands were often granted to individuals or communities, large areas remained in governmental hands, and measures were taken, albeit sporadically, to prevent encroachment on them, and to assure their use for the good of the state. When Scipio needed fir trees to make masts for his fleet against Carthage, he found them in "forests belonging to the state."[36] A limitation of the timber harvest in these areas at times by wise administrators may be assumed; Theophrastus says this was the case in the city-states of Cyprus, where the rulers "used not to cut the trees...because they took great care of them and managed them."[37] He goes on to note that later owners of the island reaped the benefit of their predecessors' restraint; Demetrius Poliorcetes cut timber of marvellous length there for his ships.

The state should take measures to keep water pure and regulate its supply from the hills, advises Plato in the *Laws*,[38] and he recognized the connection of these efforts with preservation of forests and the planting of trees. The abundant archaeological evidence of dams, tunnels, terraces and drainage canals all around the Mediterranean reveals what a laborious struggle, successful or unsuccessful, was maintained against flood and erosion. In addition, tree plantations were encouraged by some governments. Seedling trees were started in public nurseries. The plantations were protected by laws regulating the felling of older trees, the cutting of branches, and the removal of fallen trees, and excluding sheep and goats from areas where young trees had been planted. Unfortunately, many of these efforts were stopgap measures, undertaken in vain. Roman dams and canals in North Africa stand in dry *wadis* (watercourses) today, as witness to the fact that the underlying conditions of deforestation and dessication were unaltered.

A Roman consul who directed the construction of an aqueduct thought only of supplying potable water to the city, not of the possible effect on streamside ecosystems below the point of diversion. The aedile who issued a license to an equestrian consortium to strip the trees from the same watershed did not consider whether the water in the aqueduct would become muddy or its flow less dependable. When the same aedile imported lions from North Africa for the arena, the thought that wild goats in the absence of predators might strip the vegetative cover from hillsides on the margin of the advancing Sahara never crossed his mind. This is not to condemn the Romans and other ancient peoples, but simply to point out their lack of some ecological insights which, due to the advance of research in modern times, ought to be accessible to city planners today.

One of the most obvious concerns of ancient city governments was the provision of timber for military needs. So much is known on this subject that only a brief outline can be given in an article of this length. The leaders were forced to develop a "sylvan strategy" during times of war directed toward obtaining forest products and ensuring safe transport, since few cities had adequate forests nearby. While we hear most about timber for shipbuilding, it is likely that ancient land armies required even more for machines, weapons and firewood.

If a city needed forests, one way to get them was to

conquer them. As Alcibiades told the Spartans, this was one of Athens' major purposes in launching the Sicilian campaign.[39] Areas both strategically located and rich in forests, like Cilicia and Cyprus, were often the object of conquest by those who wanted to build ships. Colonies were deliberately established in forested regions to assure the founding cities' timber supplies. This was the reason for Athens' founding of Amphipolis on the river Strymon below heavily wooded mountains, and also for Augustus Caesar's foundation of Nicopolis, a Roman Colony in forested Ambracia.

International diplomacy was often directed at obtaining shipbuilding supplies. Gifts of timber from one state to another constituted both diplomatic bargaining chips and war measures in themselves. Pharnabazus, the Persian Satrap of Phrygia, helped to sway the course of the Peloponnesian War by giving the Spartans access to the forests of Mt. Ida, telling them "not to be discouraged over a lack of ships' timber, for there is plenty of that in the King's land."[40]

Treaties were signed governing the timber trade for naval purposes. The texts survive of a short-lived one between Athens and Perdiccas in which the Macedonian king promises that wood suitable for oars will be exported only to Athens, and a later one between Amyntas and the Chalcidians that requires the latter to obtain the king's permission and pay duties to export fir timber for ships' masts, while allowing them to trade less strategic lumber freely.[41]

The realities of warfare forced states to protect their own sources of timber against enemies, potential or actual, and to attempt to seize the areas that supplied their enemies. The Etruscans, who were exploiting the forests of Corsica, thwarted the attempt of the Phocaeans to found a colony there. The northern campaign of the Spartan general, Brasidas, was intended to cut off Athens' timber supply from that region and direct it to Sparta and her allies. "The Athenians were greatly alarmed by the capture of Amphipolis. The chief reason was that the city was useful to them for the importation of timber for ship-building."[42]

Armed conflict took its toll of the forests. Vegetius lists numerous uses for wood by the army; detachments of soldiers were regularly ordered to cut wood for use in fortifications and as fuel. The Spartans brought wood all the way from Asine to Pylos for engines, and Caesar; during the sieges of North African towns, had to send to Sicily for timber to reconstruct his engines.[43]

Deliberate destruction of forests often occurred in warfare; Xerxes burned the woods during his invasion of Greece. The Aetolians set forest fires to harry the troops of the Athenian general Demosthenes, who later used the same weapon against the Spartans on Sphacteria. Similar examples could be enumerated to show that warfare was a major cause of the depletion of the Mediterranean forests. Efforts at preservation and replanting were frustrated by the frequency of military emergencies during many of the ancient centuries.

In turning from the activities of war to those of peace, it is well to be reminded again of the positive ancient attitude toward trees and the appreciation for their beauty which is so evident in Greek and Latin literature. One of the practical ways in which ancient cities gave expression to these feelings was in the provision of public gardens and parks. The prominent politician Cimon was influential in this respect in Athens, getting the city to accept his gift of plane grees to shade the marketplace, and converting the exercise-grounds of the Academy to a well-watered grove with shaded walks. He also opened his private garden to the public.[44] Apparently the later flamboyant leader, Alcibiades, who disagreed with Cimon in most things, agreed with him in this and vied with Cimon's memory in providing parks for the enjoyment of the common people. The Persians had long followed the custom in planting fine gardens with shade trees, whose name in their language came into English as "paradise." The satrap Tissaphernes named his most expensive pleasuring park "the Alcibiades" after the Athenian. Theophrastus says that the paradises in Syria protected especially fine, large Lebanon Cedars.[45] Specimens of exotic trees were imported and planted in these arboreta, but they were not simply curiosities. Apollonius advises Zeno to plant three hundred fir trees in the paradise at Philadelphia, Egypt, "for the tree has a striking appearance and will be of service to the king."[46] By service, he no doubt meant they would eventually be felled for timber.

The Romans created an impressive series of private and public gardens to improve the quality of life in the city. Public gardens surrounded by colonnades eventually stretched across the Campus Martius and other sections of the city. Roman gardens were formal, consisting of geometric lawns and flower beds, polygonal pools of water, symmetrical fountains and waterfalls, with trees and shrubs clipped into fantastic shapes. They constitute a major attempt to make nature conform to the patterns of human art. Groves of trees were planted in provincial cities to honour Roman emperors.

A similar provision of city administrations allowed for the designation, planting, and protection of sacred groves around temples and other holy places. The initial and sustaining motive for this was popular religious feeling, but in addition the practice received legal sanction and enforcement from local governments. Thus a pious sentiment was enforced by laws carrying penalties that were not negligible. The association of a great number of gods with trees and forests was multifaceted and intimate, so that at the sight of a particularly impressive grove of trees, an ancient observer might exclaim, "There's a god in there!"[47] As Pliny indicates:

> Trees were the first temples of the gods, and even now simple country people dedicate a tree of exceptional height to a god with the ritual of olden times; and we...worship forests and the very silences they contain.[48]

Such were considered to be places where a god might speak; at Dodona and elsewhere the god's voice was heard in the rustling of leaves. Groves were the actual places of worship; the temple buildings that were erected in them were at first simply protective shelters for the images of the gods. The altars were still outdoors under the trees. So sacred groves were set aside as precincts, consecrated with carefully marked boundaries. Many, and in the cities most of them, were special plantations of parklike appearance. Some of the groves were quite large. As a result of the protection given to them, the individual trees often reached remarkable size; an oak at Corne reached 34 feet (10 metres) in circumference, and the huge cypresses at Psophis overshadowed a hill.[49]

The rules to prevent injuries to sacred groves were many; almost any act that would tend to produce environmental change was forbidden. The most serious prohibition was against felling the trees, or breaking or cutting branches from them. Removal of any part of a tree, even if it had fallen by itself, such as broken boughs for timber or firewood, or leaves, was not allowed. Setting fire was a grave offense. Generally, domestic animals could not be brought in, except for sacrifice. Tilling the soil and sowing grain were prohibited, and in some groves no iron object such as an axe or saw could be introduced. There was considerable variation in rules from place to place; not all groves had all these prohibitions, and some had other special rules.

The laws against violation of sacred groves were administered by the local magistrates who had jurisdiction over religious matters; in Athens it was the archon called the **basileus** (king). The priest of the grove, or indeed any witness, was expected to report the infractions to the appropriate official, and there were penalties for witnesses who failed to do so.

The penalties exacted were moderately severe; slaves or aliens might be whipped, and Plato additionally recommends imprisonment. Citizens were generally fined an amount sufficient to deter any attempt to make illegal profits from the groves, and sometimes mandatory sacrifices were assessed, mounting to not inconsiderable fines in themselves.

To these legal penalties should be added ritual curses and the far more intimidating ones that were believed to be exacted by the outraged gods and goddesses to whom the groves were sacred. Trees were believed to be inhabited by dryads. Each of these nymphs was believed to live only so long as her tree, and to die when it was cut down. Anyone who ignored the pleas of a nymph and felled her tree risked terrible retribution, like Erysicthon, who was stricken with hunger that could never be satisfied; perhaps a uniquely appropriate punishment for one who had contributed to deforestation.[50] A Roman senator was once believed to have been killed by the gods because he had cut ships' timbers in a sacred grove.[51]

If religion threatened penalties, however, it also offered expiation in the form of prayers, sacrifices, and acts of restitution. The replanting of trees in a grove, whether they had succumbed to decay, lightning, or the woodman's axe, was regarded as a religious duty, and was specifically required in the rules of the Arval Brethren. It was also written into leases. In terms of maintaining the forests, this form of expiation is to be commended. But the prayers and sacrifices seem only to have eased the consciences of those who found it expedient to use the groves for their own purposes. Cato advises the sacrifice of a pig with an all-purpose prayer in order to obtain permission from a god or goddess to cut wood or to till the earth in a sacred grove.[52] Felling timber in a grove for a sufficiently religious purpose was evidently allowed, with the proper sacrifice. A tall cypress, taken from the precinct of Apollo on Carpathos, was sent to Athens to use in the re-building of the temple of Athena, and the Athenians were grateful enough to put up an inscription honouring their benefactors.[53] Since "wood for the altars" is perhaps the most regular item of expense in ancient temple records, it may be assumed that the priests cut wood in the groves from time to time, to avoid having to purchase it elsewhere, although the latter was assumed to be the regular practice.

Sacred groves were used for many purposes other than those that might be considered religious in modern times. They often contained buildings other than temples, including baths, spring houses, arenas, gymnasiums, exercising grounds, schools, and the ancient equivalents of hospitals. In Greek and Roman eyes, each of these had a religious purpose and was regarded as a conforming use, although they cannot have enhanced the sylvan qualities of the groves. But sanctioned use of the holy precincts for purposes that can hardly be called sacred also occurred. There was evidently a common practice of renting out groves to private entrepreneurs. We hear complaints that in Rome, the sacred precincts are rented out to foreign squatters. It seems clear that although some religious motives might have tended to preserve at least certain designated forest lands and individual trees, there were other attitudes and practices typical of the ancient world that weakened this effect. Philosophers such as Pythagoras and Empedocles postulated that trees have souls like, or identical with, human souls. Therefore they concluded that cutting down trees was a kind of murder. As Porphyry puts it, "Why should the slaughter of an ox or sheep be a greater wrong than the felling of a fir or oak, seeing that the soul is implanted in trees also?"[54] This was not the dominant view of philosophy. Aristotle regarded the vegetative souls of plants as distinct from animal and rational souls.[55] Some denied that trees have souls. Pliny, though scarcely a philosopher, follows Aristotle's opinion that animals and plants exist to serve mankind when he says, "it is for the sake of their timber that Nature has created...the trees."[56]

When the choice had to be made between a human activity and the rights of trees, the decision was clear, as the following story illustrates. A tree growing in front of the temple of Saturn in Rome began to upset a statue. After appropriate sacrifices, presided over by the Vestal Virgins, the tree was cut down; the statue was not moved. It was a statue of Sylvanus, god of forests.[57]

Thus the subject of deforestation, which was mentioned above as a major result of urbanization, returns. Destruction of forests began, as would be expected, near the centres of greatest demand: the urban centres and mining districts. The earlier Mediterranean cities and civilizations flourished in the eastern and southern parts of the basin: Egypt, Syria, Phoenicia, Asia Minor and Greece, and therefore these sections experienced more advanced deforestation before other areas. Since the east and south were more deficient in rainfall (as example, Genoa, in northern Italy, gets 52 inches per year, Athens 16 inches, Alexandria only 8 inches), the forests there were less abundant to start with, and recovered less easily from heavy use. The neighbourhood of Athens was mainly bare by Plato's time, and Euboea, whose relict forests show that island to have been heavily forested in early times, later produced only inferior timber because the demands of the silver-mining complex at Laurium has stripped the island of accessible wood. To generalize, deforestation progressed from the east toward the west, from the south to the north, with the similar movement of civilization. The more limited and fragile forests of drier areas were the first to disappear. And the more accessible forest lands were denuded before the more isolated; in general, lowlands lost their trees while the mountains preserved theirs: the steeper and higher they were, the longer exploitation was in coming. The areas most often mentioned and praised as sources of good timber at the height of Greek and Roman classical times, therefore, tend to be northerly or westerly lands, mountainous and with heavier than average rainfall. But even these forest lands eventually suffered the effects of the axe and saw.

Finally, let us consider the role of deforestation and erosion in the decline of ancient urban civilization. Did the denudation of the earth make it impossible for the classical cities to continue? In the present state of our knowledge, the answer must be a qualified "yes". We have examined enough evidence of the importance of these forms of environmental deterioration and their crucial interrelationships with other factors to make a preliminary judgement. And that judgement is that the ancients who described deforestation and erosion as serious problems in their own time were correct. With reinforcement from other environmental and social processes, those problems operated as major causes of the political and economic demise of the ancient

There is a close interconnection between ruined cities and ruined land. The fact that the broken statues and scattered column drums of the centres of ancient civilization have a deforested and eroded landscape as their setting does not seem to be an accident. The general impression of synchronicity, the contemporaneous ruin of ancient societies and the ancient environment, is inescapable. Forests provided almost the only fuel energy source of the classical world, and as the source was depleted, an energy crisis occurred. It was almost certainly not the first such energy crisis in world history, and we know it was not the last, but the pressures on the ancient economy were nonetheless real. Timber was the major material for construction of many types. As forests retreated, that material decreased in availability and quality and increased in price, fuelling the ruinous inflation that plagued late antiquity. Competition for scarcer forest resources ignited military conflicts which themselves created demands for timber. Erosion weakened the agricultural base of societies which were always predominantly agrarian, and exacerbated the population decline that made it ever more difficult for Greco-Roman civilization to resist the incursions of the barbarians from beyond the frontiers. Forests which formerly moderated the climate and equalized the water supply were stripped away, permitting the desert to advance. The image of the cities of North Africa, from which olive oil and timber were exported in ancient times, buried beneath the blown desert sand, seems deservedly to epitomize the environmental factor in the decline of civilization. Perhaps the swamps along the northern Mediterranean margin, from which malaria spread to debilitate the population, should do the same. Without in any way discounting the importance of other causes of the passing of classical culture and its replacement by its less glorious successors, we must say that the cities of antiquity were consuming their own future as they felled their forests and allowed their own land to bleed away.

NOTES

1. Joshua 17, 17-18.
2. Pliny the Elder, **Natural History** 13.19 (65).
3. Livy 9.36.1.
4. Strabo, **Geography** 5.2.5 (C223).
5. Fairfield Osborn, **The Limits of the Earth**, Westport, Conn.: Greenwood Press, 1971, pp. 11-12.

6. Fairfield Osborn, **Our Plundered Planet** (Boston: Little, Brown, 1948), p. 67.
7. Henry David Thoreau, **The Writings of Henry David Thoreau**, 10 vols., ed. by Horace Elisha Scudder, et al., Boston: Houghton, Mifflin, 1884-94, vol. 9, p. 281.
8. Theophrastus, **Historia Plantarum**, 5, 3.7.
9. Lucretius, **De Rerum Natura** 5, 1370-71.
10. Dionysius of Halicarnassus, **Antiquitates Romanae** 20.13.
11. Macrobius, **Saturnalia** 7.5-9.
12. Ovid, **Fasti** 5.93-94.
13. Dion. Hal. **Ant. Rom.** 3.43.1.
14. Allan Chester Johnson, "Ancient Forests and Navies," **Transactions and Proceedings** of the American Philological Association 58 (1927): 199-209; Herodotus 7.183, 188; Claudius Ptolemy, **Geography of Claudius Ptolemy**, tr. and ed. by Edward Luther Stevenson, New York: New York Public Library, 1932, p. 87.
15. Vitruvius, **De Architectura** 2.1.1.
16. Martial, **Spectacula** 12.18.
17. Plato, **Phaedrus** 230D.
18. Cicero, **De Natura Deorum** 2.39 (99).
19. Horace, **Epistles** 1.10, 14.
20. Plato, **Laws** 5.741C.
21. Virgil, **Eclogues** 7.49-50.
22. Virgil, **Georgics** 2.431-32.
23. Alfred Zimmern, **The Greek Commonwealth**, Fourth Edition, Oxford: Clarendon Press, 1924, p. 278.
24. Columella, **De Re Rustica** 11.1.12.
25. Plato, **Critias** 111B-D.
26. Strabo 5.2.5 (C223).
27. Seneca, **Epistles** 90.9; Juvenal, **Satires** 3.254-56.
28. Livy 35.41.10, 40.51.6.
29. Russell Meiggs, **The Athenian Empire**, Oxford: Clarendon Press, 1972, pp. 143, 619.
30. Aristotle, **Politics** 6.
31. **Code of Theodosius** 13.5.10.
32. Strabo 14.6.5 (C684).
33. Sheldon Judson, "Erosion Rates Near Rome, Italy," **Science** 160 (1968): 1444-46.
34. Plato, **Laws** 8.843E.
35. A. S. Hunt and C. C. Edgar, **Select Papyri** vol.2, London: Harvard-Heinemann, 1934, no. 210.
36. Livy 28.45.18.
37. Theophrastus, **Historia Plantarum** 5.8.1.
38. Plato, **Laws** 6.761B-C, 8,845E.

39. Thucydides 6.90.
40. Xenophon, **Hellenica** 1.1.24-25.
41. Marcus Niebuhr Tod, **A Selection of Greek Historical Inscriptions**, Oxford: Clarendon Press, 1933, vol. 2, no. 111.
42. Thucydides 4.108.
43. **Bellum Africum** 20.3.
44. Plutarch, **Life of Cimon** 10.
45. Theophrastus, **Historia Plantarum** 5.8.1.
46. Michael Rostovtzeff, **The Social and Economic History of the Hellenistic World**, 3 vols., Oxford: Clarendon Press, 1941, vol. 1, p. 357.
47. Ovid, **Fasti** 3.295-96.
48. Pliny, **Natural History** 17.1 (3-6).
49. Ibid. 16.91 (242); Pausanias 8.24.4.
50. Ovid, **Metamorphoses** 8.738-878.
51. Dio Cassius 51.8.3; Valerius Maximus 1.49.
52. Cato the Elder, **De Agricultura** 139-40.
53. Tod, no. 110.
54. Porphyry, **De Abstinentia** 1.6.
55. Aristotle, **De Anima** 412, 415.
56. Pliny, **Natural History** 16.24 (62).
57. Ibid. 12.2(3); Virgil, **Georgics** 1.20.

FOURTEEN

Bela Gertig

The Effect of Urbanisation on Tourism in Hungary

HUNGARIAN TOURISM IN THE 1930'S

Hungary is situated in Middle-Europe in a basin surrounded by mountains of the Alps and the Karpathians. Two thirds of her territory (93 thousand square kms) are plains. one third is hilly and mountainous ranging between 500-800 m of height. The climate is continental; mean temperature of the summer months is over 20' C, sunlit hours are between 200-290 and days with rainfall are only 8-10. Our winter is not too cold; mean value for January: 0' C., snow persists in higher mountains only, even skiing is not possible every year. The water temperatures of our rivers and lakes reach 18-24' C. The largest sweetwater lake in Middle-Europe is Lake Balaton with a rich natural flora and fauna.

Before 1945 Hungary was a capitalist society, agrarian-industrial of medium development. More than the half of wage earners worked in agriculture. The income of peasants and workers alike was low. Majority of population lived in villages. 42 per cent lived in towns (in 1941, 50 per cent), and half of the urban population was found in Budapest.

During the 25 years before 1945, without the proper conditions for development, tourism in and beyond the frontiers of the country was slowly spreading. The number of places for accommodating tourists was hardly more than fifty thousand in 1937. Though half of the above places belonged to hotels, yet their quality—apart from those in Budapest and major towns—fell below the international standards. Both places for accommodation and their geographical distribution were out of proportion. Majority of the turnover of tourists was distributed between Budapest and Lake Balaton, even towns of considerable touristic attraction and value had an insignificant share.

Distribution of touristic turnover was uneven also throughout the year. Besides the spatial bias to Balaton and Budapest, a temporary improportionateness was seen in budapest in the main season and by Lake Balaton for a very brief "peak period".

In tourism in the country only members of the ruling and the middle classes could participate. Majority of the workers or peasants would not have thought of spending holidays travelling. They could afford brief excursions only-for a day or two.

Hungary had also a little share in international tourism during the period under survey. As late as at the end of the thirties less than half a million foreigners chose Hungary as a destination for a journey; the number of Hungarians travelling abroad was half of the above figure–2 per cent. of the population. Most foreign tourists came to Budapest–a town of beautiful situation, rich of attractive pieces of architecture, medicinal spas, restaurants and other places for entertainment. Lake Balaton attracted few foreign tourists then.

TOURISTIC TURNOVER BETWEEN 1945-1980

Hungary after 1945 began her way of building socialism. Results of our social-economic changes which have definitely affected tourism can be summarized as follows:

To make up for losses in economic development industrialization was necessary. When establishing new industrial units a rational and proportionate planning was followed also in terms of regional distribution.

With the development of industrial productivity large-scale farming also became possible with a lesser need for human work. Labour power set free by agriculture was fully absorbed by industry in towns as well as by the tertiary sector.

As a result of development in the second half of the sixties Hungary belonged to industrial-agrarian countries of average level of development. National income in 1980 was five times more than in 1950. Real income per person in 1980 was 3.5 times more than in 1950.

Almost half of the total population is active wage earner (47 % in 1980). During the development distribution of numbers of active wage earners has greatly changed. Number of those working in industry, transport, telecommunication and in trade increased twofold. On the other hand, the number of those working in agriculture became less than 20 per cent.

Differences in incomes have been becoming less marked--both in a territorial and in an occupational distribution.

As a result of development population of several villages increased: their institutions became more, their infrastructure spread, their leading role in the surrounding settlements was becoming more apparent—they became towns. The number of towns in the period under survey increased from 58 to 92. More than half of the population in 1980 lived in towns (53.2 per cent). Also as an effect of logical regional industrial planning the population of Budapest increased to a lesser degree than of other towns. Thus, Budapest's share of the urban population fell from 46 per cent in 1941 to 36 per cent in 1980.

The number of active wage-earners shows a higher rate both among men and women in towns than on the average in the country.

The population over 14 years with a little exception, completed the 8th class of the primary, so called "general" school. Almost a quarter of the population completed a branch of secondary education and 5.9 per cent had a university or college degree—six out of a hundred. In towns the rate of population with a degree is 50 per cent higher than the national average.

In the considerable increase of tourism urban population has a great, major role, because of the fact that town-dwellers spend by far greater part of their income on holidaying as tourists. Cooperative farming population, partly because they have their own houses and gardens, and partly due to continual duties to be done there, spent a very small part of their income, 0.4 per cent, on going away for holidays as tourists.

Majority of the population with weekend-houses (116, 500, 1980) also live in towns. Two thirds of them are doing

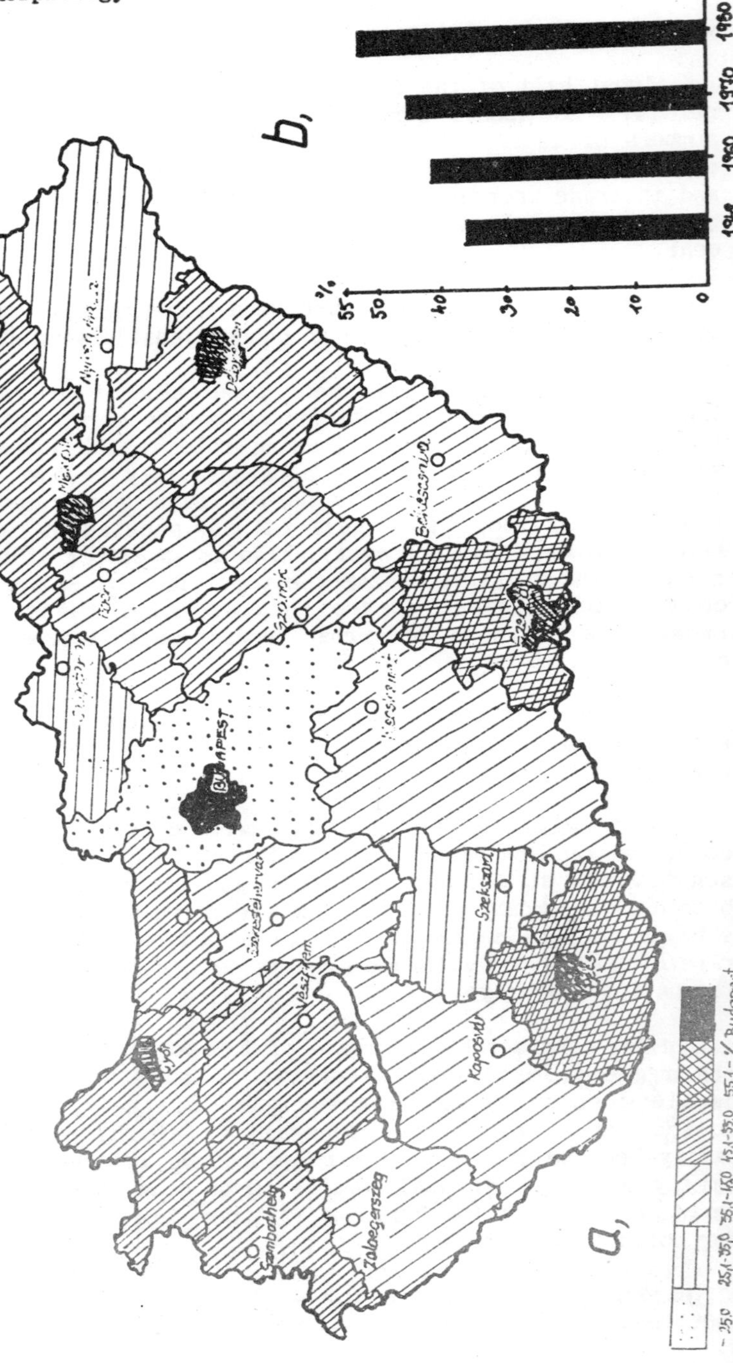
a,
b,
BUDAPEST
Szombathely
Zalaegerszeg
Kaposvár
Veszprém
Szekszárd
Szolnok
Miskolc
Debrecen
Eger
Békéscsaba
- 25,0 25,1-35,0 35,1-45,0 45,1-55,0 55,1- % Budapest
%
55
50
40
30
20
10
0
1949
1960
1970
1980

FIG. 14.1

brain work one third is worker proper. Co-operative farmers have a share of 2 per cent in the sum total.

With the development of our society our country pays greater and greater attention to developing national and international tourism. The period under consideration both as regards geographical distribution and the number of accommodation places can be divided into two, markedly different periods: 1945-1960 and 1960-1980.

Main characteristics of tourism between 1945-60

Our foreign tourism developed slowly in the above period because most of the places for accommodating tourists were destroyed during the war, and among those not affected some were made use of for different, but non-touristic purposes. Because of this the number of places after the war was half of the figure for 1937. Finances during the war were also damaged and what we had were primarily used to restore basic industry, transport network and re-building of family houses. The population was also trying to make up their own losses and could spend little money for holidaying and tourism.

During the years directly after the war first the so-called socio-touristic places were restored. In the fifties those numbers of accommodation places were increased which helped organized holidaying of the people outstanding in work and development of commercial accommodation places followed in the second half of the decade.

With the reconstruction of hotels and the building of new, commercial accommodations (motels, campings), as well as with the increase of paying-guests places supply was improved in qualitative and quantitative ways alike. The places we could offer for tourists in 1960 were still considerably below the level of pre-war period. Yet the distribution of this figure considerably improved: 51.3 per cent were so-called "other" commercial accommodation places.

Territorial distribution, however, did not change considerably, because social-touristic places were also established in the region of lake Balaton and in Budapest.

Main characteristics for accommodation places are as follows for 1960:

FIG 14.2

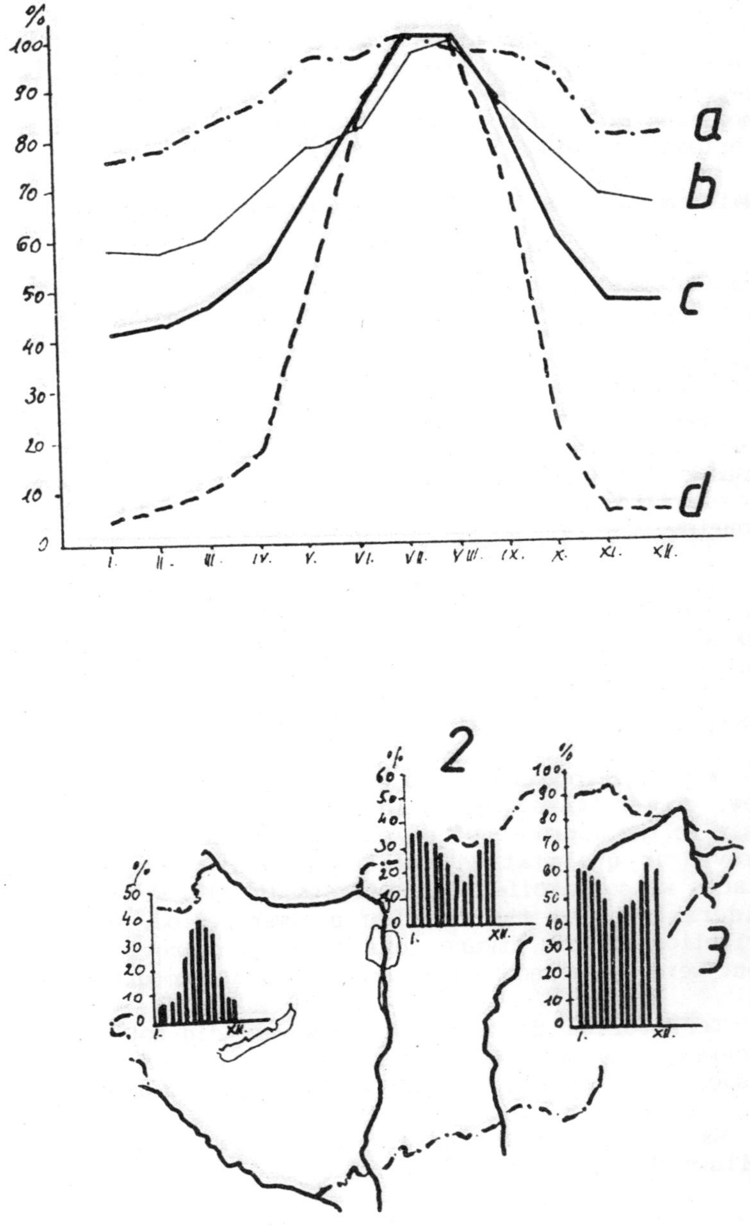
%
100
90
80
70
60
50
40
30
20
10
0
I.
II.
III.
IV.
V.
VI.
VII.
VIII.
IX.
X.
XI.
XII.
a
b
c
d
2
3

(a) the number of accommodation places was 1.5 times of the figure for 1937;

(b) though the figure increased, it was still very low: 85 beds for 10 thousand inhabitants;

(c) two thirds of the above were socio-cultural places/beds;

(d) territorial distribution did not change;

(e) holidaying places with accommodations were operated only during the peak season.

The turnover of tourists increased in pace with the growth of the number of accommodation places: in 1960 2.1 million guests were received who spent over ten million "guest-nights" in the country.

Temporary division was still out of proportion: two thirds of guests arrived and stayed during the peak season.

Distribution of nights spent at holidaying places as well as the rate of foreign and Hungarian guests appear to be even less balanced. Nine out of ten of the guests were Hungarians and their share of the nights spent at holidaying places is even higher. The share of socio-touristic and commercial accommodation places from the turnover of tourists was to a lesser extent different from the number of beds available. This is explained partly by the fact that lengths of stays were different and holidaying places were not operated according to the same pattern. While socio-touristic beds operated by trade unions, firms, co-operatives were available mostly in the peak-season bringing a much lower share of tourists' turnover, their share of the number of nights spent at holidaying places is by far greater because, guests coming with a reference from their firms stayed on the average-four times longer. (Compare: 2.5 nights of stay as an average with 11.2 nights of socio-touristic places.)

Hungary joined the international touristic activity only in the second half of the fifties. In 1960 we received more than half a million tourists from abroad and that year had one per cent share of European tourism. Most of the visitors arrived in the peak season, half of them were tourists and another half transit passengers. Though tourists from abroad used (with a few exceptions) commercial accommodation, their

FIG.14.3

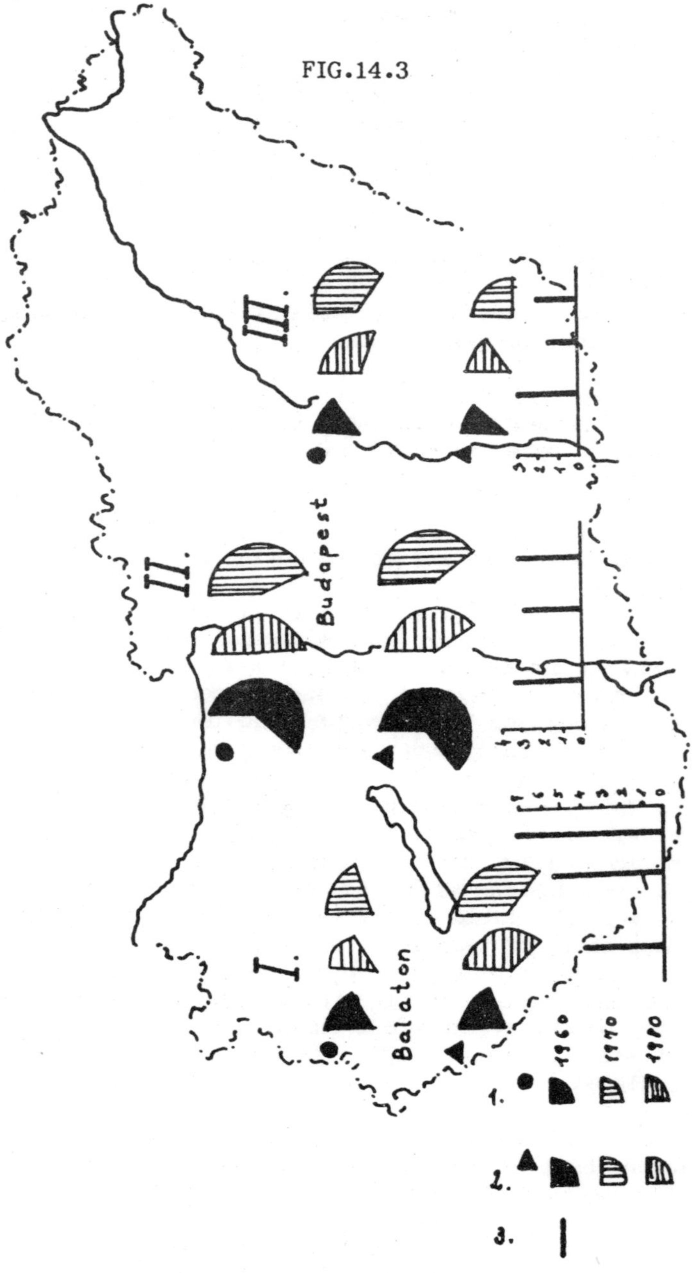

share of the total touristic turnover was little: 13.1 per cent of the total number of visitors and 17.9 per cent of nights spent in the country.

Territorial distribution of touristic turnover was uneven: two thirds of guest-nights and half of the number of guests stayed in Budapest, by Lake Balaton and the Danube-Bend.

There was a marked difference between turnover at socio-touristic and commercial places. Half of the guests at socio-touristic accommodation visited Lake Balaton. Budapest and the Danube-Bend together had a share of less than 20 per cent and other territories of the country had only 30 per cent altogether. Distribution of commercial accommodations was somewhat more favourable: Budapest Lake Balaton and the Danube-Bend had 40 per cent of guests and 50 per cent of nights spent there.

During the period under survey the number of Hungarian tourists going abroad also increased. At the end of the fifties nearly 300 thousand Hungarians were abroad. Their majority left for socialistic countries and in the peak touristic season and their supply of foreign currency could be provided from our national income from tourism.

Main features of our tourism between 1960–1980

Both national and international travels during the above period increased at a far greater pace than in the preceding one. Mainly the urban population spent greater and greater part of their income on travelling: at our resorts or abroad. Because of the development of railway and road-network travelling times became shorter and the number of people going away for a weekend or for excursions also grew considerably. The greater amount of free time and the number of cars becoming higher also had a role in the increase of tourism.

Our active tourism increased at a greater speed than that of Europe. With a figure of 10 million tourists coming from abroad our share of the European sum total was ten times higher than in 1960. Most of them still arrived in the holidaying season, rather during the peak time.

Distribution according to countries they came from did not change essentially: four out of five arrived from

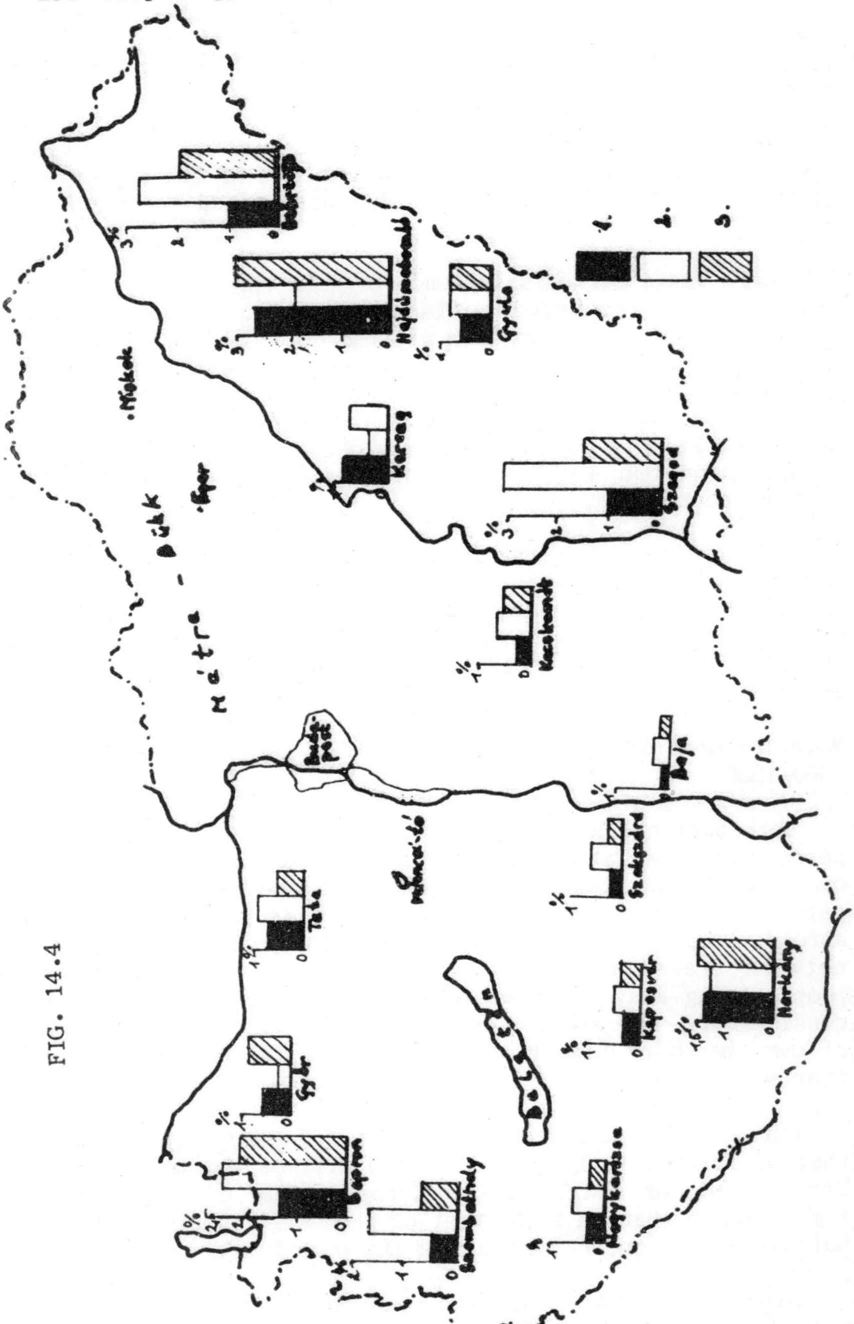

FIG. 14.4

socialistic countries and most of the remaining 20 per cent from Austria and the German Federal Republic. Distribution according to staying or/and transit passengers changed considerably (Table 14.1).

TABLE 14.1

Active and passive tourism in Hungary between 1960-80

Year	(a) Foreign tourists in Hungary -in thousands-			(b) Distribution in %		
	Tourists	Transit	Total	Tourists	Transit	Total
1960	244	280	524	46,5	53,5	100,0
1980	9413	4353	13996	67,3	32,7	100,0
	(c) Our share of European tourism /%/		(d) Number of Hungarians abroad -thousands-		(e) Their share of European tourism /%/	
1960	0,44	0,51	0,95	299	0,54	
1980	4,52	2,09	6,61	4942	2,37	

The number of tourists staying at commercial accommodation-places decreased. In 1960 nine out of ten, in 1980 two or three out of ten stayed at the above places. These figures seem to prove the inefficient services at these places (Table 14.2).

TABLE 14.2

Foreign tourists at Hungarian commercial touristic accommodations

Year	Number of tourists -thousands-	No of tourists at commercial accommodations	% of total number
1960	244	215	88.1
1980	9413	2448	26.0

Problems arising in connection with Hungarian and foreign tourism demanded great care and no little finances. The money invested, however, turned out to have been placed well as the immense increase of tourism had considerable cultural, political and economic importance. Our income of foreign tourism in 1980 was over 10,000 million forints and our balance was nearly 6,000 millions (Table 14.3).

TABLE 14.3

Incomes from tourism, millions

Year	In	Out	Balance
1960	180.4	208.4	28.0
1980	10250.0	4268.0	5982.0+

+ Calculated at non-commercial rate of exchange.

At the end of the period studied number of touristic beds was fourfold of and that of guest nights three and a half times of the 1960 figure (Table 14.4).

TABLE 14.4

Touristic beds, turnover of tourists and guest-nights in Hungary between 1960-80

Year	No. of beds	Guests (thousands)	Guest-nights	Beds	Guests	Guest-nights
				Index:	1960= 100	
1960	84.536	2.149	9.777	100	100	100
1980	354.513	6.556	35.876	419	305	367

The change of touristic accommodation places (beds)

As special care was taken during the period under consideration to explore and realize touristic potentials of different regions, in 1980—as compared with less than 300 of 1960—at 500 places (16 per cent of the number settlements in the country) were there already touristic accommodation places available. The number of beds increased more rapidly: the 32,000 of 1980 was eightfold of the 1960 figure. This immense increase was explained by favourable changes in the paying-guest system. Thus the rate of place per bed changed to 11 in 1980—half of the figure for 1960.

The number of beds per 10,000 inhabitants also changed—this value was 331 in 1980, but the figure holds good only for the holidaying season—outside this season the figure falls to one third. (Great part of holidaying places settled by waters, Balaton, Lake Velence, the Danube-Bend, do not operate in winter.)

There was a major change in the rate of socio-touristic and commercial accommodation places in the country. Commercial places increased sevenfold while socio-touristic ones became only 2.5 times more. Accordingly, in 1980 two thirds of touristic beds were operated by commercial interests. Besides their number their quality also improved. When qualifying these international standards were considered for comparison.

Distribution of accommodation places also varied according to who operated them and of what type they were.

At the end of the period in more than 200 towns and other settlements socio-touristic places of accommodation were available. The number of their beds was over 130 thousands. Operators being trade unions, firms, co-operative farms, they developed these places at different pace, thus, their share of total number of beds changed: trade unions and institutions came to have fewer, co-operatives and firms more beds for accommodating their guests.

The period for utilizing the capacity of these places changed according to demand. One fifth of them were open all the year round, half of them in the touristic season, and one third only in the main or peak season.

The quality of accommodation places also underwent a change. While the number of those providing full board and lodging in permanent buildings, or just lodging, increased, the number of tents and other camping places decreased. Weak-end resort places showed little change.

The number and distribution of places with commercial accommodation also changed. (In 1980 400 towns and villages offered some kind of accommodation for tourists.) In 1960 hotels and other places had a share of 50-50 per cent. In 1980, other commercial places had a share of five out of six–their numbers increased by far more rapidly than hotel-beds. Distribution of individual commercial accommodation places also changed (within the category of "other"). In 1980 paying-guest places were the half of "other" places and campings had a share of 20 per cent. Weekend-houses built since the sixties were already twofold in 1980 of tourists' hotels (Figure 14.5).

Not in the season time, when less than one third of "other" places operated and only three quarters of the hotels also, the above rates necessarily changed. Then

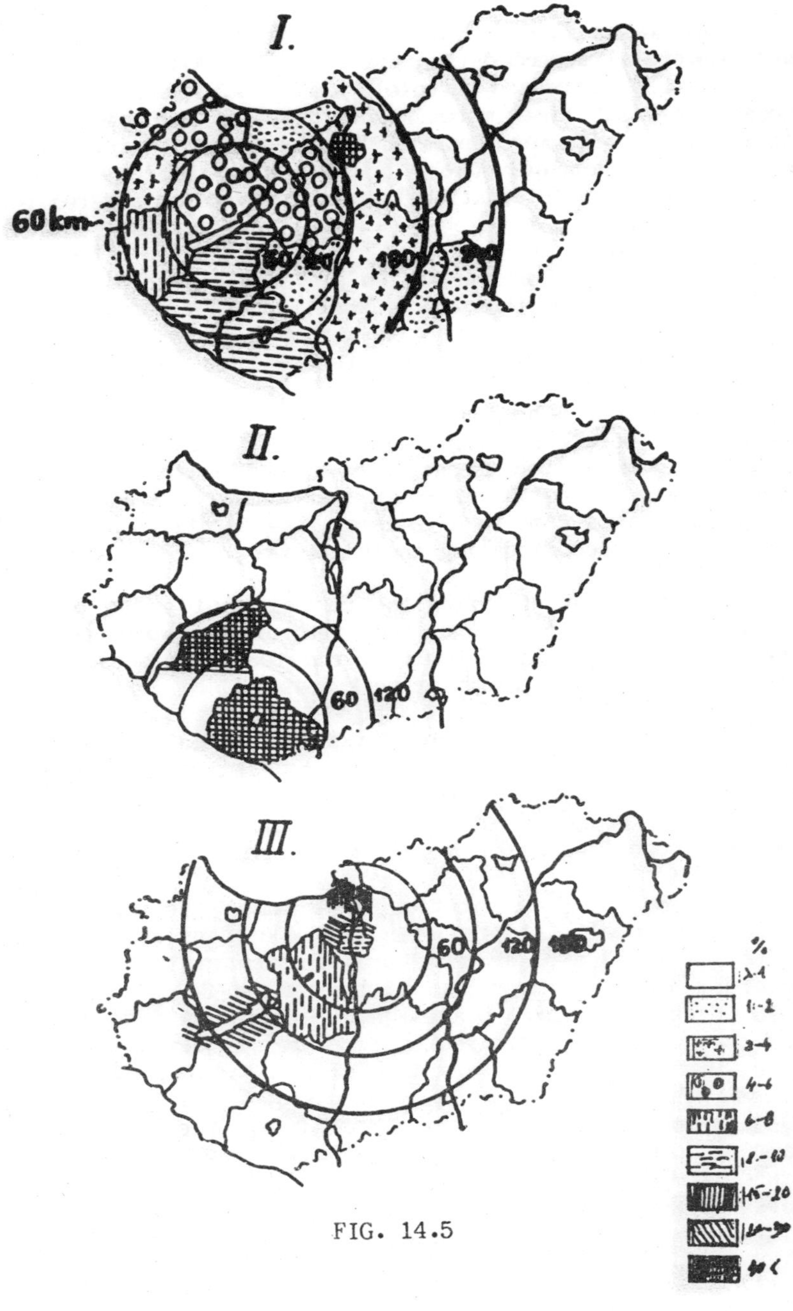

FIG. 14.5

hotels had a share of 40 per cent, while other commercial places 60 per cent of the beds provided for tourists.

Operators of commercial accommodation places also changed. Hotels were no more managed directly by the state but by hotel-associations like Hungarhotels, Pannonia, Danubius and the other commercial accommodation places were managed by travel bureaux.

TABLE 14.5

Distribution of commercial accommodation places in 1960 and 1980

Year	No.of beds	Hotels	OTHER Tourists' hotels	Week-end h.	*	COMMERCIAL BEDS Camping	Pay.g.	Total	Sum Total
1960	31.669	48,7%	11%	--	--	11,0	29,3	51,3	100,0
1980	226.067	15,0%	2,8%	5,9	6,0	21,2	49,1	85,0	100,0

* Contributory accommodation.

To make proper use of finances when building new places for accommodation the following were considered:

- Volume and composition of the holidaying region;
- What demand does and will the place meet ? (cultural, medicotherapeutic, excursion place, etc.)
- The role of the place in the national and foreign tourism (i.e; demand for the place).
- Conditions and quality of infrastructure.

Because of the above said geographical concentration of accommodation places continued, in the form of complex accommodation units, and in 1980 two thirds of the total number of beds belonged to these units, which had hotels, other commercial, and socio-touristic places of accommodation. Such units, however, were available only in one tenth of Hungarian towns and villages (so-called: "complete units of accommodation").

Other, non-complete units of socio-touristic and commercial nature were available in one fifth of our towns and villages.

Geographical distribution of units of touristic accommodation is characterized by a further shift towards lake Balaton. The demand for the lake is best shown by the fact that—in spite of the relatively brief season—half of beds available in the country for tourists were available around the lake. Budapest had one fifth in accommodation facilities of the figure by lake Balaton. Other holidaying regions in the country had altogether a figure similar to that of Budapest. If the number of touristic beds available is studied in view of main factors attracting tourists, river, and lakeside resorts catered for half of the tourists though the territory of lake and riverside holidaying regions in Hungary is only 5 per cent of the full territory of the country. Mountainous regions (Mecsek, Matra, Bukk) provided accommodation for one tenth of tourists.

Other territories not classified under either lake Balaton, Budapest, Danube-Bend of Mountain-regions have considerable role primarily in inland tourism, because our resorts supply (meet) considerable regional demand also. Their role is increasing in Hungarian tourism. Medicinal spas have a marked turnover of foreign tourists also.

Supplies in beds for tourists are characterized geographically by their being detached. But, when considering factors attracting tourists, their concentration is considerable: medicinal and thermal spas account for one quarter of touristic accommodation. Mountain-regions provide beds for one tenth, major places along transit routes for one twentieth of tourists. Other places about three hundred towns and villages have a share of the one third of national total. This rate, with the development of urbanisation and the increase towards village tourism will definitely increase. Other territories will necessarily be made use of continually because of the overload in demand for particularly preferred territories and regions.

Turnover at accommodation places made specifically for tourism

The turnover increased slower than the number of beds available. Yet the division between socio-touristic and commercial places changed significantly between 1960 and 1980. Figures for the two years and for the two kinds of accommodation practically "changed places": while in 1960 socio-touristic places received more, eight out of ten tourists, and commercial places the remaining twenty per cent; in 1980 85 per cent of guests and 70 per cent of guest-nights were provided by commercial accommodation places. In 1980 com

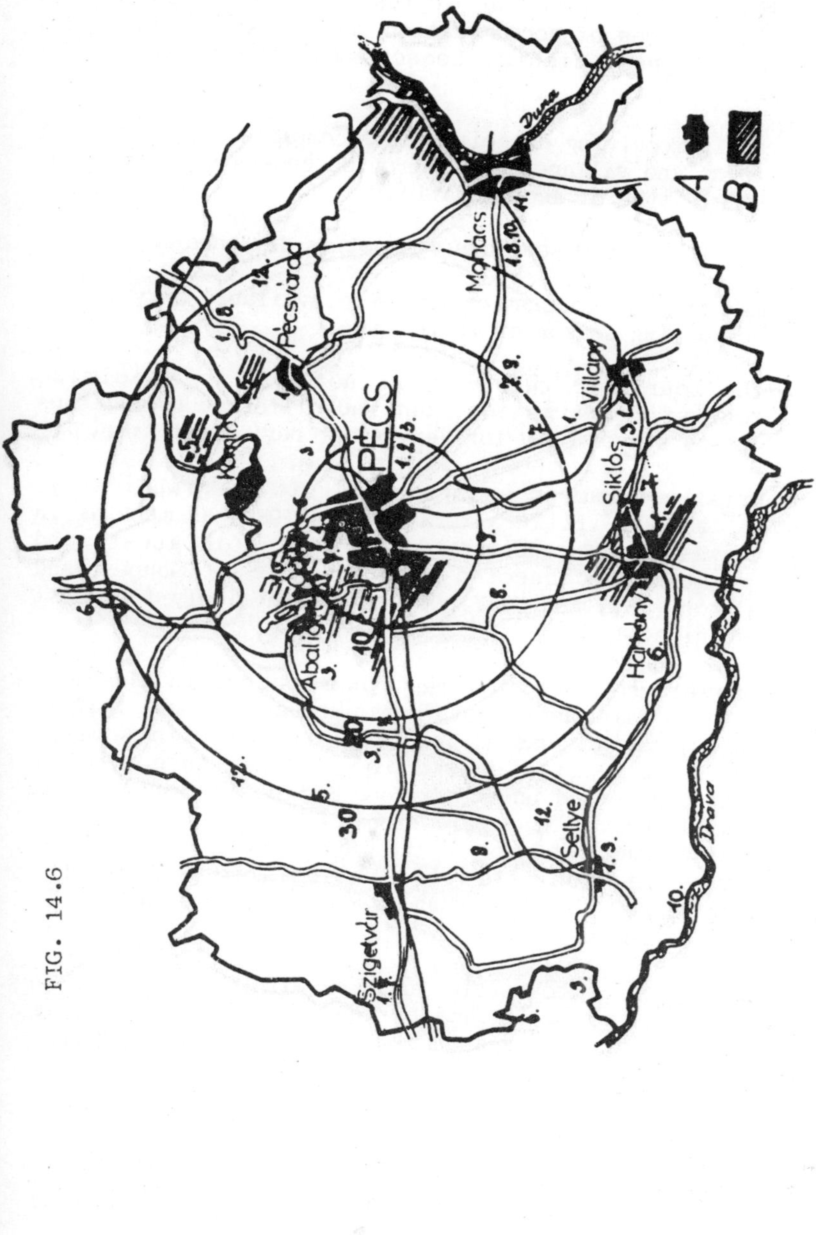
PÉCS
Pécsvárad
Mohács
Villány
Siklós
Harkány
Sellye
Szigetvár
Abaliget
Komló
Duna
Drava
A
B

FIG. 14.6

plete units of touristic accommodation, meeting the demands of guests at a high level, received the 70 per cent of the guests and had a share of also 70 per cent of guest-nights. On the other hand nine out of ten towns and villages with incomplete places of accommodation had a share of less than a third of guest-nights. Reasons for the above are as follows:

(i) their receiving capacity was incomplete; two thirds of towns and villages could provide guests with only one single type of accommodation;

(ii) quality of the services was not as demanded;

(iii) majority of touristic beds were available only in the holidaying season or in the peak;

(iv) the touristic turnover was not due to specific, touristic attraction, but had different roles, thus guests stayed only for very short periods of time.

Touristic turnover and guest nights geographically, however, showed little alteration. In 1980, as much as in 1960, it was highly concentrated. Half of both guests and guest-nights are connected with the name of Budapest and Lake Balaton (46.0 and 57.7 per cent respectively for guest and guest nights).

Turnover of tourists was concentrated in the main season. Three quarters of both guest and guest-night fell to the main holidaying season. Touristic places with several factors of attraction showed a more even turnover all throughout the period under survey. Budapest, mountainous regions with medical and recreational qualities received the two thirds of their guests in the main season, but the number of visiting tourists was considerable outside the holidaying season also. Lakes Balaton and Velence had guests in the holidaying season mainly.

Distribution of touristic turnover within the season in Budapest was less uneven than by the above lakes. Turnover in the main holidaying season in Budapest was 8-10% higher than in periods preceding and succeeding the peak. Visitors went to the lakes during two months about as many as in the remaining ten.

Distribution between Hungarian tourists and foreign visitors also changed brought about by the increase of tourists from abroad and by the uneven growth of commercial accommodation places. Turnover of Hungarian tourists showed a twofold increase in guests and a threefold one in guest-nights, while figures for tourists from abroad are tenfold for both guest and guest-night. An insignificant percentage of tourists from abroad availed themselves of socio-touristic facilities, hence here only guests of trade unions and official visitors of particular firms and institutions were allowed to stay (95-98 per cent for commercial places of accommodation).

In Budapest and by Lake Balaton the share of commercial accommodation claimed and used by foreign tourists was still higher. In hotels both guest and guest-night figures showed high values in Budapest and by Lake Balaton: 85-91 per cent and 75-82 per cent respectively.

In other holidaying regions and other territories the share of commercial places of guests and guest night was similarly slower for foreigners than the national average (25-25 per cent respectively).

With a reasonable propaganda of factors attracting tourists to places at the moment not properly discovered would contribute to an increase of our guests.

The above also indicate the highly concentrated nature of Hungarian tourism in Hungary geographically. While Budapest and Lake Balaton together had a share of three thirds of foreign guests in Hungary both in 1960 and 1980, they respectively had very different contribution to the above figure. Budapest had 45 and 40 per cent of guest turnover and guest night respectively, while by the lake 35 per cent was the figure for guest night and 19 per cent for the number of guests. Tourists stayed by Lake Balaton twice as long as in Budapest which latter offered a great variety of programs for entertainment (7 and 3.5 nights as an average for guest-night). Other territories received one third of the guests and had a share of one fourth of the guest-nights. Tourists from abroad spent two nights (on the average) at commercial places of accommodation.

With the increase of the population of our towns weekend houses in personal property also grew in number. The weekend houses whose figure was well over the 100 thousand mark in 1980 (counting an average of five beds or persons in each) meant two and a half times more than touristic places can accommodate. Though the majority of these places cater for the families themselves, there is an increasing tendency that in the peak season more and more families let out part of or the whole building. The touristic turnover (estimated figure) at these privately rented places is two thirds and the number of guest-nights is approximately the same as at commercial places of accommodation.

CONCLUSIONS

Tourism in Hungary is limited to a season. Both Hungarian tourists and visitors from abroad during the past thirty five years under survey arrived in the main season, many of them in the peak of the season. Accordingly, it is not very likely that we are in any way able to modify holidaying habits of people wanting to spend their holidays by the lakes and in the Danube-Bend.

The number of beds for accommodating tourists at commercial places should be increased. At the moment they are not able to meet the demand in the main season.

Among these hotel accommodation forms should be encouraged, hotel beds increased. With the improvement of services at paying guest places their receiving capacity could and should be increased.

New touristic places should be established considering demand, constitution of the turnover of guests, utilization of beds at and near the region, as well as whether it is economic to invest there or not.

Besides all these geographical, territorial distribution should also be altered-against the over-concentration of touristic places of attraction. The over-loaded nature of a few regions—which is already undesirably crowded in the season (Lakes Balaton and Velence) could be changed by establishing of **new and complete** areas. Both inland and foreign tourism would benefit from an increase of accommodation places and an improvement of services at medicinal and thermal spas (Buk, Zalakaros, Fonyod, Taska-Csisztapuszta, Igal, Karcag-Berekfurdo, Hajduszoboszlo, Gyula).

Regional demands could best be met through improvement of waterside resorts (Fadd-Dombori, Szelidi-lake, Toserdo, Martely, Szarvas, Gesztely) developing near urban agglomerations.

SECTION FOUR

URBAN LANDUSE IN HILLY TOWNS, INDIA

FIFTEEN

P.C. Sharma

Factors Affecting the Morphological Patterns of Hilly Towns

A case study of Himachal Pradesh

The State of Himachal Pradesh spreads from 30° 22' 30" N to 33° 13' N Latitudes and from 75° 23' 24" E to 79° 00' 50" E Longitudes[1]. It is a mountainous state with its elevation ranging from about 450 to 6900 mtrs a.m.s.l. Its total area is 55673 km^2, and population is 34,60,434 as in 1971 and 4,237,569 (1981) with an average density of 76 persons per sq km (1981). In 1971 its total urban population was 2,41,890. And there were 35 towns in the State in 1971[2].

The following factors have been influencing the evolution of the morphology of these hilly towns.[3]

PHYSICAL CONTROLS

Locational factors

The towns located in the southern parts of the State have experienced expansion because of the cultural influence of the neighbouring states like U.P, Punjab and Haryana. Such towns are Paonta Sahib, Solan, Nalagarh, Una etc.

These towns grew larger because they could procure the supply of material from the towns of plains for redistribution to their own population or to that of surrounding areas. The impact of this aspect of their closer location to such material is reflected in their building material also.

The general elevation a.s.l. has also influenced the expansion of towns. The following table shows that about 42.8 per cent of the towns of H.P. lie in 2000 - 4000 ft. elevation group. The towns which are on an elevation below 2000 ft. a.s.l. have greater areal expansion and resemble the towns of plains.

TABLE 15.1

Altitudinal Location of Himachali Towns

Range	Towns	No. of towns	Percentage
Above 6000	Jutogh, Manali, Simila Theog, Dagshai, Dalhousie & Dhalli	7	20%
4000-6000'	Dharmasala, Bakloh, Jogindernagar, Kasauli Palampur, Sarahan, Solan Kulu and Sabathu	9	25.7%
2000-4000'	Arki, Bilaspur, Chamba, Kangra, Ghamarwin, Sundernagar, ShriNaina Deviji, Hamirpur, Mandi, Pandoh, Nagrota, Nurpur, Yol, Rampur and Nahan	15	42.8%
below 2000'	Una, Santokhgarh, Paonta Sahib, and Nalagarh	4	11.5%

The location and nearness to plains have influenced the functions of the towns also. All the industrial towns of Himachal Pradesh have easy accessibility to plains. Paonta Sahib, Nalagarh, Nahan and Solan are main industrial towns. The newly built up big industrial town of H.P - Parwanoo—is just on its southern boundary, and is almost joined to the township of Kalka (Haryana). Parwanoo township came into existence very recently i.e., after 1971.

In the interior parts of Himachal, there is no possibility of industrial development, nor the interior attracts the outside people for business. Therefore, only smaller service centres have grown there. The interior areas of Pangi and Bharmaur tahsils of Chamba district and the districts of Lahaul and Spiti and Kinnaur are entirely rural; there is not even a single town. Even the district headquarters of these districts are located in the villages of Kelong (Lahaul and Spiti) and Kalpa (Kinnaur).

Site control

Availability of Flat land

So far, availability of the flat land has been the

single important factor which influenced and controlled the origin, growth and evolution of the towns in the State. The towns of Paonta Sahib, Nalagarh, Una and Santokhgarh developed in open areas.

Chamba is sited on the 'Chowgan' between river Ravi and the hills. In Simla also the famous 'ridge' is important heart of the town and the nucleus. Likewise, Mandi is sited on a plateau on the left bank of river Beas. Nahan also had its nucleus near its 'Chowgan'

Ridge site

Some towns of Himachal Pradesh grew and expanded around a ridge. Simla developed around its first nucleus near the ridge at the foot of the Jakhu hill which is the main attraction in Simla for the outsiders even now.

Spur Site

Dharamsala experienced its expansion on a Spur of Dhauladhar Lower Dharamsala - from college and Sainik Sarai area to Kotwali Bazar cover the gentle slope of the spur with an average height of about 1300 mtrs with sunny and almost deforested tract, while the upper Dharamsala - Cantonment, Forsytheganj, and Mcleodganj are on higher elevation with cold climate. Dalhousie is also sited on the Spur of Dhauladhar.

Valley site

Most of the Himachali towns are sited in the valleys. Kangra, Nagrota (Bagwan), Yol, Palampur are the main towns in Kangra Valley, Sundernagar is sited in Bahl valley.

Hill-top

Nurpur grew and developed on the top of a small hill infront of the Fort.

'Sri Naina Deviji' is the smallest township of the state. The only nucleus here is the Temple of the Goddess Naina Devi which is on the top of a conical hill.

River site

Rivers have provided favourable site to a considerable number of towns in Himachal Pradesh. Good examples are Rampur, Kulu, Manali, Bilaspur, Paonta Sahib, Chamba, Pandoh and Mandi.

Rivers have also been a very significant factor in controlling the growth and expansion of the towns. The expansion of the towns of Chamba and Mandi remained restricted to the one side of the rivers in early days. It was only after the 14th century that Mandi shifted and expanded to its present main area. The towns of Kulu, Rampur and Bilaspur grew and expanded on one side of the river.

Thus it is observed that 8 towns (23%) of this state are sited on rivers. An equal number is of the valley towns. 8.5 per cent of the towns are in the foot hill areas. The number of hill top towns is 7 which are 17.2 per cent of the total towns. The ridge towns are 6 in number (17.2%) and 3 (8.5%) are spur towns in the state.

Climatic Control

Climate has been playing an important influencing role in the origin, growth and in determining the morphological patterns of the towns in Himachal Pradesh.

The odd and severely cold climate with harsh and fast winds hampered the growth of Sarhan (Bushahr) and Bharmaur (Chamba). It was the main reason that the kings of these erstwhile princely states searched for better sites. The King of Bushahr state ordered placing of live lamps on several spots in the night to test and find out a calm and cosy place for his capital. The site of present Rampur was the place where the lamp kept on burning for the whole night.[5] Thus the capital of Bushahr state was shifted to Rampur. The capital of old Chamba state was shifted from Bharmaur to Chamba. So these two new settlements came into existence due to climatic reasons.

The influence of climate is clearly visible on the morphology of Dharamsala also. The growth and expansion in Dharamsala could not take place in upper Mcleodganj and Forsytheganj area due to severe climate, and all functional as well as main residential areas developed in Lower Dharamsala.

Yol camp was developed in 1944 for the Italian prisoners of war because of the suitability of climate of the place for the Italians.

It has also been observed that in the hilly towns the sunny sides, and the areas not subject to the fast winds, are more developed. Simla, Dharamsala, Dalhousie and Arki are all examples of this. The great crescent arc of Simla is the sunny and calm zone of Simla. Similarly in Dharamsala and Dalhousie the developed areas are the sunny southern slopes of Dhantadhar. The whole township of Manali developed away from the thick coniferous, deodar flora in an open, sunny, spacious area.

Geological control

Among geological forces the only important element influencing the growth of towns appears to be earthquake which has occasionally resulted in destruction of built-up areas particularly in the towns like Kangra and Dharamsala. From such towns there has been migration of people to safer sites. The earthquake phenomena has also sometimes forced new constructions. Hot water springs and springs of mineralised water and gas (as in Jawalamukhi) have also effected the growth and expansion of a few settlements.

Natural Beauty

It is the scenic beauty of the places and their commanding view which has attracted the people and led to the growth of some towns. Such towns grew either on the top of hills. e.g. Simla, Dalhousie, Kasauli, Nahan and Nurpur or on the banks of rivers like Chamba, Kulu and Manali.

People selected sites for their houses in such places which have beautiful and attractive view in their vicinity. The scenic beauty plays important role in selection of a site for tourist centre, hotels, residences of officers and the rich people. Simla, Kulu, Manali and Dalhousie have considerable growth due to their beautiful surroundings.

The Availability of Water

In the beginning, the towns grew close to some source of water, such as springs (Baoris), rivulets, streams and rivers. Water schemes were introduced in the post-independence period, in some towns, but still these are inadequate and people have to depend on natural source of water. In Kangra, Paonta Sahib, Nurpur, Una, Santokhgarh and Kulu there are some wells also. Lack of water hampers the growth of many Himachali towns. It also leads to dirty and unhygienic living conditions.

The water supply points or sources have effected the shape and growth of towns like Kangra, where Gupta Ganga Achhra-kund, Chakra kund and Suraj-kund have added beautiful attractive structures__temples, shades, houses and ashram type buildings. Gupta-ganga and Chakra-kunds are famous spots worth a visit in Kangra. Suraj-kund has been converted into restricted water supply place in Kangra.

CULTURAL CONTROLS

The cultural factors are the resultants of human efforts put into geographical environment. And they have also played very significant role in determining the morphology of urban settlements of the state. The detailed study of their influence is revealed as follows:

Impact of the Transport and Communication

Most of the towns in H.P. have developed along the highways. Since the journey in mountainous region is always tedious, tiresome, expensive and risky, only those townships have been developing fast which are within the easy human approach. Examples are Paonta Sahib, Nalagarh, Solan, Simla, Nahan. The population of Solan increased from only 61 persons in 1901 to 10,120 in 1971. Likewise the population of Simla increased from about 13000 in 1901 to 55368 in 1971, and that of Paonta Sahib from about 400 in 1901 to 3692 in 1971.[6] These towns are expanding at comparatively faster rate than the towns of interior such as Rampur, Kulu, Manali, Dalhousie and Chamba. And the remote parts of interior are without any township.

Even the character of houses varies away from roads within a town. The road side houses are generally double or triple storeyed and perform commercial and recreational functions. Roads and lanes form the skeleton of a settlement. The improved roads have helped in the growth of the town. The good roads also add to its beauty and attractions. The great attraction in Simla and Kasauli is the Mall.

Business areas and industries have also developed in towns on the main roads. The peripheral development, due to centrifugal forces, took place in the areas linked by roads.

All the roads in Himachali towns run around its main centres. Generally the roads follow the contour lines. In hill top towns the roads have developed in circular pattern e.g., the circular roads of Nahan and Dalhousie and the Cart road of Simla.

Functional Impact

In Himachal Pradesh the towns are small and perform almost all the urban functions but on a very small scale.

The towns have been performing various functions through their respective functional zones viz., residential, commercial, industrial, administrative, educational, recreational, religious, medical and transport areas.

In Himachal Pradesh, at present there are only 3 towns with large scale industries. These are Nahan, Solan, and Nalagarh. Twelve towns have cantonments/defence areas. Six of these towns have cantonment boards, and other six have civil administrative bodies with separate defence areas. These defence areas caused growth of towns and provided them with bungalows, barracks, shooting ranges and open training grounds. The capitals of the erstwhile princely states grew around a fort or residences of the rulers and subsequently there grew a marketing zone in such settlements. At this stage centripetal forces led to the over-crowding around the main market in the core of the settlement. Administration, residence and business have been the main functions of these settlements. In Chamba, Rampur, Mandi, Nalagarh, Nahan, the residences of the rulers are surrounded by residential houses and markets.

The rulers were orthodox and religious minded, yet fond of recreational activities. They erected famous temples and developed recreational places like'chowgan' in Chamba, park in Mandi, Melaground (fair ground) in Rampur and Chowgan in Nahan. They also built temples like "Laxmi Narayan" and other temples at Chamba, Bhootnath, Tarna and Shiv temples at Mandi; Raghunathji Temple at Kulu, Goddess temple at Kangra and Jagannath temple at Nahan.

There came the next phase of the growth of the Himachali towns in the modern age after 1820 A.D. when the British started settling in the hills of Himachal Pradesh. The trend of open, spacious and bungalow type residential houses with proper places for towns etc and parks and open grounds in the towns brought a change in their morphology. In about A.D 1860 many settlements were developed on modern lines (though not planned) with a cantonment area e.g. Kasauli, Dagshai, Sabathu, Jutogh, Dharamsala, Bakloh and Dalhousie.

The modern educational system was also introduced in some places. British attaches, officials, tourists and missionaries went to all parts of the state and propagated the idea of better education and improved ways of living with changed standards and values. At the same time, the Indian leaders and the then rulers from these hill areas also went out-side and grasped new ideas. The Raja of Nahan happened to visit Bombay in about 1870 and brought the idea of underground drainage system, which was materialised in the town. Thus Nahan was the first town in Himachal to have underground drainage system. A municipal committee was formed in Nahan in near about the same time.

The new phase of development is characterised with the growth of additional functions in the towns and resulted in the growth and extension of these towns. There had been drawbacks of odd climate, difficulty of acquiring land, steep gradient, river valleys, bottlenecks in conveyance, yet the towns developed in all possible directions. The new administrative zone (Govt. quarters) in Chamba, the College and P.W.D. colony in Rampur. Govt. Hr. Secondary School in Paonta Sahib, Govt. departments and Resin Factory at Nahan, developed areas in Dhalpur Maidan in Kulu, new colony on the other side of the Beas in Mandi, all together are some of the impressive examples of the expansion of the towns under this phase.

The state capital Simla is visited every year by about 1,00,000 tourists. It has a high court, headoffices of all the departments, Indian Institute of Advance Studies and a University. It is a big transport centre and is linked to important places outside the state - such as Kalka, Chandigarh, Delhi, Dehradun, Hardwar, Amritsar, etc. It has developed from a hut (the first house by Capt. Kannedy) in 1821 to an urban area of 19.55 km^2 in 1971[7]. Now Simla is also famous for its seed potatoes and apple market. It has many hotels, inns, and restaurants. It is the only town in the state with 4 cinema houses, ice skating rink, and golf ground (though golf ground is outside urban town limits at Naldera).

Impact of Educational Institutions on the Morphology

In the modern period some of the Himachali towns are equipped with big educational institutions of higher learning and famous English and Public schools. Some of these have nationwide fame. The public schools are run in very congenial atmosphere with sufficient space and good hostels, in open areas in peaceful atmosphere away from the congested residential and business areas. The St. Bedes College, Bishop Cotton Auckland, Tara-Hall of Simla, Dagashai Public School, at Dagshai, and Sacred Heart School and College at Dalhousie are some of the examples. In addition to these there are residential Dharamsala and Kendriya Vidyalayas (Central Schools) at Simla and Yol. Besides these, the training and technological institutes have also added to the town-morphology. These training institutions have hostels and facilities for games. The Small Industries Service Institute at Solan has some students even from abroad. Similar examples are Teachers Training Institute, and College of Agriculture (Solan), Institute of Secondary Education for Nomadics at Theog, University complex at Summer Hill, and the Indian Institute of Advance Studies housed in the famous Viceregal Lodge (Rashtrapati Niwas) at Simla. Though these institutions are also handicapped by limited area at their command, they have helped in the growth and expansion of the towns on modern lines.

Impact of trading and commercial establishments

Some of the towns of Himachal Pradesh are growing fast because of the growth of trade and commerce. There have grown business centres in the central parts of Simla along the mall, in the lower Bazar and along the cart-road, and have added crowded business zone and administrative areas. In Simla the Business and Transport areas have become so over crowded that in the Simla Master Plan, it is proposed to shift the whole-sale market and export import agencies to 'Sheogi' - a settlement place (also a railway station) some 13 kms from Simla towards Kalka on Simla-Kalka road and railway line. Likewise the business areas form significant crowded parts in other towns also.

The impact of industries

The towns of Himachal Pradesh have mostly small scale cottage or medium size industries like 'carpet making' by Tibetans in Dalhousie, and shawl weaving in Kulu. But some towns - like Nahan, Solan, Paonta Sahib and Nalagarh have some big industrial concerns and industrial estates. Recently big industrial centre - New Township of Parwanoo has come up by taking the advantage of nearness to the plains and Kalka railway station.

The industries are mainly located outside the main

residential areas and away from administrative and educational zones. 'The Mohan Meakins Brewery' at Solan is at a distance of 3 kms from the main town. It has a big complex with shops, canteen, its own school, temple and railway station. And in between the Brewery and the town lies the industrial area of industrial estate at Chambaghat. There are various industrial units including T.V. factory, Neon signs, weaving centres, automobiles. Some hotels and shops have also come up in the area.

In Nahan The 'Nahan Foundary Works' which was once outside the congested town area, is now surrounded by residences and offices of various departments due to the expansion of the town. The other two big industrial concerns - 'Sirmaur Foundary Works' and the 'Rosin Factory'__are at a distance of about 3 kms from the main town.

At Nalagarh the 'Hypine Carbons Ltd' was set up in August 1972. And other industries - woollen and cotton textiles__ were going to be set up. With these the town is growing fast and needs new buildings for workers. Paonta Sahib is another town where some big factories like cement factories are coming up. And another future industrial town of Himachal Pradesh will be Mehatpur near Nangal.

The industries add to the growth of trade and commerce, job opportunities and income prospects attract large number of people who require new residences.

Impact of administrative functions

Most of the earlier towns of the state grew to perform administrative functions because these were the capitals of the erstwhile princely states. In British and post-independence period govt. offices were added. In district and tahsil headquarters well marked administrative zones have sprung up.

In Bilaspur there are two administrative sectors with the residences of officials and govt. offices. In Dharamsala the police lines, courts, P.W.D offices, and govt. colony are in the lower Dharamsala. In Simla the residences and offices of most of the departments are along the Mall. The Secretariat is in Chhota Simla on the Highway. In Kulu govt. offices and residences are in Dhalpur Maidan. In some towns like Solan and Nalagarh all district or tahsil level offices are housed in one big administrative building built for this purpose as administrative block. Thus the establishment of these units has also added to the growth and expansion of towns.

Impact of the policy of the government

As a result of the policy of the present govt. planned colonies are being added to the existing towns and new townships are being established, rivers are being bridged and their interlinking is being carried on. Thus the towns have better future prospects of growth.

Impact of the feeling of regionalism

The people of Himachal have been living in comparatively isolated environment and have a strong feeling of regionalism. They do not mix up very freely with outsiders, and do not encourage the outsiders to build up their property in their towns, though they welcome the visitors and treat them with hospitality. The towns are of local character. Even the people of one area feel out of place if they happen to be in another area. The dialects also differ from valley to valley. The local people of Chamba talk in Chambyali, people of Mandi talk in Mandyali, of Kangra in Kangri, of Nurpur in Dogri and the people of Kulu in Kulu dialect. The languages of the people of Lahaul & Spiti and interior parts of Kinnaur are of completely different type which resembles more the Tibetan type and style. This feeling of regionalism has resulted into a slow pace of development of the towns.

An analysis of the geographical controls makes it clear that the towns of Himachal Pradesh resemble dynamic organisms constantly in the process of evolution. The layout and builtup of these towns may be taken as an expression of their origin, growth and evolution of functions. Some old established functions of these towns are being modified while the new functions are being added to them under the influence of various physical and cultural forces, which are, in many cases interwoven.

The impact of town forming forces

In Himachali towns both of the town forming forces - centripetal and centrifugal__are primarily the situational forces and the forces of the social evaluation. These are still predominant and are causing haphazard and unsatisfactory functional spacing and alignment of various functions in different zones and particularly in the old central parts of the towns. There are also examples where spatial forces and site forces are playing not less important role. These are causing congestion in the old town centres and thereby setting an impulse of outward movement.

There is also sufficient evidence to show migration of functions from one zone of the town to the other. In these towns each activity appears to seek a site at which it may flourish best and the people of the community appear to determine how they wish the land to be used. Now Master Plans of some of the towns like Simla, Solan, Nahan, Chamba and Mandi are prepared and control over the past practice of haphazard growth is being exercised. Let us hope and wish for the best possible growth of these towns in the healthy natural surroundings.

NOTES

1. Census of India, **Himachal Pradesh**, Vol. 20, 1961, Pt. 1. A General Report, Supdt. of Census Operations, Simla, 1965.
2. Census of India, **Himachal Pradesh**, Final Population Totals, 1971, Sr. 7 Paper 1 of 1972, Director of Census Operation H.P. Simla, 1972.
3. Census of India, Population figures for 1981 collected personally from various sources like daily news-papers and books on General Knowledge.
4. Phool Chand Sharma, "Morphology of Hilly Towns - A case study of Himachal Pradesh," An unpublished Ph.D thesis of the Meerut University, 1977.
5. Phool Chand Sharma, **ibid** pp. 72.
6. Rahul, Shankrityayan, **Kinnar Desh**, Kitab Mahal Allahabad, 1955, p. 14.
   I. Important Statistics of Himachal Pradesh, issued by Directorate of Economics and Statistics, Himachal Pradesh, 1972-73.
   II. Census of India, Figures personally collected from the Census Office, Himachal Pradesh, Simla, 1971.
7. Edward J. Buck, **Simla Past and Present**, Thacker Spink & Co, Calcutta, 1904.

SIXTEEN

Mahadeb Pal and Jyotirmoy Sen

Siliguri

A Study in Urban Land Use

INTRODUCTION

Siliguri, a corruption of "Siliguri" or "collection of rocks", stands on the piedmont plain of the Himalayas. It is one of the Sub-Divisional towns of Darjeeling district, West Bengal and is the most important town of North Bengal. It is difficult to imagine today that even upto the first decade of the present century, it was a small malarious village with a population of only 784 in 1907. It was constructed as a non-municipal town in 1931 and on the 24th May, 1949 the local administration of the town was made over to the municipality.

Table 16.1 shows that the growth of population in 1951 was due to a huge influx of displaced persons from the then East Pakistan since independence. The town received strategic importance during the Chinese war in 1962. With the geographical problems created by the partition of the country, Siliguri came under a major focus in the transport and commerce lines among South Bengal, North Bihar, Assam, Sikkim, Bhutan and Nepal.The present paper studies some of the problems associated with huge growth of population vis-a-vis the land use of the town.

LAND USE

Residential

Land for residential purposes is used along Nivedita Road (Gurungbustee) near Panchanoi river (Ganganagar and other slums), in the extreme northern part of municipal area i.e., at the junction of Hill Cart Road and N. H. 31 (Mallaguri), Netaji Subhash Road (Subhash Palli), near Town RailWay Station, Deshbandhu Chittaranjan Road (Deshbandhupara), Aban Thakur Road (Babupara), Satyen Bose Road (Milan Palli), Bhagat Singh Sarani, Saradamani Road, Najrul Sarani (Ashrampara), Atul Prosad Sarani (Purba Vivekananda Palli), Kabiguru Sarani (Rabindranagar), Pritilata Road and Prafulla Chaki Road (Bharatnagar).

FIG. 16.1(a)

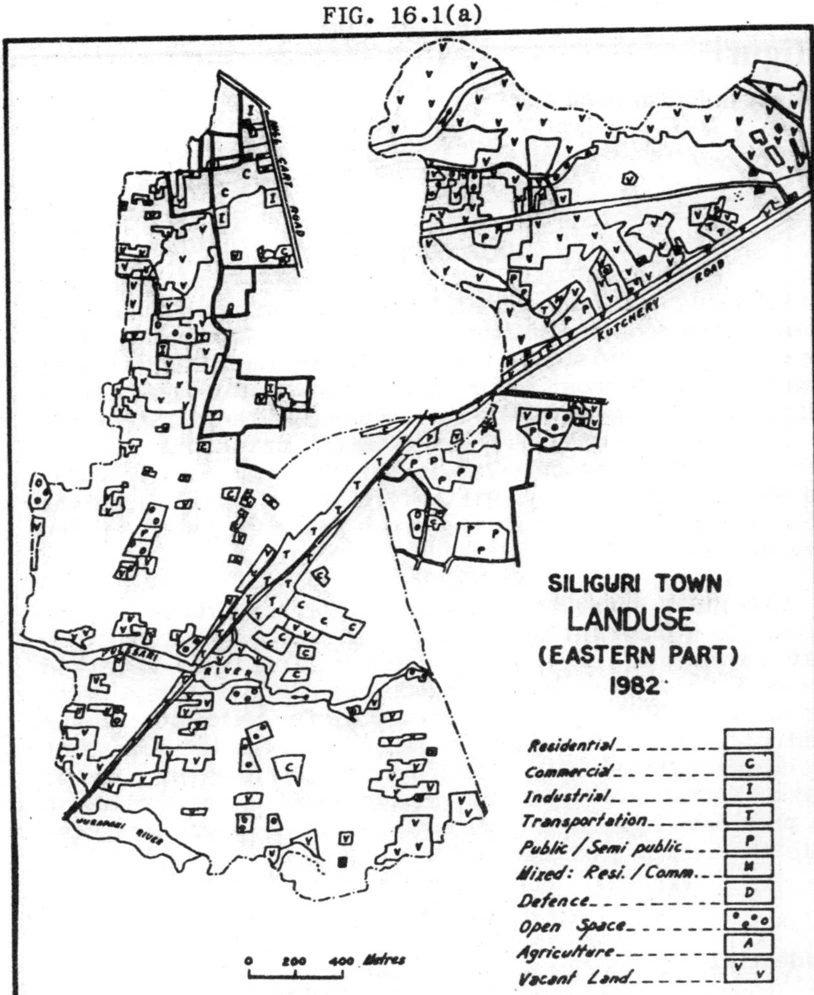

fig 16.1(b)

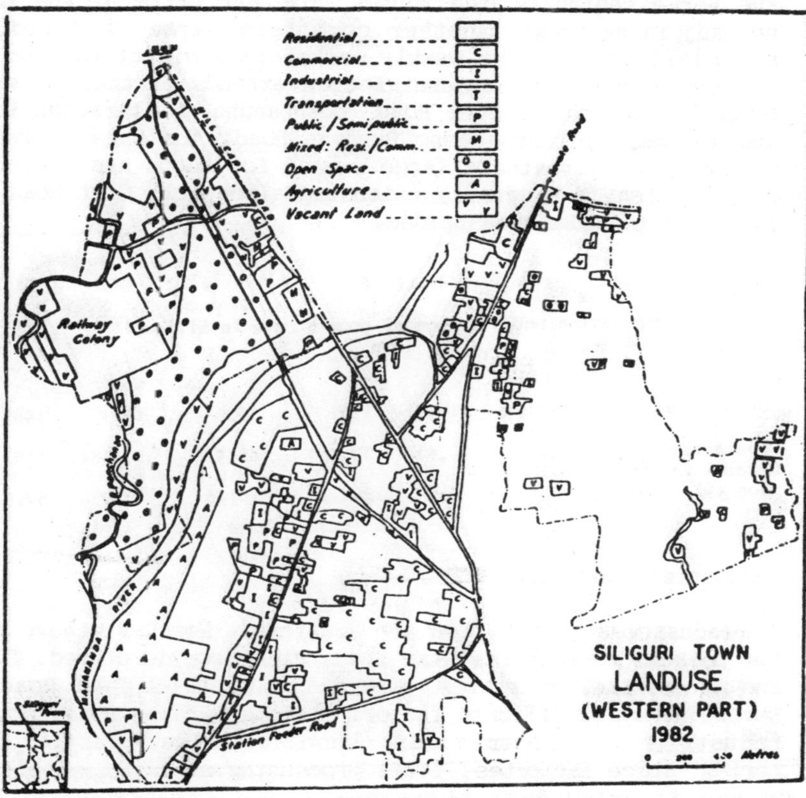

Residential areas may be divided into old and new groups. Old residential section in the west is congested. The town of Siliguri is expanding fast and new residential sections have sprung up in the eastern part. This area shows some planning. The roads are broader. In the very recent years, the town is expanding in the extreme south eastern part. This area was formerly vested land where the government rehabilitated the displaced persons. In 1980, there were very few brick-built houses, the roads were unmetalled. The railway colony in the north-western part of the town borders the Mahananda river in the south and Hill Cart Road in the west. This is a newly constructed planned colony.

Commercial

Commercial activities of the town have been concentrated in the mid of the town. The triangle formed by Hill Cart

Road, Bidhan Road and Sevoke Road is the most important commercial area. This area is advantageously located and is in the nerve centre of the routes from all parts of the town and adjoining areas. Another commercial area is found at Mahabirsthan. The bi-weekly market is a big attraction of the area. Then the commercial area extends further in west along the Station Feeder Road, Deshbandhu Chittaranjan Road and in small patches along Burdwan Road. The huge increase of population created a large demand for shops and the commercial area is gradually extending along Hill Cart Road to the north of Mahananda Bridge.

TABLE 16.1

Population and its decadal growth rate in Siliguri Town

Census Years	1931	11,941	1951	1961	1971	1981
Population.	6,067	10,437	32,480	65,471	97,484	1,53,825
Decadal variation (%).	-	72.8	209.7	101.6	48.9	57.8

Industrial Landscape

Industries of the town are scattered. However, there are two pockets where particular industries have developed. They are automobile industries, saw mills along Bidhan Road - Sevoke Road and Silicate factories along Burdwan Road. Other industries are flour mills, shoe factories, plastic potteries, spice factories, fruit processing etc.

Transport and communication

These include bus terminals, auto rickshaw terminals, bus garages, railway station and railways. These are located at Kutchary Road, Bidhan Road, Hill Cart Road, Siliguri town Station and the line connecting New Jalpaiguri with Siliguri Junction Station.

Public and Semi Public

These include schools, colleges, banks, libraries, hospitals, clubs and religious institutions. These are mostly developed: in collegepara Subhaspally is most developed as a number of schools, colleges etc. have sprung up there.

Defence

It has already been noted that the growth of Siliguri town was partly due to its strategic importance. Hence, defence plays a part in urban land use. Such land-use is found in two pockets along Nivedita Road and Hill Cart Road.

Open Space

These include parks, fields and the like. They are scattered all over the town.

Mixed Use - Residential/Commercial

In this case lower storey is usually used for commercial purpose and the upper storey for residence. The quadrant formed by the Vivekananda Road in the north, Station Feeder Road in the south, Deshbandhu Chittaranjan Road in the east and Burdwan Road in the west is most important in this respect.

Vacant Lands

These are scattered all over the town. However, a large extent of this sort of land is found along the Mahananda river. The vacant spaces in between the residential areas is being filled up for dwelling.

Agriculture

This type of land is dominant along the Mahananda river where paddy cultivation is carried on. Elsewhere, in the residential area, mainly kitchen gardens are laid out.

WARD-WISE LAND USE

Ward No. 1

It is a mixed area of residence, transport, Public & Semi Public Institutions, Defence, Residential cum Commercial place, Agricultural and vacant land. Residential and vacant land occupy almost equal share. A part of the area is inhabited by the Nepalese (Gurung Bustee). Here few development works have been taken up. In fact, this part is gradually being settled by people. Still now low-income groups are the residents of this locality. A few retired employees have settled here the Western part of Ward No. 1 is a developed one. Siliguri junction Railway Station, Offices and railway colonies are located here. The railway colonies are spacious and show some sort of planning.

FIG. 16.2

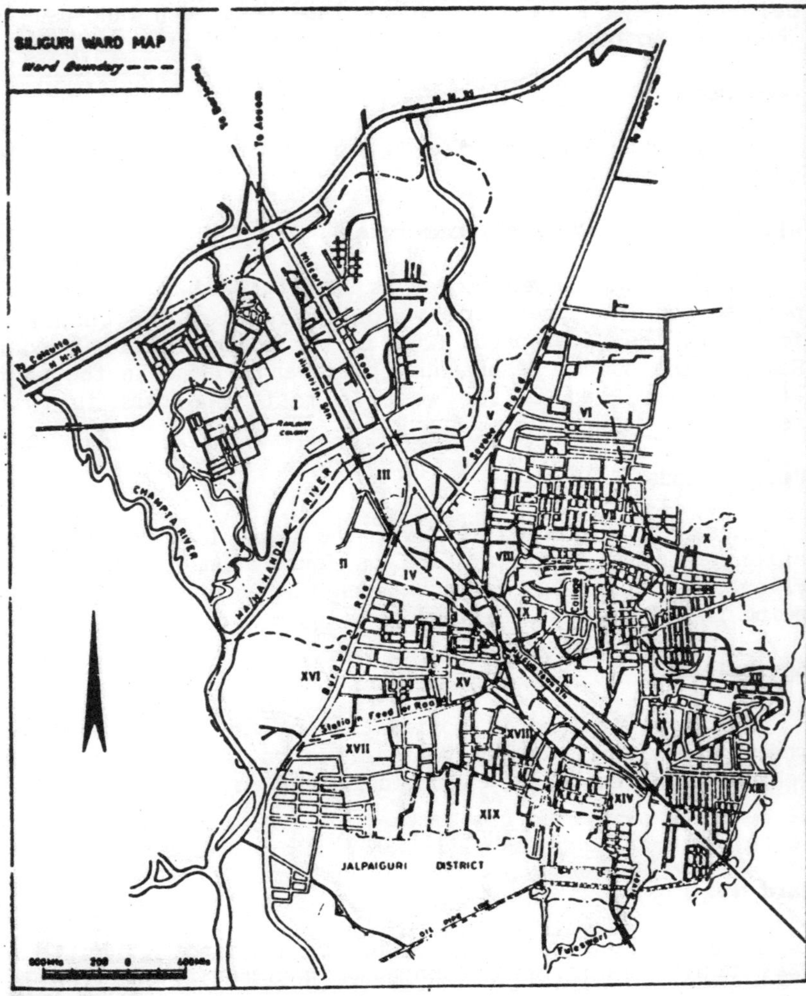

Ward No. 2

Located in between the Mahananda river in the West and Burdwan Road in the East, this is a mixed area of residence, industry, public semi-public Institutions, vacant land and agricultural land. Residential and agricultural lands share almost equal area. This is an area settled by low income groups as well as solvent families. Some Silicate Factories are located here. This is one of the least developed parts of Siliguri Town.

fig 16.3

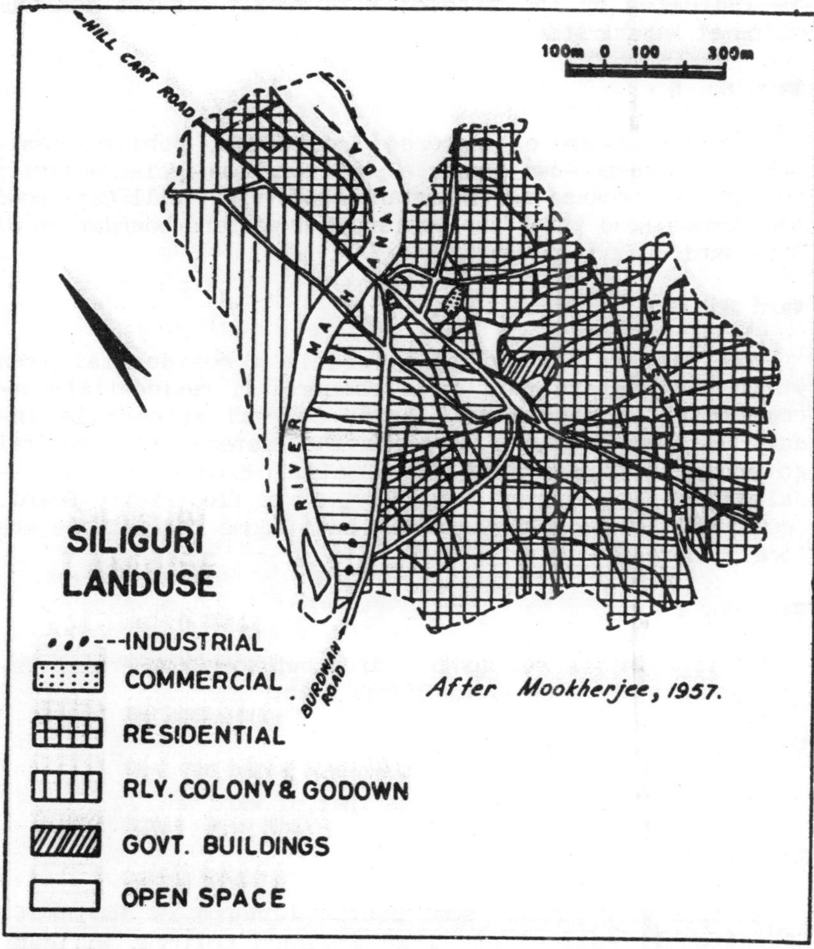

Ward No. 3

This is mainly a commercial area and the central Business District (CBD) of the town. A varieties of shops, retail and wholesale, cater to needs of the people. The area behind Hill Cart Road, i.e. Churel Road-Nabin Sen Road has developed by leaps and bounds within a span of three years, as a commercial-cum residential area.

Ward No. 4

Residential-cum-commercial land use is most dominant use of this ward. Importance of commercial land use of the area is indicated by the site of a bi-weekly hat and numerous ships at Mahabirsthan.

Ward No. 5

Mixed landscape of commerce, residence, public, semi-public, residence-cum-commerce. However, commercial activity is dominant because two important roads viz., Hill Cart Road and Sevóke Road touch the eastern and western boundaries of this ward.

Ward No. 6

The eastern part of this ward is a residential area while the western part is a commercial, residential-cum-commercial and industrial area. Several automobile industries have developed here. In the eastern part, several government offices like the Central Excise, Siliguri-Jalpaiguri Development Authority, State Electricity Board, Gestetner, Indane Gas, Sales Tax and Income Tax Offices are located here.

Ward No. 7

It is mainly a residential area but some commercial establishments are seen along Bidhan Road.

Ward No. 8

Here the land use is same as that of ward No. 7.

Ward No. 9

In this ward public, semi-public landuse is dominant. Educational institutions like Siliguri College, Siliguri Boys' High School, Siliguri Girls' High School and Hakimpara Balika Vidyalaya, Municipal Library, Bangiya Sahitya Parisad, Town Hall (under construction) and Offices like Indo-German Fertiliser Education, Information and Culture, Food Corporation of India are located.

Ward Nos. 10, 11, 12, 13 and 14

The main landuse of these wards is residential. The only notable commercial activity centre is around the Subhaspalli daily market (road side) which is located in ward No. 11.

Ward Nos. 15, 16, 17, and 18

These are also residential areas. There are patches of vacant land in these areas (public and semi-public landuse) Jyotsnamoyee Girls' High School and Hindi High School that are found along station Feeder Road are the examples of (public and semi-public landuse). In the western part of the area commercial and residential-cum-commercial land use is dominant.

Ward No. 19

The land use of this ward is residential. In the extreme South (Central Part) is inhabited by the low income group people. This is one of the least developed areas.

CHANGES IN LAND USE

Since Mookherjee's survey in 1957 (Map. 16.3) some notable changes in land use have taken place at the present day. These are as follows:

(1) Mookherjee (1957) noted that " a thin band of commercial development is seen on both sides of the Hill Cart Road and extends north to the Mahananda Bridge. Here tiny congested shops are owned by refugee population, providing facilities for all kinds of retail trade". He also observed that the main commercial activity was then in the West of town Railway Station. In recent years commercial activities of both the areas have enhanced in varieties and volume. Moreover, commercial areas in both the areas have expanded. This is particularly marked along Hill Cart Road, Bidhan Road and Sevoke Road which is the CBD of the town. Instead of tiny congested shops owned by the refugee population, spacious sophisticated shops, market, super market and mini market have developed here.

(2) He also noted "some twelve big mills" scattered over the town. Some new mills have been established. With the development of roads, automobile industry has come into prominence and it has developed along a particular locality. The same localisation is true in the case of timber industry.

(3) Town area and municipal area have expanded in the South. Mookherjee in his survey (1957) observed the Municipal area as 3.60 square miles (9.29 km^2). But, at present the municipal area measures 15.54 km^2. The huge increase of municipal area by 6.25 km^2 has changed the land use to a great extent.

LAND VALUE

A comparative study of land value of the different wards (Appendix-I) shows that Hill Cart Road, Sevoke Road, Bidhan Road, Station Feeder Road, Kali Mandir Road, Deshbandhu Chittaranjan Road comprising Ward Nos. 2, 3, 4, 5, 7, 15, 16 and 17 command high value than the other wards. Localities like Subhaspally (ward Nos. 9 & 11) Collegepara, Hakimpara (ward No 8), Ashrampara (ward Nos. 5 & 6), Vivekananda Pally (ward No. 7) provide easy access to market, hospital, place of work, schools, college etc. They are mainly used for residential purposes. These areas command high land value. The third Zone of high land value lies in the South. Land is used here as residential-cum-commercial purposes.

Appendix-I brings to light that during the last ten years, land value of some particular localities of Siliguri has increased abnormally. This is due to:

(i) huge increase in population and consequent heavy pressure on limited land. To keep pace with this ever-increasing population, semi-urban localities like Rabindranagar, Dabgram, Rathkhola, Prodhanagar, Bharatnagar and Gurung Bustee have been rapidly urbanised. A few years back, these were low-lying areas inhabited by low-income groups. With the rapid urbanisation, land transactions in these areas have been faster and the low-income groups are being replaced by middle and high income groups. appendix shows the ward-wise distribution of population of the town.

Since December, 1980, when the Siliguri-Jalpaiguri Development Authority under-took land use survey, most of the then open spaces have come under miscellaneous uses, for instance, Sevoke Road, where a number of automobile industries have come into being. It has also been observed that there has been an encroachment on public land.

(ii) Establishment of tea auction centre and resultant

growth of many tea ware-houses, ply-wood factories and a significant growth of transport-based and its allied industries over the last few years have enhanced land values.

(iii) The other factor is speculation in land. It has become a source of income for some of the rich people of Siliguri. A piece of land is purchased by them. It is substantially fragmented into several plots and sold at high prices. This speculation has caused an artificial crisis in the availability of land.

DISCUSSION

The town itself was not built according to any plan; it is really an "over-grown village" (Mookherjee, op. cit). This seems to be true when we think of congested part of Mahabirsthan, uneven development of the town, presence of agricultural land within the town, lack of drainage system and potable water in most parts of the town, encroachment of bazar on roads etc.

From the study it appears that:

(i) there is an unbalanced land-man ratio and the core area is most developed. In order to redress the unbalanced land-man ratio and to get ample space in the core of the town, attention should be paid to develop the outer fringes of the town such as Dabgram, Rathkhola, Gurung Bustee and Prodhannagar. It is a happy sign to note that the Government has undertaken a proposal to develop a satellite town in the western part. It will lessen congestion over the town.

(ii) Slums cover many parts of the town. A model low-cost housing scheme on the basis of long-term plan should be undertaken by the government in order to rehabilitate the growing number of people of the town (Pal, Dutta and Chakraborty, 1965).

(iii) The narrow Station Feeder Road and Deshbandhu Chittaranjan Road at Mahabirsthan are very congested. Rail movement augments this congestion. An overbridge at the railway crossing near Mahabirsthan is essential to avert congestion and ensure smooth traffic movement.

(iv) The Bazar at Subhaspally is held along Kabiguru Sarani and this causes congestion on road. Shift of this market from road-side to a suitable place or a market building can solve this problem.

REFERENCES

Mookherjee, D., The urban pattern of Siliguri, **Geographical Review of India**, Vol. 19, No. 3, 1957, pp. 15-20.

Pal, A., Dutta; M.K. and Chakraborty, P.K. ; Siliguri - A case study for urban Redevelopment, **Geographical Review of India**, Vol 27, No. 4, 1965, pp-195.

Pal, M., and Sen, J.; A comparative study of two towns in North Bengal, **Geographical Review of India**, Vol. 45, 1983.

APPENDIX I

Siliguri Municipality
Average land value in Rupees per Khata

Ward1975 No.	1976	1977	1978	1979	1980	
1	412	1125	4600	1700	12130	2300
2	375	10000	4500	3200	8300	4800
3	5500	4000	4300	2100	19000	5500
4	2300	3400	13300	7000	6800	3700
5	1840	14300	13500	17000	18000	5500
6	1340	7800	8100	3550	13928	6500
7	4426	5500	5600	4500	4400	5150
8	2900	1700	7600	6330	15100	5800
9	2700	2800	4600	2900	5100	5250
10	1100	560	1950	2150	3300	3200
11	NA	4200	4300	5200	2200	6500
12	"	550	4600	750	2600	1840
13	600	950	1450	850	1530	1300
14	NA	75	1700	NA	3500	NA
15	NA	NA	7500	16200	6250	5000
16	NA	10350	25400	5300	15400	10200
17	550	2550	3300	2300	3500	8300
18	NA	1500	3200	4100	1000	6150
19	1436	1700	5200	1500	2250	2500

APPENDIX II

Wardwise Population of Siliguri Municipality-1981

Ward No.	Male	Female	Total
1	13,343	10,197	23,540
2	4,774	3,954	8,728
3	2,834	2,077	4,911
4	2,278	1,372	3,650
5	2,952	1,766	4,718
6	4,783	3,957	8,740
7	4,499	3,971	8,470
8	2,789	2,721	5,510
9	2,672	2,402	5,074
10	3,644	3,419	7,063
11	3,704	3,304	7,008
12	3,056	2,754	5,810
13	2,546	2,449	4,995
14	5,984	5,259	11,243
15	3,070	2,075	5,145
16	7,887	6,064	13,951
17	4,982	4,183	9,165
18	1,841	1,486	3,327
19	4,106	3,684	7,790
			1,48,838
Flying1,856	782	2,638	
International	2,079	170	2,249
Total Population of S.T.		1,53,825	

Appendix II

Wardwise Population of Siliguri Municipality-1981

Ward No.

SEVENTEEN

J.P. Singh

Shillong

An Urban Survey

Shillong, the capital of Meghalaya, is one of the large cities of North-eastern India. In the recent past, it had the privilege of functioning as the capital of Assam and the headquarters of Arunachal Pradesh. It functions at present also as the headquarters of the North-Eastern Council, of the North-Eastern Hill University and of the Eastern Command of the Air Force. Situated some 103 km south of Gauhati, the gateway of North-Eastern India, Shillong at an elevation of 1,500 m above sea level is considered to be the 'Queen of Hill Stations'. To some Western writers, it is the 'Scotland of the East'. Surrounded by the beautiful pine trees and spreading over a wide valley, it looks like a city estate.[1] Shillong is an agglomeration of six towns - Shillong Municipality, Shillong Cantonment, Nongthymmai, Mawlai, Madanriting and Pynthorumkhrah - which together cover about 25 sq km of area and have a population of 175,180, according to 1981 Census.

Located at 25°34'N Latitude and 90°53'E Longitude, Shillong in the north is linked with Gauhati by a metalled road. On the east at a distance of 65 km is Jowai, the district headquarters of the Jaintia hills. On the south are situated Cherrapunji (51 km) and Mawsynram (53 km), the two rainiest places known all over the world. It has road links with all important places of North-eastern India. For broken topography, however, it has no rail link; the nearest railway station is Gauhati. Umroi, about 22 km north of Shillong, near Barapani, is the nearest aerodrome for the city.

Shillong urban agglomeration is rectangular in shape. The Shillong Municipality, however, is star-shaped. The municipality like a mother occupies the centre of the urban agglomeration and the rest of the towns like children agglomerate round the former. The municipality shares 62.3 per cent of the total population of the city. The rest of the population are distributed as follows : Nongthymmai 12.8 per cent, Mawlai 11.5 per cent, Pynthorumkhrah 6.1 per cent, Shillong Cantonment 3.8 per cent and Madanriting 3.5 per cent.

PHYSICAL SETTING

The city occupies a valley called the Shillong Valley. About 45 sq. km in area, the valley is bounded on the south by the Shillong range (1,900 m), on the north-east by the Mawpat hills (1,600 m), on the east by the water divide of the tributaries of the Umkhrah and Umkhen rivers, on the north by the Umkhrah-Umshing water divide, and on other sides by minor water divides. The valley is drained primarily by the Umkhrah and Umshirpi rivers, and through the Wah Ro Ro ultimately into the Umiam (Barapani). The tributaries of the Umshirpi take their origin in the northern slopes of the Shillong range. Barring a few, the tributaries of the Umkhrah flow from the Laitumkhrah-Mawkhar upland. The physiographic characteristics and the drainage pattern of the valley suggest that it originated as a result of the creation of a number of faults, probably at the time of the Tertiary uplift.[2]

Location to the north of the Tropic of Cancer and in the central part of the Meghalaya plateau has made the climate of Shillong mild and equable. It is neither muggy like that of Gauhati nor raw like that of Cherrapunji. It is ideal, characterised by warm wet summers and cool dry winters. The pleasant summer accounts for its charm as a hill resort. The mean daily maximum temperature in summer is about 24°C and the mean daily minimum in the winter months is 4°C. The mean annual rainfall is 242 cm, two thirds of which comes during the four monsoon months of June to September. Some 130 days in a year are rainy, some of the days getting over 40 cm of rain in 24 hours. The relative humidity all the year round is over fifty per cent.

The heavy rain of the monsoon enriches underground water resources - the major source of drinking water for the city. The rapid surface run-off often causes heavy damage to roads and steps. An umbrella or a rain-coat is a must in the rainy season. Warm clothes are essential in winter. Hills and forests that surround the city make its natural beauty superb.

EVOLUTION OF THE CITY

Shillong is pronounced by the Khasis as 'Shyllong'. It is said that Shyllong was a man in the Khasi hills, who discovered God in the highest peak of the district now known as the Shillong peak. The city derives its name from the peak.

After the British entered the north-eastern region of India, they were very much attracted by the hills. The reasons seem to be both political and climatic. They were interested in the central part of the Khasi hills, and they got a health centre constructed at Nongkhlaw, the headquarters of the famous Tirot Singh's Syiemship. For unavoidable reason, however, they moved to Cherrapunji, in the southern part of the district. A health resort and a jail for the prisoners were constructed at Cherrapunji, but the unpleasant climate with heavy rain was found unsuitable for the British soldiers. An intensive search for a good health resort was made, and out of a number of places, the table land near the Shillong peak was found suitable. It had a central location in the Khasi and Jaintia hills suitable for military post and civil station, had an easy access both from the Surma and the Brahmaputra valleys, and had a sufficient supply of water.

For the establishment of the district headquarters at Shillong, the British Government purchased large tracts of land from the Syiem of Mylliem in December 1863. The district headquarters was formally transferred from Cherrapunji to Shillong in 1864. The total transfer, however, came by the end of 1866. The military cantonment was established in 1866. In February 1874, a new province of Assam was constituted and the next month Shillong was made its capital. The major considerations for its selection as the capital were the central location and a good climate for the European Officers and tea planters.

Shillong was constituted into a municipal station in November 1878. Mawkhar and Laban, two densely populated and growing villages, located to the north and south of British Shillong, were also included in the station as the sanitary improvement of the town was impossible without them. In 1905, a new province of Eastern Bengal and Assam was created, and Dacca was made its capital. Shillong was its summer capital. The town thus did not lose its importance and it continued to receive waves of human migration. Shillong became a full fledged municipality in 1910. Assam in 1912 was constituted into a full fledged province with Shillong as its capital. Shillong with a legislative council became, politically, more important. The municipal boundary further extended.

In early 1910, Laban, European ward, Police Bazar and Mawkhar were the four wards of the Shillong Municipality. The same year Mawkhar was split into Jaiaw and Mission Compound, and Goalapatti and Southern Mawkhar. After the extension of the Municipal boundaries in 1910, Laitumkhrah, Malki and Mawprem were constituted into three new wards. In 1929, there were eleven wards of the municipality - three in the so-called British area and eight in the native, or non-British Syiemship area. The British wards were European Ward, Police Bazar and Jail Road, and the non-British Wards were Kench's Trace, Laitumkhrah, Malki, Mawkhar-Proper, Mawprem and Jhalupara, Mission Compound and Jaiaw, South east Mawkhar and Garikhana, and Laban. In 1931, Laban was split into Laban, and Lumparing **cum** Madan Laban. Since 1931 the Shillong Municipality did not create or add any new wards. After independence of the country, a large number of central and state Government offices were established in Shillong, and consequent upon it a large number of people in search of Government jobs and other employment came to the city. People even across the international border could reach and find jobs in Shillong. Prior to independence the buildings in the town were mainly single storeyed. Later constructions added considerable number of multistoreyed buildings. Vacant lands in Laitumkhrah, Laban, Kench's Trace, Malki, and Mawprem were filled with new residential areas. The Municipality could not provide enough accommodation and consequently new residential colonies outside the municipal limit came up. Risa colony, Motinagar and Rynjah (Umpling) grew around Nongthymmai. Mawlai group of villages, to the north of the Municipality, changed their rural character to become an urban place in 1961. Even these towns could not provide sufficient space for residences, and Pynthorumkhrah and Madanriting continued to grow to become urban places in 1981.

Happy Valley, Umlyngka, Upper Shillong, Nongkseh, Lowsohtun and a few nearby villages are rapidly growing around urban Shillong. They have considerably developed suburban characteristics. Ribbon growth on Gauhati-Shillong, Shillong-cherra, and Shillong-Jowai roads are easy to be noticed.

The over-all growth of Shillong both in terms of time and space has not been uniform. From the District Commissioner's Office, the centre of 1878 Shillong, the town has expanded mainly to the north, north east, south-east, south-west and north-west. The expansion in other directions has been either negligible or nil. The presence of the protected forests on the northern slopes of the Shillong range and the location of the cantonment and long distance from the administrative areas have been two major causes for the slow or no growth of the city to the south and the west. The improved bus services in recent years are likely to help expansion of Shillong even to the west of the cantonment.

DEMOGRAPHIC STRUCTURE

At the time of the formation of the Municipal station in 1878, the population of Shillong was 2149. In 1981 there was a population of 4,288 which increased to 6,720 in 1891. Table 17.1 shows the growth of population in Shillong since 1881.

TABLE 17.1

Growth of population in Shillong urban agglomeration

Year	Persons total	Decennial-per cent	Variation
1881	4,288	-	-
1891	6,720	+ 2,901	+ 56.76
1901	9,621	+ 2,901	+ 43.17
1911	13,636	+ 2,018	+ 41.76
1921	17,203	+ 3,564	+ 26.13
1931	26,536	+ 9,333	+ 54.25
1941	38,192	+ 11,656	+ 43.93
1951	58,512	+ 20,320	+ 53.20
1961	102,398	+ 43,886	+ 75.00
1971	122,752	+ 20,354	+ 19.88
1981	175,180	+ 52,428	+ 41.08

Source: (i) Census of India 1891, Assam Vol II.
(ii) Census of India 1971, Meghalaya, Part II-A.
(iii) Census of India 1981, Meghalaya, Paper I of 1981, Provisional Population Tables.

Except 1911-21, and 1961-71, during which the growth of population was low, the growth in the population of Shillong has always been high, above 40 per cent. The growth of population in the early years of the town was good on account of various employment and business facilities which brought in more people. Widening educational scope, developmental works associated with the Government of India Act of 1935 and the outbreak of the Second World War created more job facilities and thereby population increase continued at a high rate[3]. After independence, expansion of the existing departments and opening up of new ones led to an increased in-flow of people from the Brahmaputra valley and other parts of India. High inflow of refugees mainly Hindus from erstwhile East Pakistan (now Bangladesh) is also responsible for high post-independence growth of population.

Since 1951, ward wise population data are available for the municipality. The decennial growth of population during 1951-1961 and 1961-1971 has been very unequal in different municipal wards. The highest growth within the municipality was in Mawprem, 55 per cent; Laban, Kench's Trace and Jail road experienced very low growth of less than 2 per cent. The great diversity in the growth rates has been mainly due to 'pull' and 'push' factors which operated differently in different areas. Comparatively low house rents and close location in relation to Bara Bazar were major pull factors in Mawprem. Spacious and cheap rental areas of Mawprem, Mawlai and Nongthymmai, in spite of their location away from the administrative district attracted people in large number during 1961-1971. Laban, Police Bazar, Mawkhar and South-East Mawkhar appear to have reached saturation point as the space for future expansion is almost negligible in these localities.

The distribution of population by Isopleth method shows three centres of population in Shillong Agglomeration. These centres are Mawkhar Police Bazar, Laban and Malki. The first one is the largest centre while the other two are very small. The population centre does not coincide with the commercial centre of the city.

Shillong as a whole is a city of 'other services'_non-categorized activities. In 1961, over 70 per cent of the total workers were engaged in other services and this percentage stood at 55 in 1971. A comparative study of the 1961 and 1971 censuses shows a general increase in the share of categorized services like industry, trade and commerce, and transport. As per 1971 census, there are two concentrations of industrial workers - one in the north from Mawkhar to Mawprem and another in the south from Laitumkhrah to Madan Laban. There are three concentrations of commercial workers within the municipality. They are (1) Police Bazar, including Jail Road, Mawkhar, Jaiaw and Mawprem, (ii) Laitumkhrah and (iii) Laban. There are two clear-cut areas of transport workers - the northern area comprising Mawprem, Mawkhar, and Jaiaw, and the southern area comprising Laitumkhrah, Malki and Laban. The people engaged in other services are more or less uniformly distributed.

Shillong has been a non-tribal town in a tribal setting. Mawkhar, Jaiaw, Malki and Mawlai, however, remained perfectly tribal areas. The reasons for Shillong being a non-tribal town are its establishment by a foreign government which brought in early years almost exclusively non-tribal people, in-migration of Bengalis and Nepalis, waves of business communities, in-migration of Assam Government officials and in-migration of people from different parts of India for Government and non-Government jobs. After shifting of the Assam and the Arunachal Pradesh Government offices and officials the position has changed greatly. Among the tribals, the Khasis including Jaintias form the biggest group. Other tribal groups are the Mizos and the Garos.

PATTERN OF LAND USE

For the study of the pattern of land use, the author conducted a detailed house to house survey in the summer of 1972. The following discussion is based on his findings.[4] About three fourths of the area of Shillong is built-up. The residences account for seventy four per cent and defence fourteen per cent of the built up area (Table 17.2). The commercial, educational and administrative uses rank third, fourth and fifth respectively.

TABLE 17.2

Areas and percentages of major land uses in Shillong 1972

Land Use Types	Area in hectares	Percentage of total land use
Residential	1155.0	74.0
Commercial	55.1	3.5
Industrial	30.3	1.9
Educational	40.4	2.6
Administrative	37.2	2.4
Medical	15.1	1.0
Defence	213.3	13.6
Recreational	15.1	1.0
Total in urban use	1561.5	100.0
Vacant	565.5	-

Source: Field work by the author.

The residential areas of Shillong vary in character with the number of amenities and congestion of houses. The whole of Lumparing, large parts of Mawlai and some parts of Mawprem have only a few amenities. Motinagar, La Chaumiere, etc. have good water supply, good educational institutions close to them and good road facilities. Police Bazar, Mawkhar, South-east Mawkhar and Malki with over 36 houses per hectare are congested wards. Laitumkhrah, Lumparing cum Madan Laban, Kench's Trace and Rilbong, European Ward, Jail-road, Shillong Cantonment, Nongthymmai, and Mawlai with less than 20 houses per hectare are spacious. Based on general conditions of houses in terms of construction, building types and maintenance, the residential houses of Shillong can be classified into four groups of good houses, fair houses, poor houses and dilapidated houses. Various classes of residential areas have developed in sectors.[5] High class residential areas are located in the eastern sectors while most of the slums are located in the old part of the town, near Bara Bazar and Garikhana. Majority of the slum dwellers are Punjabis and Nepalis.

The high increase of population in the city since independence has created an acute housing shortage. The construction of houses could not keep pace with the growth of population. In 1961, on an average, 5 persons lived per residential house in the Shillong municipality. Most of the house-holds in the city, however, occupied one or two roomed accommodations. About 21 per cent of the house-holds occupied four or more roomed accommodation. It seems that the housing shortage in Shillong is partly because of the occupation of large houses by a considerably high percentage of families. After the shifting of the capital of Assam to Dispur and of the Arunachal headquarters to Itanagar many people have emigrated and the housing problem has eased to a great extent. The city in recent years, however, has experienced a high rise in house rents.

Like the urban growth, the commercial growth of Shillong has also passed through different phases. In the early years the business establishments were concentrated at Bara Bazar. Later on shops were opened in Laitumkhrah, Laban and Garikhana. Recently the business areas are getting decentralised.[6] In 1974, the author identified twenty-four commercial centres in the city and conducted a shop survey. According to the survey, there are in all 4344 shops, of which 14.5 per cent belong to grocery, 12.2 per cent to clothiers, 10.4 per cent to general stores, 11.1 per cent to hotels and restaurants, 4.8 per cent to personal services, 7.7 per cent to meat and fish, 7.7 per cent to vegetables and fruits, 10.3 per cent to betel leaves and nuts, 1.9 per cent to handicrafts, 2.4 per cent to hardware, 2.5 per cent to jewellery and watches, 3.2 per cent to auto repairs, 2.2 per cent to foot-wear and leather goods, 1.9 per cent to medical stores, 0.5 per cent to financial offices, and 6.7 per cent to others. Of the twenty-four market centres, Bara Bazar, Police Bazar, Laitumkhrah and Laban are considerably large, sharing together 69 per cent of the number of shops of organised markets (Table 17.3). Bara Bazar and Police Bazar together form the central business district with 56 per cent of the total shops of organised markets. There exists a hierarchy of business structure though it does not conform to Christaller's model.

TABLE 17.3

Number of shops in the organised markets of Shillong, 1974

S. No.	Markets	No. of Shops
1.	Bara Bazar	1993
2.	Police Bazar	463
3.	Laitumkhrah	321
4.	Laban	200
5.	Race Course	170
6.	Garikhana	141
7.	Mawlai	129
8.	Nongthymmai	113
9.	Mawprem	107
10.	Malki Point	99
11.	Jalaw	94
12.	Mawkhar.	92
13.	Umpling	90
14.	Phudmawri	50
15.	Jhinking	49
16.	Keatinge Road	43
17.	Jail Road	34
18.	Nongrim Hills	30
19.	Arbuthnot road	27
20.	Motinagar	23
21.	New Colony	22
22.	Dhankheti	22
23.	Bishnupur	18
24.	Fire Brigade	14
	Total	4344

Source : Field work by the author.

Convenience goods are sold in almost all the markets, but in the isolated store clusters and neighbourhood markets the percentage of such goods is high. The shopping goods are sold mainly in the central business district and regional market centres where the area of sale is large and which are situated conveniently at or near the centre of the town and which can be easily approached in comparatively less time from all or large parts of the city. The wholesale business is localised in Bara Bazar and its fringe.

Most of the offices in the city are situated near the Deputy Commissioner's office. These offices form the major administrative district. This district is characterised by tall building, up to five storeys, and non-residential houses. It is characterised also by an inflow of population during the day time and ebb of the same during the evening. Shillong is well known for good educational institutions. It has ten colleges, the North-Eastern Hill University and a number of schools. Though the educational institutions are scattered in different parts, most of them are localised in Laitumkhrah. The city does not have any large industrial establishment. It has some printing presses, saw mills, furniture and fixture manufacturers, metal works, motor vehicle repairing establishments and bakeries.

Shillong being an important place in North-Eastern India and also a hill station, has several hospitals. The Pasteur Institute, the Khasi Hills Presbyterian Hospital, T.B. Hospital, Nazareth Hospital and Civil Hospital are conveniently located to serve the city. Recreational places of Shillong include cinemas, clubs, parks, playgrounds, race course, golf links, water falls and auditoriums. There are five cinema halls, over ten clubs, two public libraries, two large parks, about half a dozen playgrounds, six waterfalls and two public auditoriums. The Golf Links and the Race Course are located in the eastern part of the city. Most of the recreational places are located in the central part of the city. Shillong is an important centre of the Christians and, therefore, churches dominate the religious landscape of the city. The cultural institutions namely Namghars, Brahmo Samaj, Ravindra Bhawan, Seng khasi, etc. have a scattered location. In Shillong most of the city buses ply between Bara Bazar and Nongthymmai. The bus traffic flows between Mawlai and Laban via Bara Bazar, between Bara Bazar and Umpling, and between Bara Bazar and Happy Valley are particularly heavy.

Suburbs around Shillong have grown in sectors. The suburbs are located to the east and west of the city and no suburbs have developed to the north and to the south. The role of physiography in controlling their location and of the transportation in assisting their growth seems to have

been significant. The establishment of non-farm villages to the east and west has also helped suburban development. The suburbs are marked by agricultural farms, defence establishments and recreational grounds.

PROBLEMS OF PLANNING

The city has considerable misuses of land, which are partly the product of the past. An inspection note of 1929 bears the fact that 'a large number of ramshackle houses are built of temporary materials' and most of them were constructed 'without any regard to building regulation'. In many parts of the city the buildings were erected, the alignments of roads made and drains set out long before the area could be included within the Municipality.[7] There are two easily identifiable misuses - one is the growth of Shillong on the northern slopes of the Shillong range, in Lumparing **cum** Madan Laban, and the other is the close location of the Cantonment to Bara Bazar. Moderate to steep slope in case of the former is a grand misuse of land as the construction of roads is very difficult. Bara Bazar is an old market, older than the town and the Cantonment. In the absence of any forethought given at the time of the establishment of the Cantonment, today with increased customers, vehicles, traffic volume etc., the roads along the Bazar have become very congested and the traffic flow very slow. In spite of some measures taken by the Town Planning Department for the diversion of vehicular traffic, the problem has not been sufficiently resolved. Some residential misuses exist in certain parts of the city. Lumparing **cum** Madan Laban, for example, has grown on steep slopes. So is the case with Malki. Mawkhar, South-east Mawkhar and Jaiaw have very congested houses without parks and playgrounds. As most of the shops of Shillong are located in Bara Bazar and Police Bazar, heavy vehicular congestion exists. There is need for the dispersal of business centres. The industrial misuses are seen along the Keatinge Road and the Laitumkhrah Main Road. The Meghalaya Road Transport Corporation Office and Bus Depot at Police Bazar is a misuse in the present context as it creates traffic jam. The space is suitable for the business use. The Fish Dale, South of St. Edmund's College, is under the Agriculture Department of Meghalaya but it is suitable for a park. In some of the suburban villages the houses are built on agricultural lands which need to be conserved.

For effective planning of the city, the Shillong Municipality must extend its limited jurisdiction. multiplicity of local bodies namely the Syiems, District Council, the Municipality and the State Government create problems in areal extension. Commissioner G.D. Walkar of the Surma Valley and Hills Division wrote in May 1937 that the Shillong Municipality found itself unable to extend its boundaries because the Government had no inclination to over-rule the objections of the Syiem of Mylliem to such extension. Unless the Government extends effective municipal control over Shillong and its environs, the sanitary and other improvements in the capital cannot be made.[8] Besides, there are rules framed by the District Council which pose other difficulties in land acquisition.

A tentative plan[9] for the development of Shillong is suggested by the author for a period of 25 years. New residential colonies with neighbourhood facilities should be developed within the present urban limit and in the suburbs. In order to provide uniform marketing facilities some community and neighbourhood civic centres are proposed to be established in and around Shillong. The marginal shifting of government offices and defence establishments is also suggested. Decentralisation of schools and colleges is required for equal educational opportunity to different areas. Two areas, one on the Jowai Road and another on the Gauhati-Shillong Road, should be developed into industrial districts. The Fish Dale should be converted into a park. Large cheap hotels and more rest houses are required in order to develop tourism in the city and the state.

NOTES

1. J.P. Singh, Shillong: A Geographic Analysis of Internal Variations, in Goswami, B.B. (Ed), **Cultural Profile of Shillong**, Anthropological Survey of India, Calcutta, 1979, p. 64.
2. J.P. Singh, **Urban Land Use Planning in Hill Areas**, Inter-India Publications, New Delhi, 1980, p. 39.
3. K.D. Shah, The Study of Communitywise Distribution and Growth of Population in Shillong, **Cultural Profile of Shillong**, op.cit., p. 12.
4. J.P. Singh, Pattern of Land Use in Urban Areas: A case Study of Shillong, **Indian Geographical Studies**, Bulletin No. 6, 1976, pp. 25-32.
5. J.P. Singh, Residential Use of Land in Shillong, **Geographical Review of India**, Vol 39, 1977, pp 232-40.
6. J.P. Singh, Commercial Structure of Shillong, **Geographical Review of India**, Vol. 42, 1980 pp 62-72.

7. J.P. Singh, **Proceedings of the Government of Assam**, Local Self Government, A, September 1929, p. 7.
8. J.P. Singh, **Proceedings of the Government of Assam**, Local Self Government, B., December, 1940, p. 6-38.
9. J.P. Singh, Details of the Plan may be seen in the author's **Urban Land Use Planning in Hill Areas**, op. cit.

EIGHTEEN

Jagdish Kaur

Badrinath : Hindu's Super Pilgrimage Resort on the Himalaya

A Study in site Character, Pilgrim Patterns and Process of Modernisation

Badrinath is Hindus' super-pilgrimage resort (Dhama). located in the higher Himalayan region of Chamoli (Garhwal-Himalaya). Amongst the four most sacred pilgrim destinations of the Hindus, Badrinath singly represents the Himalayan majesty, the rest three (Dwarka, Jagannath Puri and Rameshwaram) look towards the Arabian sea, Indian Ocean and the Bay of Bengal respectively. Spectacular landscape, superb ecological features, sanctity and religiosity must have been some of the site attributes in the establishment of this highly revered and most ancient of the dhamas[1] that now attracts about two hundred thousand pilgrims/tourists every year from far off Indian States and territories, despite strenuous hill journey of 301 km from Rishikesh rail-head. The challenge of the Yatra was far more formidable when rail road network left Himalaya inaccessible and forbidding, leaving it to its savagery and primitiveness.

Badrinathpuri is a small township with ribbon settlement along the bank of turbulent Alaknanda that flows southwards, embracing the Rishiganga to the south of the township. Located in 30°44'-56" N 79°-31'-20" E, it runs longitudinally into a spacious valley (4 1/2 km long and 1 1/2 wide), opening up north wards to the Bhotia village of Mana the last human settlement of this region. In elevation, it is 3122^{m} (10244') above the sea level.

Badrinath landscape is undulating, with encircling high black mountains super-posed by snow-clad ranges and lofty peaks. The mount Narain, in the west, slopes down abruptly eastwards into the Alaknanda whereas mount Nar, eastwards, leaves adequate space for human settlement. The two mountain ranges embody in them Hindu mythological belief and breathe Puranic faith.[2] The Nilkant peak, mysteriously lonely, peeps out majestically from the west, where the Rishiganga has her source. The Badrinath surroundings with adjoining meadow, and Vasudhara fall are no less enchanting. In fact, the Badrinath township should not be studied in isolation. It is a religious belt[3] spreading from Kanav Ashram[4] to Satopanth - 23 km north of present Badrinath which is considered highly sacrosanct for religious pursuits where sages and saints devoted major part of their lives. This religious belt has often been alluded as Badrivan or **Badri-ka-Mandal** in Puranic literature. According to Singh[5] Hindu Missionaries had a purposeful design in assigning pilgrims itinerary along the sacred Alaknanda in the Badrinath circuit, having the sublimest mountain scenery and the noblest river aspects, particularly river junctions (Prayagas), the five (panch) **Badrees** and the five **Kedaras.** A sacred journey to Badrinath is invariably linked up with Kedarnath and its adjuncts. Considering outstanding religious-cum-scenic resources of this belt, the Hindu expertise seems at its best in **Tirtha** planning and in placing pilgrim centres, in hierarchical order, climaxing in Badrinath. Presently road system has altered the prescribed pilgrim scheme and has interfered with traditional itinerary. None was, indeed, allowed to visit Badrinath at the first instance. This is not so now.

The Himalayan pilgrimages in Garhwal were ordained to be performed from west to east[6], viz., Yamnotri, Kedarnath and Badrinath, after completing visits to their satellites on a definite time scale. All these pilgrim centres had unusual physical background though difficult of access which perhaps lent them more enchantment. Puranic references support the fact that selection of **Badri-ka-Ashram** was no accident. The hectic efforts of Dharmas"[7] progeny for the choice of an ideal religious space led to the establishment of the five **Badrees** in the **Gandhmadan** region[8], Raj Badree (present Badrinath) being the crowning glory.

Badrinath acquired fame during **Mahabharata** times for its environmental values, and for being the 'hermitage of the perfect'. Sages and saints, priests and pundits, scholars and savants all flocked to the Hindu Elysium, braving the hazards of the journey.[9] Popular belief, anecdotal myths and some oral history, make believes that puranas were composed in this Gandhmandan[10] environment. There are references to the effect that many founders of the Hindu schools of philosophy received inspiration in this divine wilderness.

FIG. 18.1

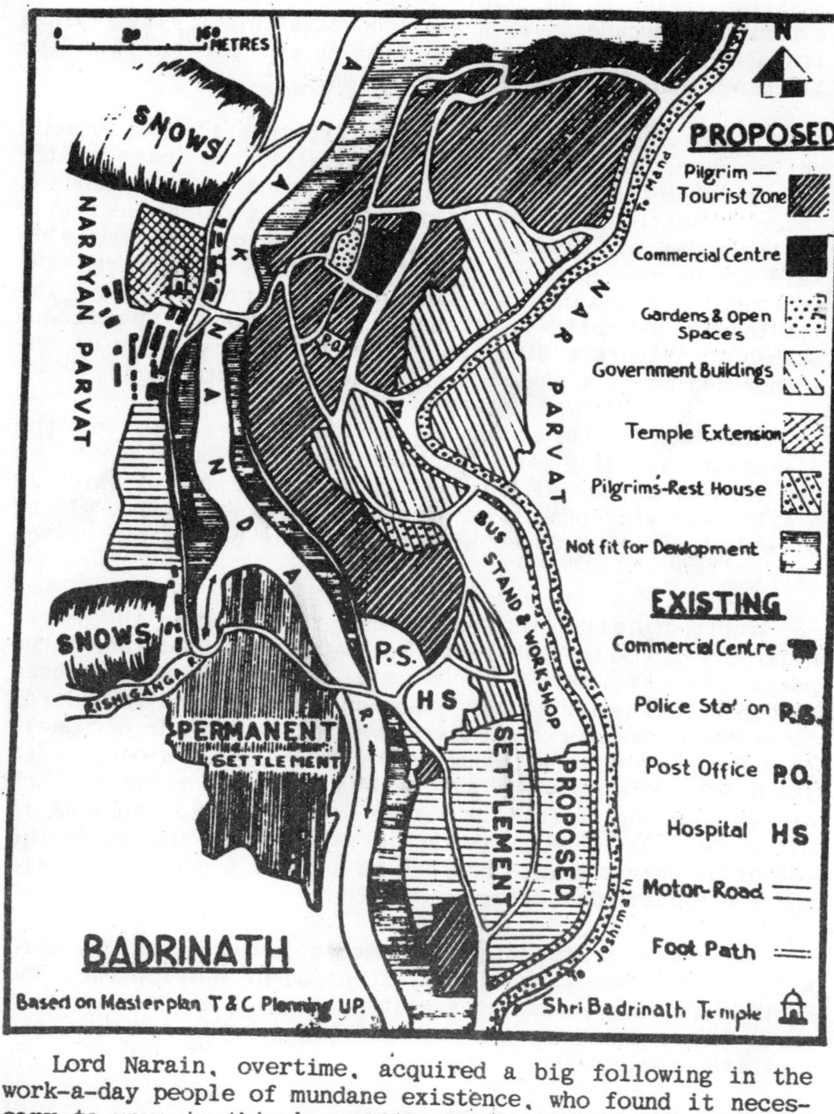

Lord Narain, overtime, acquired a big following in the work-a-day people of mundane existence, who found it necesary to move to this beautiful Himalaya, both for religious merit and for change from humdrum of life and living. Religious benediction bestowed upon the laity led a movement of pilgrimage a **yatra** tradition. This movement of people of Garhwal Himalaya suffered a severe setback when Buddhism had its sway in this region and a queer mix of cults Tantricism,

Shaktism, Saivaism and magic began to be practised. This was a period of decadence when the iconoclastic activity reached its acme. The image of Lord Vishnu was thrown into the Alaknanda and the temple was demolished.[11]

It was around the eighth century that a young Brahmin philosopher, Shankaracharya, who installed the image in the 'Garur Gufa' (near Tapt Kund), having found it in Naradkund. Later, tradition has it, it was removed to the present site by the ruler of Garhwal. The gold canopy of the temple is said to be the gift of queen Ahilyabai. This marks the period of renaissance in Badrinath pilgrimage, when the temple was dedicated to **Vishnu, Shiva, Surya, Shakti** and **Ganesh** to integrate Hinduism and to restrict worship of unauthorised gods, a practice which had come into vogue.

The Temple is situated on the right bank of the Alaknanda, standing over 15^m high from the base, built in the form of a cone with small Cupola on the top of which is a gilt ball and spine. The main body is made of flat blocks of stone and plastered with cement that belies its antiquity.

Architecturally, the temple has taken after the early Nagar Style[12] with a definite hill stamp. Divided into three parts (a) Garbhgarh (the sanctum sanctorum), (b) Darhsan Mandap (rectangular shaped where puja is performed) and (c) Sabha Mandap (outer hall where devotees stand for darshan), it has square plan with number of graduated projections in the middle of each side that lend it a cruciform shape. Much of its form has suffered a change on renovators' hands as it often fell to the invasion of avalanches and men. The colourful entrance gate has put on a Turkish cap, camouflaging the traditional exterior.[13]

The temple stands high on "Puri's" dense religious core with little space around for extension or development. The shrine with its attendant services occupies an area of 0.39 acres being the 1.18 per cent of the developed area - the planners predicament.

Religious-Cum-Recreation Resources

Essentially a religious destination, Badrinath attracts both religious and secular visitors; the latter are steadily on the increase. With the process of modernisation and better facilities in transport and accommodation, Badrinath with its multiple outdoor recreation resource endowment promises an up-coming tourist destination. In fact, the Badrinath Yatra has been responsible in opening up this area for tourism. The Badrinath recreational-cum-religious resource may well be studied in two parts, the one which exists within the township and immediate surroundings and the other that may be developed on a tourist complex planning base on a time scale. It is pertinent to discuss the first one here for inclusion in tourist itinerary.

In the vicinity of the temple are hot and cold cisterns (Kunds), Ghats, engraved boulders and geologic forms. Of these, Taptkund[14], a hot spring having a temperature of 130°F, and closely Suryakund are user-based resources, associated with Panch-Tirth sacrament.[15]

Five giant formations known as "Panch-Shilas"[16] are linked up with religious myth and puranic legends. There are huge sized boulders that are worshipped and enjoyed as 'sites' by the visitors.

The Ganga Ghat where Mahatma Gandhi's ashes were consigned to the holy waters of the Alaknanda, is another point of visitors' attraction. This is located midway between Brahma Kapal and Taptkund.

Away from the temple (1.6 km) is Shesh Netra, a boulder with an engraving of a legendary snake's eye, a geological fossil phenomenon.

Nilkantha is a pyramidal snowy peak (21,650') which towers above Badrinath and present a most enchanting sight, best enjoyed from the left bank of the Alaknanda.

Charan Paduka is a beautiful meadow, about three kilometres west of Badrinath, towards the foothills of Nilkantha Peak. In this emerald green environment are found the footprints of the Lord. As July approaches, this beautiful meadow is carpeted with flowers.

The Mana Valley has many potential touristic attractions, viz., 'Vyas Gupha'- a rock-cave where sage Vyas is said to have compiled puranas; 'Keshav Prayaga' the confluences of the Alaknanda and the Saraswati and the natural bridge, "Bhimpul". The Mana Valley with Bhotia settlement and with their unique lifestyle is itself a scurce of attraction.[17]

Vasudhara is an enchanting site of a waterfall at an

elevation of 3658 m from where the water jumps from a height of 111 m in a trans-inducing manner. It is situated 5 km. from Mana.

Alkapuri, about 8 km further north of Vasudhara, is the source of the Alaknanda. Alkapuri, from where the river gushes out from the glacier snout of Bhagirath-Kharak and Satopantha, much like Gaumukha, the source of the Bhagirathi. The Satopanth lake, with its serene water, is a potential tourism resource for trekkers and trailors. Poet Kalidas presumably alludes to this point in his famous play 'Meghdoot'.

Pilgrim Traffic and Patterns

The Badrinath pilgrimage lasts for six months, mostly in summers and rains (May-November). May-June being the drier months the majority (35%) take to pilgrimage during this period to safeguard against inclemency of weather and road breaches.

On an average, over 1000 pilgrims visit Badrinath every day. However, peak is touched in June when 2000 to 3000 visitors come in a single day.

August, normally, visitors will be lowest as it will rain and threaten landslides; slope failures are not uncommon then on the mountain roads. But it picks up again in September when weather is fairer, sky is clearer, hills are greener and journey is more rewarding. With the onset of snows November traffic begins to fade out. Finally, doors of Badrinath are closed and the chief priest moves to Joshimath, the winter seat of Badri Narain.

Badrinath attracts pilgrims/visitors from all over the country and a few tourists from overseas. Results of interviews, conducted by the Institute of Himalayan Studies and Regional Development, Srinagar, showed that the largest number of visitors originated from West Bengal (560), Uttar Pradesh (310) and Gujrat (220), followed by Andhra Pradesh (120) and Rajasthan (117). Only a few came from Kashmir (2), Assam (2) and Meghalaya (3). Of the 108 foreigners interviewed at the Tourist Rest House, Srinagar, the largest number was of Australians (28), Japanese (13), Britishers (13), West Germans (7), Americans (6), French (3). The fewest were Dutch (4), Belgian (2). However, Nepalese were 29. A few of these foreign visitors entered purpose of their visit as 'pilgrimage' and styled themselves as "Yatrees". Many were expeditionists, or field scientists.

Another study, conducted by the U.P. Town Country Planning Unit of Srinagar[18] in 1979 revealed that out of the total visitors to Badrinath 11.3 per cent originated from Garhwal region, 17.5 per cent came from other States of India (outside Uttar Pradesh). Majority of them (74%) belonged to 30-60 age group. About 78 per cent of the total visitors in 1979 had motivation for Badrinath as destination, whereas 22 per cent of them had Kedarnath, Gangotri, Yamnotri, the Valley of Flowers and Hemkund as their destinations.

Surveys conducted by the Town Planning Unit of Srinagar reveal that the visitors' income group varies considerably, though the majority falls into lower and lower middle class. However, 15.5 per cent belonged to Rs. 801 to 1000 and 4.1 per cent were found in students category.

While the Himalayan pilgrimage have gateways in Kotdwar and Rishikesh, almost 91 per cent visitors prefer entry from Rishikesh, both for transit facilities and en-route attractions, particularly Devprayag. The 310 km long journey is completed in one halt, Joshimath on the onward and Srinagar on the backward journey. Both the stopovers have developed adequate accommodation facility. Average two-day stay at Badrinath has been registered. However, Master Plan Report revealed that of the total visitors to Badrinath, 18.5 per cent stayed at Badrinath only for one day, 58.5 per cent stayed for two days; 19.9 per cent 3 days and 3.1 per cent stayed for 4 days[19]. It may be observed that length of stay is directly proportional to recreation resource attraction, facilities, hospitality and travel costs. Badrinath being mainly a religious destination, would take sometime to cater to the tourist needs, though the trends have set in.

Visitors' influx to Badrinath shot up after 1968 when metalled road reached Badrinath for the first time.

The Badrinath road provided fresh opportunities for opening up new areas for tourism promotion. The Valley of Flowers, accessible enroute, caught-up the market and developed an independent destination in its own right. Many other micro regions are receiving the attention of the developers, particularly the Garhwal Regional Development Corporation and U.P. Tourism. The problem of right kind of facilities is the foremost.

TABLE 18.1

Badrinath Visitors 1976-1979

Year	Visitors	Percentage growth
1976	174,000	7.49
1977	196,000	+12.6
1978	144,000	-26.5
1979	180,316	+25.2

Source: Badrinath Temple Committee

THE HOSTING TOWN

Badrinath faces many constraints in meeting market demands. The major problem is geographical in nature. A town goes live only for six months, May to November, and the rest is the sway of snows. This hard seasonality of character is further accentuated by limited land use adequacy. Man-power resource is another limiting factor for taking up any enterprise which may confirm benefits locally or regionally. A hosting town shall reveal enormity of the situation. Badrinath has a resident population of 1398 people, dwelling in three Mohallas of Badrinathpuri (883), Bamni Village (223), Nar Parbat (292), constituting 278 families[20]. Badrinath Puri being the oldest settlement forms the core where the shrine has cluster of Panda population and services. Here, practically every inch of ground has been used for religious purpose. Of the 225 houses, about 140 are in this Mohalla. As a whole,township has only 140 shops[21]. Of them, 33 per cent shops are devoted to hoterliering, eating and sweets stores, and 31 per cent sell cloth, medicine or religious souvenirs.

In terms of civic services, such as water supply, electricity, hospital and toilets, Bamni is poorly served. Leaving Bamni, tap water and electricity is supplied to the rest of the town. Bamni receives 100 per cent water supply from the river Rishiganga. The following table 18.2 provides classified information on water supply.

Struck by avalanches, Bamni has been deprived of electric lights; 'Puri' and 'Nar' have 46.6 per cent and 25.50 per cent electric supply respectively. Street lights are available to 49.7 per cent of the Puri families. Considered as a whole, 35 per cent families have street lights.

TABLE 18.2

Water Supply in Badrinath (1979)

Moh/Village	Total families	Percentage River	Private taps	Public taps
Badrinathpuri	185	29.7	2.2	68.1
Bamni village	46	100.0	-	-
Nar Parvat	47	4.2	20.8	75.0
Total	278	18.6	23.2	58.2

Source : Badrinath Master Plan (1979) p. 11

Badrinath has only two public toilets; one near the bus stand and the other in 'Puri'. Use of septic tanks has been introduced and the 'Jal Sansthan' has started laying sewerage lines in the town.

Badrinath has only two public hospitals__one Allopathic and the other Ayurvedic. Together they can attend 60 patients per day. The town has one Post Office, one Telephone Exchange, one Police Station and one Information Centre.

These facilities, however modest, look pretty, impressive for a semi-mobile township of 278 families that stay hardly for seven months. But considering the vast floating population of about two hundred thousand pilgrims/tourists and their heterogeneous needs, these services are all too meger, besides being wanting in grade. The town falls short miserably in accommodation, the foremost destination facility.

Accommodation facility

Badrinath can accommodate 53290 visitors in its 36 accommodational units[22] having 525 rooms. A large number of these units came up after 1960 when road to Badrinath began to be constructed.[23] The Parmarth Niketan has the largest capacity (40 rooms) providing 7.62 per cent of total accommodation, followed by the Bhajan Ashram (35), the Manav Kalyan (25), Sant Nivas (23), Ashtakshri (23), Devlok Tourist Rest House (22), Jalan Tourist (22) and Shankracharya (20). Many of them do not have basic facilities such as bath, toilet, kitchen and electric light.[25] Nevertheless a few of them have standard facilities and obviously they are quite expensive stay places.[26] On the contrary there are many 'expensive' stay places with the Pandas who look after their clients on a traditional style[27] and charge exorbitantly though at the 'sweet pleasure' of their clients the Hindu Way of life.

Since many stay places are without bath, toilets and other basic facilities, and that Badrinath township has only two public toilets, the environment suffers the worst from litter and waste, responsible for health hazard and infection that inflict the visiting community who helplessly carry it to other places.

Most agonising feature of the Badrinath pilgrimage is the difficulty in getting a chance to have a look or **darshan** at the deity. The premises of the temple are too small to accommodate even 200 pilgrims at a time. Pilgrims wait in endless queue from the small hours of the morning till afternoon.[27] In fact, the township faces serious challenges for the development of an adequate pilgrim-cum-tourist service system, particularly the constraint of limited land use at the Narain piedmont, close to the temple, to which are tied up superstition and attachment of the local people. Across the Alaknanda beneath the mount Nar, is adequate space for organisation, an opportunity that the town planners have seized upon. It needs some discussion here as the new structures have started coming up, giving a modernised look to a far-flung Himalayan shrine resorts, deep in tradition and religious history of the country.

The master plan

Physical land surveys completed by the Town Planners reveal that the township between Nar and Narain has only 125.90 acres of land available of which about 92.82 acres is 'undeveloped' and 33.08 is suitable for development. The latter should include residents zone, visitors housing, commercial and official zones, transport and community services, besides the religious zone of the Temple. The following table provides details of the land use.

While Pilgrim Zone has been created mainly to the right bank of the Alaknanda, the new township with pronounced tourist zone is emerging on the eastern side beneath the mount of Nar. A separate commercial zone has been created here. Proposed area along Nar has been divided into three sectors:

TABLE 18.3

Badrinath Master Plan Land Use 1979

Undeveloped Land use	Area	Percent -age	Developed Land Use	Area	Percentage
Agriculture	34.14	36.78	Residents' Housing	9.02	27.28
Open Space	32.40	34.90	Visitors' Housing	6.60	19.96
Low Land	7.18	7.75	Commercial Govt. Offices	2.12 3.12	6.42
River Sides	19.10	20.57	D.G.B.R. area	2.52	7.62
			Community Services	0.75	2.27
			Transport Zone	8.56	25.83
			The Temple	0.39	1.18
	92.82 73.2	100.00		33.08 (26.28) percent	100.00

Source: Badrinath Master Plan 1979, p. 25.

(i) Northern Sector: Extends from northern boundary to Hotel Devlok, purporting to be a regional commercial centre.

(ii) Middle Sector: To serve as CBD, rendering town and regional services. This extends from Hotel Devlok to the Hospital.

(iii) Southern Sector: Having a regional outlook it shall have bus stand, petrol station and the like.

The best land has been reserved to the south of Joshimath-Mana road for tourist accommodation and services. This would also be close to the transport zone. Optimal connectivity with tourist service zone and community service centres has been planned. Master plan envisages development of all important activities on a horizontal axis, keeping off the bus stand to the southern outskirts to screen off noise and congestion.

Joshimath-Mana highway (66' wide) shall pass through the middle of the new town with links to various zones. The only other motor road shall link the PWD rest house to the Manav Kalyan Ashram. There would be recreation parks social/cultural centres and green belts on the skirts.

NOTES

1. Of the four **dhamas**, Badrinath is supposed to be established earlier than Dwarka and Rameshwaram (Vishnu Puranas, 5.24, 6).
2. Indian scriptures, particularly the **Mahabharata** and the **Vishnu Puranas** have the parables how Arjuna and Lord Krishna, in the disguise of a recluse-Nar and Narain, performed penances over these ranges, given the name of **Gandhmadan.**
3. This region has been given the name Vaishnav-ka-Kshetra, which according to Atkinson comprised a dozen micro-regions (Kshetras) of which Badri-Kshestra was supposed to be most holy. (Atkinson Vol. III, page 24.)
4. There is a controversy about the location of 'Kanva Ashram'. Govind Prasad Nautiyal and others locate it near Nandprayaga while others place it near Kotdwara where rivulet Malini flows by; the latter has also been recognised by the Department of Tourism, U.P., and a forest has been reserved as sanctuary.
5. Singh, Tejvir, Badrinath: 'A Study in Himalayan Pilgrimages' In Tourism and Tourist Industry in U.P. (India), New Heights, Delhi, 1975.
6. Hindu tirtha itinerary followed a circulatory mechanism in clockwise order (Bharadwaj, SM: **Hindu Places of Pilgrimage in India : A Study in Cultural Geography**, Thomson Press, Delhi. 1973 p. 43.
7. According to Vishnu Purana, Dharma had two sons, Nar and Narain who were divinely inspired to set up **ashramas** in the **Gandhmadan** where ultimately they chose their abode. Since they desired to spread their religious activities on a larger scale, they needed spacious valley in this part of the higher Himalaya. In their search for an ideal, they set up **ashramas** at different places of natural beauty, viz., **Vridhbadree, Yogbadree, Dhyan- badree** and **Bhavish Badree.** Conclusively, they found the present Badrinath more suitable for having hot and cold springs besides the

Alaknanda waters. In time, their devotees gave form to the settlement.

8. Yet another tradition has it that Lord Vishnu alongwith espouse Laxmi left Thuling (now in China) as the place got corrupted by meat eating monks and licentious priests. He set up his **ashrama** 4 km. south of the village Mana, beside the Alaknanda. Laxmi, finding her husband exposed to inclemency of weather assumed the form of **Badree** tree (Jujubi) protecting him with her foliage. Having been pleased with her devotion, Lord Vishnu named the place **Badri-ka-Ashram.** Atkinson holds that there used to be jujubi forests (Badree Van) here, but they are not to be found now. (Atkinson; E.T. op cit., Vol III Part I, p. 23.)
9. Kaur, Jagdish, "Pilgrims' Progress to Himalayan Shrines: Studying the Religious phenomenon." In Singh, T.V., Kaur, J. and Singh, D.P. (eds) **Studies in Tourism Wildlife Parks and conservation**, (1982) Metropolitan; Delhi.
10. Expert opinions find the Gandhmadan area in the higher Chamoli close to Badrinath environs. Atkinson associates Badrinath group of peaks with the Gandhmadan (Atkinson Vol. III, P. 283). Ali does not seem to be sure of the exact location but finds support in **Vayapurana and Matsyapurana** where Gandhmadan is placed on the west and south of Mount Meru respectively (Ali, M. **Geography of Puranas** p. 58). However, Bharadwaj puts it in proximity to Badrinath (Bharadwaj S.M; **Hindu Places of Pilgrimage in India**, Thomson, 1973, p. 72).
11. The temple structure must have also suffered the ravages of avalanches and earthquakes which are not uncommon in this area.
12. Nagar Style of temple architecture exhibits distinct varieties and ramification in different localities and geographical regions, conditioned by different lines of evolution and elaboration that each locality/region chose for itself. The cruciform plan and crucilinear tower are common to every medieval temple.
13. Recently business magnet Birla's efforts for temple renovation invited severe comments, and had to be stopped.
14. Dr. Heim discovered it to be a ferruginous calcareous water containing very little sulphur and having a temperature of 130° F; the volume of the flow is about one gallon per second.
15. **Panch Tirth** include (i) Tapt Kund (Bahri Tirth); (ii) Prahlad Kund (Lukewarm Dhara near Tapt Kund), (iii)

Narad Kund (a recess in the bed of the Alaknanda forming a pool, close to Tapt Kund), (iv) Kurma Dhara (a cold water stream associated with tortoise legend and (v) The Rishiganga, cascading down the Nilkantha and meeting the Alaknanda at Badrinathpuri.

16. **Panch-Shilas** in Badrinath are (i) Narad Shila (after the sage Narad), (ii) Varha Shila is a huge boulder amidst the Alaknanda waters that commemorates the return of Varha to Badrinath after killing Hiranayaksha, (iii) Garur Shila- is a rock dedicated to bird-god Garur who became the vehicle of Narain, (iv) Markandeya Shila is after the sage Markandeya who is said to have performed austerities here, (v) Narsimha Shila after the Lord Narasimha who resorted to Badrinath after slaying Hiranyakasipa.
17. Recently it has again been declared as restricted area being the border area. Mana, the last village of the region, has road and is very rich in Bhotia culture.
18. Badrinath Master Plan p. 21.
19. Badrinath Master Plan, op. cit.
20. 273 households are of Garhwalis, 4 of Uttar Pradesh and one outside U.P. 86.6 per cent of the population is engaged in tertiary sector; of them 40 per cent are engaged in Panda Services.
21. Imagine these handful of shops serving over 200,000 people. During peaks, essential service centres face crisis.
22. 12 dharamshalas are owned by the temple committee, 2 by Garhwal Mandal Development Corporation and 17 are owned by tourist or private agencies.
23. 5 dharamshalas were constructed upto 1947, 7 from 1948 to 1960 and 17 from 1961 to 1970 and 7 from 1971 to 1978.
24. Kali Kamli, Sant Niwas, Nepali Jaipuriya, Bhurimai.
25. One has to pay Rs. 120 per day per room in Alwasia Dharmshala.
26. On the face, the Pandas do not charge for their all-inclusive services, except the tip or **dan** that his 'Jigman' or client would like to offer in the name of Vishnu. But all that he extracts from him by religious promise, coercion or threat amounts to fleecing a Panda malaise found universally on all Hindu places of pilgrimage, only with a difference of degree.
27. **Darshan** is facilitated on a promise of offering "Chhota Darshan" or "Bara Darshan".

NINETEEN

Pranab Kumar Chakravarti

Darjeeling

The Queen of the Hill Stations

"For natural beauty Darjeeling is surely unsurpassed in the world"

— Sir F. Younghusband

Darjeeling (6864' ft) nestling among the Himalayan foothills is, undoubtedly, a tourist's paradise. It commands a thrilling view of the towering snowcapped peaks – Kanchenjunga and others. "The town is modern, elegant and sophisticated by all standards, offering all the amenities of civilised life. But beyond it lies nature, unbroken and untamed in hills, valleys and jungles."[1] The scenic beauty, bracing climate, rich flora and fauna, all have attracted tourists, holiday makers, healthseekers, adventurists, globetrotters alike since long. The majestic kaleidoscopic view of the hills have aptly named the famous hill resort as "the Queen of the Himalayan Hill Stations".

The town, it is said, has derived its name from three probable sources, viz (i) Tibetan source where 'Dorji' meaning thunderbolt and 'ling' place. Hence it is "the place of thunderbolt"; (ii) Sikkimese source where 'Dorji' a Sikkimese deity and 'ling' i.e., Shivalinga were installed side by side at the Observatory Hill. Hence this name; and (iii) Sanskrit source where it derived its name from a sanskrit word "Dorjayling" meaning invincible God Siva who is considered as the presiding deity of the Himalaya.

Darjeeling came to be what it is from a very obscure origin. In the early part of the nineteenth century it was a part of Sikkim and assailed frequently by the Gurkhas from Nepal in the west. This aggression led to the famous war of

1814 wherein the Raja of Sikkim was reinstated by the East India Company. Sikkim including the present district of Darjeeling, became a buffer state between Nepal and Bhutan. In 1824 trouble started again between Nepal and Sikkim and in 1823 Captain Lloyd was deputed along with J.W. Grant to settle the dispute. These two Britishers proceeded towards the place through unknown mountain regions and were attracted in course of their journey by the position of Darjeeling. The position and bracing climate of the place attracted them most which was ideally suitable for adoption of Darjeeling as a sanatorium. Sir Joseph Hooker in his Himalayan journal also referred "children's faces afford as good an index as any to the healthfulness of a climate, and in no part of the world is there a more active, rosy and bright young community than at Darjeeling". The report submitted by Captain Lloyd was approved by the East India Company and finally through the Treaty of 1835 the Raja of Sikkim donated Darjeeling to the E.I. Company - and it thus became an Indian territory. In 1839 the population was only 100 souls and within a decade it rose to 10,000 a remarkable feat indeed for which Dr. Campbell the then Superintendent must be thanked. There was a steady progress since then. Road, hotel, sanatorium, houses, bazar, jail, hospital units were all coming up slowly and cultivation of tea on an experimental basis was tried. In 1864, the formation of the district of Darjeeling was completed by the addition of the Kalimpong police station.

"Darjeeling is in deep debts to Grant, Lloyd and Campbell. Grant and Lloyd discovered the inherent possibilities of development of Darjeeling. Lloyd secured its cession and Campbell, by his wise administration, attracted people from far and near and laid the foundation of the tea industry which was to usher in an era of prosperity".[2] Lord Napier laid out the town plan and European settlements were coming up in the midst of forested hill slopes in the backdrop of the lofty mountains with snow covered peaks. "The climate and breezes are life giving and charged with ozone, and at almost every inspiration those whose health may have suffered from a long residence in the plains feel as if they were adding days to their lives".[3] Establishment of school, cinchona plantation at Mungpoo and quick spread of tea gardens - all led to the pouring in of immigrants from all directions. Development of trade based on the plantation industry resulted in rapid growth of good communication network. The Hill Cart Road and the Darjeeling Himalayan Railway's remarkable engineering feat were soon completed (1881) which opened up the entire region to the most flow of tourist traffic to the outside world. Darjeeling is connected with the rest of country by air, rail and road through Siliguri at the foothill, which is the "Gateway to the Entire North Eastern India".

For one who is going to Darjeeling for the first time, the journey by the "Toy Train" is worthwhile. The distance is 80 kms and "the beauty that reveals itself at every turn simply baffles description. Blue and green foothills sharply outlined against the azure sky, stately trees entangled with enthusiastic creepers, overhanging foliage, rocks and boulders, lovely waterfalls, extensive plains visible from time to time with meandering rivers looking like so many silk ribbons tell their respective tales. To the startlingly impressive scene which vision would feign to feast on without interruption is added the music of the beetles that in a sense enhances the solemn silence that reigns supreme in the Himalayan regions".[4]

The Town is situated on a long spur which projects to the north from the Singalia range. It rises abruptly from Ghoom to an elevation of 7886 ft at Katapaher, descending gradually to 7520 ft at Jalapahar and 7002 ft at Chaurastha which is considered to be the heart of the town. Just behind stands the Observatory Hills (7163 ft) wherefrom it is divided into the Lebong Spur and Tukvar spur. The total area of the town is nearly 5 sq miles, the difference in height between the highest at Katapahar and lowest at Lebong is about 2000 ft. The ridge is narrow at the top. The eastern slope of the ridge descends into the Rangit valley while on the western slope which is gentler in gradient most of the human settlements have been built.

The situation of the town is singularly beautiful, standing as it does on a narrow ridge that juts out in a vast basin in the heart of the Himalaya. To the west and south, it is enclosed by mountains higher than itself, but to the north and north-east the view is more open, and the eye travels past range after range of hills raising in ascending waves behind the cultivated slopes of the nearer hills, until the prospect terminates in the distant snowy mountains with their long girdle of rugged peak".[5]

Darjeeling Town is the district headquarters. The town is located in such a position that from any point the majestic view of mountains can be obtained which is unsurpassed in the whole world. The only botanical garden in the entire northeastern India, Lloyd Botanical Garden is located at the bazar area. The Natural History Museum contains valuable specimen of the fauna which are available in the entire Himalayan region. The natural beauty of the woods situated on the Birch Hill show what Darjeeling was like when it was first discovered. Close by stands the Observatory Hill where the famous deity of Mahakal is located. Among the beautiful parks within the municipal boundary are the Victoria Park, the Donvan Park and the Brabourne Park.

Beyond Ghum many roads radiate through fine forests of oak, magnolia and rhododendron, one road leads to the famous Senchal Lake (8163 ft) - the water reservoir of the town - and another runs towards the Tiger Hill from where the tourists have a glimpse of the crimson red sunrise. From this hilltop (8575 ft) one can clearly enjoy the full view of the snow capped mighty mountain chain with towering majestic peaks like Kanchenjunga, Everest, Kabru, Janu, Pandim and host of others. The play of life and shade and ever-changing cloud and mist over the valleys and tea gardens in the foreground are almost as the magnificent panorama that becomes visible when the sky clears.

Darjeeling has two tourist seasons—the spring (Mid April to Mid June) and the autumn (September and October). Rains are too nagging while the winters are quite cold. The town is fairly well provided with hotel accommodation of varying tariffs and means of recreation. Taxis ply to different places of tourist interest and fetch huge profit during the two tourist seasons. Cinema Houses, Schools, Colleges abound in the town as well as places of worship for the various communities living in the town. One of the features of the town is the market square situated on a levelled and extensive piece of ground in the middle of the town and surrounded by substantial buildings. The town has good lay out of motorable roads and fine buildings including some very tall ones. Other places of interest include the Himalayan Mountaineering Institute at Birch Hill, a Zoological Park, Lebong Race Course, The Mall, Rabindra Bhanu Bhaban within the limit of the town and Keventer's Dairy Farm, Sinchal Lake, Ghoom Monastery, Victoria Falls, Jalapahar, Batasia Loop etc., outside the confines of the Municipal limit. Some other notable places of tourist interest which can be reached from Darjeeling within a few hours are Simana, Mirik, Phalut, Sandakphu, Bijanbari, Kalimpong, Kurseong, Sukna reservoir, Teasta Bridge, Tonglu, Sukhia Pokhri etc. There are a few recognised trek routes which radiate from Darjeeling and all along the routes Dak Bungalows and Youth Hostels are located where cheap accommodation is freely available.

Darjeeling's recognition as an international hill resort is a post-independence phenomena. Increased leisure, better education, affluence, fast transport media have added to its development. Tourism has changed the physiognomy of the urban landscape a great deal and much of its original flora and fauna have been depleted by human encroachment. But this phenomenon of tourism is closely related to structure, farm, use and conservation of the natural landscape and have far reaching social and cultural effects as well.

A recent survey made in connection with the study of measurement of tourism and tourist flows at Darjeeling indicate the following characteristics:

(a) The scenic beauty, bracing climate, accommodation, amenities and good transport network with the rest of the country is a 'plus' factor for its development;

(b) 'Democratisation' of leisure pursuits (mountaineering, winter sports etc.) which were formerly the monopoly of the rich people, 'commercialisation' of many hobbies (riding, climbing etc.) and 'socialisation' of tourism (low priced accommodation etc.) made the region accessible within the reach of lower income group.

(c) Tourism being a multi-dimensional phenomenon it has contributed a great deal in the regional development, has created service and allied industries, created employment opportunities in the area. Hence its economic importance in the regional economy is noteworthy.

(d) Motivation study of the tourists reveal that they usually come here for : (i) Mental refreshment, (ii) recuperation of health, (iii) Pleasure (iv) Curiosity and culture, (v) Participation in Sports etc.

(e) It is a purely seasonal activity and has two peaks - spring (April, May, June) and Autumn (September October).

(f) The entire tourist industry rests primarily on road transport system because of the rugged character of the terrain. Hence road transport development is a must for the expansion of the tourist industry here.

(g) Tourism here, is in a great way responsible for western culture and cultural diffusion which the local inhabitants imbibe from the outsiders.

(h) With the increase of tourists during the peak season the 'infrastructure' as well 'superstructure' break down creating insurmountable problems like transport, accommodation, water scarcity, power crisis, soaring price etc, which need a careful and deft handling.

Darjeeling primarily being a hill resort it earns a huge revenue through tourism. Therefore if it has to retain its superiority some more facilities will have to be created in order to attract more tourists:

(i) Accessibility and ease of transport;
(ii) Accommodation to meet the demands of all categories of people;
(iii) Parking facilities for visitors and day excursionists;
(iv) Open spaces - Parks with floral displays;
(v) Amusement, games, shopping, catering facilities;
(vi) Seating arrangements in the Mall, toilet facilities etc.;
(vii) Enquiry office, information bureau and publicity cells.

NOTES

1. Ghosn, A.C., **Darjeeling.** Cambridge Book & Stationeries Co., Calcutta, 1967.
2. Ibid. p. 6.
3. Darjeeling, **Guide Book**, Newman & Co., Calcutta.
4. Ghosh, A.C., (Ed) ibid.
5. Ray,B., **Darjeeling**: District Census Handbook 1961. Calcutta, 1967.

Index